Teaching and Researching Autonomy in Language Learning

APPLIED LINGUISTICS IN ACTION

General Editors:

Christopher N. Candlin and David R. Hall

Books published in this series include:

Teaching and Researching Autonomy in Language Learning

Phil Benson

An imprint of **Pearson Education**

Harlow, England · London · New York · Reading, Massachusetts · San Francisco
Toronto · Don Mills, Ontario · Sydney · Tokyo · Singapore · Hong Kong · Seoul
Taipei · Cape Town · Madrid · Mexico City · Amsterdam · Munich · Paris · Milan

Pearson Education Limited
Edinburgh Gate
Harlow
Essex CM20 2JE
England

and Associated Companies throughout the world

Visit us on the World Wide Web at:
www.pearsoned.co.uk

ISBN 0-582-36816-2 PPR

British Library Cataloguing-in-Publication Data
A catalogue record for this book is available from the British Library

Library of Congress Cataloging-in-Publication Data
A catalog record for this book is available from the Library of Congress

8 7 6 5 4 3 2
08 07 06 05 04

Set by 35 in 11/13pt Janson Text
Produced by
Printed in Malaysia, LSP

Contents

General Editors' Preface

Applied Linguistics in Action, as its name suggests, is a Series which focuses on the issues and challenges to practitioners and researchers in a range of fields in Applied Linguistics and provides readers and users with the tools they need to carry out their own practice-related research.

The books in the Series provide readers with clear, up-to-date, accessible and authoritative accounts of their chosen field within Applied Linguistics. Using the metaphor of a map of the landscape of the field, each book provides information on its main ideas and concepts, its scope, its competing issues, solved and unsolved questions. Armed with this authoritative but critical account, readers can explore for themselves a range of exemplary practical applications of research into these issues and questions, before taking up the challenge of undertaking their own research, guided by the detailed and explicit research guides provided. Finally, each book has a section which is concurrently on the Series *web site* www.booksites.net/alia and which provides a rich array of chosen resources, information sources, further reading and commentary, as well as a key to the principal concepts of the field.

Questions the books in this innovative Series ask are those familiar to all practitioners and researchers, whether very experienced, or new to the fields of Applied Linguistics.

- What does research tell us, what doesn't it tell us, and what should it tell us about the field? What is its geography? How is the field mapped and landscaped?
- How has research been carried out and applied and what interesting research possibilities does practice raise? What are the issues we need to explore and explain?

- What are the key researchable topics that practitioners can undertake? How can the research be turned into practical action?
- Where are the important resources that practitioners and researchers need? Who has the information? How can it be accessed?

Each book in the Series has been carefully designed to be as accessible as possible, with built-in features to enable readers to find what they want quickly and to home in on the key issues and themes that concern them. The structure is to move from practice to theory and research, and back to practice, in a cycle of development of understanding of the field in question. Books in the Series will be usable for the individual reader but also can serve as a basis for course design, or seminar discussion.

Each of the authors of books in the Series is an acknowledged authority, able to bring broad knowledge and experience to engage practitioners and researchers in following up their own ideas, working with them to build further on their own experience.

Applied Linguistics in Action is an **in action** Series. Its *web site* will keep you updated and regularly re-informed about the topics, fields and themes in which you are involved.

We hope that you will like and find useful the design, the content, and, above all, the support the books will give to your own practice and research!

Christopher N. Candlin & David R. Hall
General Editors

A Companion Web Site accompanies *Teaching and Researching Autonomy in Language Learning* by Phil Benson

Visit the *Teaching and Researching Autonomy in Language Learning* Companion Web Site at www.booksites.net/benson to find valuable teaching and learning material, including:

www.booksites.net

- Links to valuable resources on the web
- Useful sources and resources relating to the study of Autonomy in Language Learning
- Search for specific information on the site

Author's Acknowledgements

This book is the product of a process of autonomous learning that has lasted for twenty years of teaching and research and is not yet complete. It is also the product of numerous learning conversations with other teachers and researchers – a demonstration of the fact that autonomous learners are not isolated learners. Among those whose conversation I have most valued are my colleagues and friends in Hong Kong, especially David Gardner, William Littlewood, Winnie Lor, Elaine Martyn, David Nunan, Richard Pemberton and Peter Voller. For their help in pointing me to sources for the writing of this book, I must also thank Naoko Aoki, Anne Burns, Sara Cotterall, Peter Grundy, Lienhard Legenhausen, David Little, Ian McGrath, George Jacobs, Joan Rubin, Richard Smith, Flavia Vieira and Anita Wenden. I am particularly thankful to the researchers whose work is summarised in the case studies in Section III, to Winnie Lor for her help in the preparation of the manuscript, to Hiroko Itakura and Peter Voller for their proof-reading skills and to my editors at Longman for the hard work that followed the submission of the manuscript.

Above all I am grateful to the co-editors of the series, Chris Candlin and David Hall, without whose vision and encouragement this book might never have been written, and to Hiroko Itakura, whose support and encouragement have been unfailing even at the most difficult moments of our life.

Our pedantic mania for instruction is always leading us to teach children the things they would learn better of their own accord.
Jean-Jacques Rousseau

To Kaz,
who hopes that his father will follow Rousseau's advice.

Introduction

As the theory and practice of language teaching enters a new century, the importance of helping students become more autonomous in their learning has become one of its more prominent themes. The idea of autonomy often provokes strong reactions. To its critics, autonomy is an idealistic goal and its promotion a distraction from the real business of teaching and learning languages. To its advocates, autonomy is a precondition for effective learning; when learners succeed in developing autonomy, they not only become better language learners but they also develop into more responsible and critical members of the communities in which they live.

Discussions on autonomy are, however, often characterised by misconceptions about the nature of the concept and its implementation. For example, it is often assumed that autonomy implies learning in isolation, learning without a teacher or learning outside the classroom, such that the relevance of the concept to language *teaching* is unclear. Similarly, autonomy is often seen as necessarily implying particular skills and behaviours and particular methods of organising the teaching and learning process. These misconceptions are, at least in part, a result of terminological and conceptual confusion within the field itself.

The aim of *Teaching and Researching Autonomy in Language Learning* is both to clarify and problematise the concept of autonomy in language learning and its relevance to the practice of language education. There are certain fundamentals on which researchers in the field agree: for example, autonomy refers to the learner's broad approach to the learning process, rather than to a particular mode of teaching or learning. There are other issues on which they disagree, and often agree to disagree, for autonomy is in essence multidimensional and takes different forms in different contexts of learning. This book thus aims to establish what research does and does not tell us about autonomy, so that those who wish to foster it among their learners can engage in research and practice on an informed basis.

Autonomy can be broadly defined as the capacity to take control over one's own learning. In the course of this book, I will expand on this definition, but for the moment it is sufficient to note that autonomy is not a method of learning, but an attribute of the learner's approach to the learning process. As a teacher and researcher who has been involved with the promotion of the idea of autonomy for a number of years, I take the position that autonomy is a legitimate and desirable goal of language education. Among the claims made for autonomy, three stand out as being equally important to theory and practice:

- The concept of autonomy is grounded in a natural tendency for learners to take control over their learning. As such, autonomy is available to all, although it is displayed in different ways and to different degrees according to the unique characteristics of each learner and each learning situation.

- Learners who lack autonomy are capable of developing it given appropriate conditions and preparation. The conditions for the development of autonomy include the opportunity to exercise control over learning. The ways in which we organise the practice of teaching and learning therefore have an important influence on the development of autonomy among our learners.

- Autonomous learning is more effective than non-autonomous learning. In other words, the development of autonomy implies better language learning.

In *Teaching and Researching Autonomy in Language Learning*, I argue that these are claims rather than facts and that before we accept or reject autonomy as a legitimate goal of language education, we should examine them carefully. Certain claims can be substantiated by research evidence, others remain open to research and some are non-researchable. I also argue that the best research on autonomy is often not research concerned with 'grand theory', but action research conducted by practising teachers on the specific conditions of teaching and learning within which they work and on the effects of changes to these conditions. In order to research autonomy, we must make some attempt to foster it among the learners we work with. In doing so we will frequently find ourselves in a position where we are able, through careful observation and analysis of empirical data, to contribute to theory.

The book is divided into four sections. Section I focuses on the origins and development of the concept of autonomy in language learning, definitions of key terms and research evidence that enables us to describe autonomy in terms of various dimensions of control over learning. Section II focuses on evidence for the effectiveness of practices that have been claimed to foster autonomy. Section III outlines key areas for future research and presents six case studies of action research in the field of autonomy. Section IV lists resources that will help researchers and practitioners in the field.

What is autonomy?

Chapter 1

The history of autonomy in language learning

The first six chapters in this section will...

- describe the history of autonomy in language learning and its sources in the fields of language pedagogy, educational reform, adult education, the psychology of learning and political philosophy;
- discuss definitions of autonomy and key issues in research;
- explain why autonomy is a key issue in language education today.

1.1 Origins of the concept

Second language acquisition predates institutionalised learning by many centuries and even in the modern world millions of individuals continue to learn second and foreign languages without the benefit of formal instruction. Although there is much that we can learn from their efforts, however, the theory of autonomy in language learning is essentially concerned with the organisation of institutionalised learning. As such, it has a history of approximately three decades.

According to Gremmo and Riley (1995), early interest in the concept of autonomy within the field of language education was in part a response to ideals and expectations aroused by the political turmoil in Europe in the late 1960s. Holec (1981: 1) began his report to the Council of Europe (see Concept 1.1) with a description of the social and ideological context within which ideas of autonomy in learning emerged:

Concept 1.1   **The origins of autonomy in language learning**

The concept of autonomy first entered the field of language teaching through the Council of Europe's Modern Languages Project, established in 1971. One of the outcomes of this project was the establishment of the *Centre de Recherches et d'Applications en Langues* (CRAPEL) at the University of Nancy, France, which rapidly became a focal point for research and practice in the field. Yves Châlon, the founder of CRAPEL, is considered by many to be the father of autonomy in language learning. Châlon died at an early age in 1972 and the leadership of CRAPEL was passed to Henri Holec, who remains a prominent figure within the field of autonomy today. Holec's (1981) project report to the Council of Europe is a key early document on autonomy in language learning. The journal *Mélanges Pédagogiques*, published at CRAPEL, has also played an important role in the dissemination of research on autonomy from 1970 to the present day.

The end of the 1960s saw the development in all so-called industrially advanced Western countries of a socio-political tendency characterized by a definition of social progress, no longer in terms of increasing material well-being through an increase in consumer goods and services, but in terms of an improvement in the 'quality of life' – an expression that did not become a slogan until some years later – based on the development of a respect for the individual in society.

The Council of Europe's Modern Languages Project aimed initially to provide adults with opportunities for lifelong learning. The approach developed at CRAPEL was therefore particularly influenced by proposals from the emerging field of adult self-directed learning (2.2), which insisted 'on the need to develop the individual's freedom by developing those abilities which will enable him to act more responsibly in running the affairs of the society in which he lives'.

Autonomy, or the capacity to take charge of one's own learning, was seen as a natural product of the practice of self-directed learning, or learning in which the objectives, progress and evaluation of learning are determined by the learners themselves. Among the key innovations in the CRAPEL approach to the provision of opportunities and support for self-directed language learning were the self-access resource centre and the idea of learner training. In its early days, the theory and practice of autonomy in language learning also enjoyed an uneasy association with ideas of individualisation.

1.2 Autonomy and self-access

The first self-access language learning centres, at CRAPEL (Riley and Zoppis, 1985) and the University of Cambridge (Harding-Esch, 1982), were based on the idea that access to a rich collection of second language materials would offer learners the best opportunity for experimentation with self-directed learning (Quote 1.1). The provision of counselling services and an emphasis on authentic materials were also important elements in the CRAPEL approach.

> **Quote 1.1** Riley and Zoppis on the Sound and Video Library at CRAPEL
>
> If one of our initial aims was to make sure that the Sound and Video Library would actually be able to take in all its potential users for as long as possible each week, we also wanted it to be a place where we would apply some of the pedagogical principles and strategies we firmly believe in. Foremost among these was the principle of *autonomous learning* for advanced and fairly advanced students. In our view, students who have reached a certain level in English can improve their listening comprehension, their oral expression or their written comprehension by regularly working in semi-autonomy with adequately prepared teaching material or in complete autonomy using 'raw' *authentic material*.
>
> Riley and Zoppis (1985: 287)

At CRAPEL, self-access was seen as a means of facilitating self-directed learning. In recent years, however, self-access language learning centres have proliferated to the point where 'self-access language learning' is often treated as a synonym for self-directed or autonomous learning. In many institutions, self-access centres have been established without any strong pedagogical rationale and it is often assumed, without any strong justification for the assumption, that self-access work will automatically lead to autonomy. To a lesser extent, the producers of self-instructional and distance learning materials have assumed that autonomy will be one outcome of these modes of learning. One of the important lessons of the spread of self-access over the past three decades, however, is that there is no necessary relationship between self-instruction and the development of autonomy and that, under certain conditions, self-instructional modes of learning may even inhibit autonomy (Chapter 8).

Because self-access centres have been enthusiastic consumers of educational technologies, self-access learning has also tended to become synonymous with technology-based learning. Within the field of computer-assisted language learning, especially, autonomy has become an important issue. As in the case of self-access, however, researchers on autonomy emphasise that learners who engage in technology-based learning do not necessarily become more autonomous as a result of their efforts. A great deal depends on the nature of the technology and the use that is made of it (Chapter 9).

1.3   Autonomy and learner training

Like self-access, learner training began life as a mechanism to support self-directed learning (Dickinson and Carver, 1980; Holec, 1980). At CRAPEL, it was argued that in order to carry out effective self-directed learning, adult learners would need to develop skills related to self-management, self-monitoring and self-assessment. Learners who were accustomed to teacher-centred education would also need to be psychologically prepared for more learner-centred modes of learning. According to Holec, teaching learners how to carry out self-directed learning would be counterproductive, since the learning would by definition no longer be self-directed. Instead, learners needed to train themselves (Quote 1.2). Although learners might draw on the support of counsellors, teachers or other learners, the important thing about learner training was that it should be based on the practice of self-directed learning itself. Self-direction was understood as the key to learning languages and to learning how to learn languages.

Quote 1.2 Holec on learner training

The basic methodology for learner training should be that of *discovery*; the learner should discover, with or without the help of other learners or teachers, the knowledge and the techniques which he needs as he tries to find the answers to the problems with which he is faced. By proceeding largely by trial and error he trains himself progressively.

Holec (1980: 42)

As the practice of learner training became more widespread in the 1980s and 1990s it increasingly drew upon insights from research on learning strategies, which has aimed to identify the behaviours and strategies used by successful learners and train less successful learners in their use. Although the idea of autonomy did not initially have a strong influence on this research, Wenden (1991) made the link explicit in the title of her book, *Learner Strategies for Learner Autonomy*. Like self-access, learner training has also taken on a life of its own in recent years. While most practitioners in the field see learner training as leading to greater autonomy, learner training is no longer confined to self-directed learning. Dickinson (1992), for example, views learner training as a resource to help learners to engage more actively in classroom learning, and some of the best learner training materials have been developed for classroom use (Chapter 10).

1.4 Autonomy and individualisation

Throughout the 1970s and 1980s, the concept of autonomy was closely associated with the concept of individualisation, an association evident in the titles of collections that linked the two fields (Altman and James, 1980; Brookes and Grundy, 1988; Geddes and Sturtridge, 1982). Brookes and Grundy (1988: 1), for example, suggested in the introduction to their collection that autonomy and individualisation were associated by a mutual link to the concept of learner-centredness:

> One corollary of learner-centredness is that individualization will assume greater importance, as will the recognition of the autonomy of the learner as the ultimate goal.

Individualisation and autonomy overlapped in as much as both were concerned with meeting the needs of individual learners. Self-directed learning as it was practised at CRAPEL was thus in a sense a form of individualisation, in which learners determined their own needs and acted upon them. As the practice of self-access spread, self-access resource centres were also seen as performing important functions in the individualisation of learning.

Individualisation also took the form of programmed learning – a mode of instruction in which learners were expected to work their way, at their own pace, through materials prepared by teachers. From the outset, researchers at CRAPEL took pains to distinguish self-directed learning from programmed individualised learning on the grounds that that the latter left the most important decisions in learning to the teacher rather than to the learner. Holec (1981: 6) also made a distinction between teaching that takes the learner into consideration and learning that is directed by the learners themselves:

> In a general way the extent to which the learner is taken into consideration forms no criterion for judging the extent to which learning is self-directed: individualization effected by taking into account the learner's needs, his favourite methods of learning, his level, and so on, leave the learner in the traditional position of dependency and do not allow him to control his learning for himself.

Riley (1986) similarly argued that programmed learning deprived learners of the freedom of choice essential to the development of autonomy (Quote 1.3).

Quote 1.3 Riley on autonomy and individualisation

Individualisation ('individualised learning', 'individualised instruction') is, historically at least, linked with programmed learning and based on a thoroughly behaviouristic psychology. As it is generally practised, it leaves very little freedom of choice to the individual learner. Rather it is the teacher who tries to adapt his methodology and materials to the learner, like a doctor writing out a prescription. That is, the majority of the relevant decisions are made for the learner, not by him. It is in fact individualised TEACHING: it aims at the most efficient use of the teacher and at the most effective result, but in terms of what the teacher wants the learner to achieve.

Riley (1986: 32)

The early association of autonomy with individualisation may also be largely responsible for the widespread criticism that autonomy implies the learner working in isolation. This criticism was more difficult to counter since it must be acknowledged that, although collaborative programmes for self-directed groups of learners have been designed at CRAPEL and elsewhere, much of the early work in the field of autonomy focussed on the learner as an individual with distinct characteristics and needs. In recent years, however, researchers on autonomy have emphasised that the development of autonomy necessarily implies collaboration and interdependence.

1.5 Autonomy and interdependence

It is evident in retrospect that the concept of autonomy in language learning had, by the late 1980s, begun to suffer something of a crisis of identity. Although Holec (1985a) continued to emphasise that the term *autonomy* should be used to describe a capacity of the learner, others began to use it to refer to situations in which learners worked under their own direction outside the conventional language-teaching classroom. Riley and Zoppis (1985: 287), for example, described learners working in a self-access centre as working in 'semi-autonomy' or 'complete autonomy'. Dickinson (1987: 11) defined autonomy as 'the situation in which the learner is totally responsible for all of the decisions concerned with his learning and the implementation of those decisions' and also used the term 'full autonomy' to describe the situation in which the learner is entirely independent of teachers, institutions or specially prepared materials.

The use of autonomy to describe learning situations, which is still found occasionally in the literature, has undoubtedly led to a degree of conceptual confusion within the field. Researchers on autonomy were aware that in order to develop autonomy, learners needed to be freed from the direction and control of others. At the same time, they were well aware that learners who chose, or were forced by circumstances, to study languages in isolation from teachers and other learners, would not necessarily develop autonomy. However, the argument that the opportunity to exercise autonomy through self-directed learning was a necessary precondition for the development of autonomy was interpreted by critics of autonomy as an argument that it was a sufficient condition. Moreover, the theory of autonomy had, in a sense, become framed within the practice of individualised self-directed learning, and was seen by many as irrelevant to classroom learning. The use of the term *independence* as a synonym for autonomy by some researchers has also led critics to view the field of autonomy as one in which crucial questions concerning the social character of learning are avoided (Concept 1.2).

The theory and practice of autonomy escaped from this crisis of identity largely through the efforts of practitioners who experimented with the idea of autonomy in classroom settings. Their work was influenced in part by developing views of the classroom as a 'social context' for learning and communication (Breen and Candlin, 1980; Breen, 1986) and the idea that autonomy could be developed by a shift in relationships of power and control within the classroom. Some of the most

---

Concept 1.2   Independence, dependence and interdependence

In recent years, a number of researchers, in the United Kingdom especially, have preferred the term independence to autonomy, creating two terms for what is essentially the same concept. When *independence* is used as a synonym of autonomy, its opposite is *dependence*, which implies excessive reliance on the direction of teachers or teaching materials. One problem with the use of this term, however, is that it can also be understood as the opposite of *interdependence*, which implies working together with teachers and other learners towards shared goals. Many researchers would argue that autonomy does imply interdependence. For this reason, the term independence is avoided in this book.

---

influential work in this area was carried out by Leni Dam and her colleagues in Danish secondary schools, where a model of autonomy was based on classroom and curriculum negotiation (Dam, 1995). This work has had a considerable influence on later innovations in classroom and curriculum autonomy and has also prompted a shift in the focus of research on autonomy in the 1990s towards issues of collaboration and negotiation.

One of the most challenging developments in the theory of autonomy in the 1990s has been the idea that autonomy implies interdependence. Kohonen (1992: 19) has argued the point forcefully:

Personal decisions are necessarily made with respect to social and moral norms, traditions and expectations. Autonomy thus includes the notion of interdependence, that is being responsible for one's own conduct in the social context: being able to cooperate with others and solve conflicts in constructive ways.

Collaborative decision making within co-operative learning groups is thus a key feature of Kohonen's 'experiential' model for the development of autonomy. Little (1996: 210) has also argued that collaboration is essential to the development of autonomy as a psychological capacity, stating that 'the development of a capacity for reflection and analysis, central to the development of learner autonomy, depends on the development of an internalization of a capacity to participate fully and critically in social interactions'. Such statements have provided an important corrective to the earlier emphasis on the individual working outside the conventional classroom. They have also provided a focus for research and practice on the reform of the conventional classroom to support the development of autonomy (see Chapter 11).

A second important development has been the examination of the teacher's role in the curriculum. While research in the field of self-access has tended to focus on the teacher's role as counsellor of individual learners (Kelly, 1996; Riley, 1997), researchers working in classroom contexts have explored the role of the teacher in the negotiation of the curriculum. In a review of the literature, Voller (1997: 112–13) summarises the results of this research in the form of three assumptions about teachers' roles in the development of autonomy:

> The first is that language learning is an interpretative process, and that an autonomous approach to learning requires a transfer of control to the learner. The second is to ensure that our teaching practices, within the external constraints imposed upon us, reflect these assumptions, by ensuring that they are based on a process of negotiation with learners. The third is to self-monitor our teaching, to observe and reflect upon the teaching strategies we use and the nature of the interactions we set up and participate in.

The most recent research in the area of teacher roles also addresses the issue of the teacher's own autonomy in relation to the curriculum and its implications for teacher education (Little, 1995a; Sinclair et al., 2000). The idea of negotiation, and its implications for teacher and learner roles, has informed a number of innovative curriculum-based approaches to the development of autonomy (Chapter 12).

1.6 Why autonomy? Why now?

In the course of its evolution, the concept of autonomy has become part of the mainstream of research and practice within the field of language education. This is in part due to the reported success of numerous projects associated with autonomy and the efforts of those who advocate autonomy as a goal of education to promote their ideas. However, it would be a mistake to assume that autonomy has entered the mainstream of language education independently of social and economic factors that have made language educators and those who fund their work more open to the practices associated with it (Concept 1.3).

The idea of autonomy in language learning originated in the late 1960s and drew sustenance from the social and ideological changes of

---

Concept 1.3 **The economics of autonomy**

The argument for autonomy is principally a pedagogical argument. How-ever, programmes that aim to promote autonomy are often influenced by social and economic factors. The economic imperative is often one of meeting complex educational needs at low cost. The Bell School and Eurocentre have been among the leaders in developments in self-access within the commercial sector in the UK. In both schools, meeting the individual needs of learners is an important justification for self-access. At the same time, self-access provides a focus for experimentation in the development of autonomy (Sheerin, 1997; O'Dell, 1997). The Adult Migrant Education Programme in Australia is a publicly funded pro-ject with similar economic priorities. On the one hand, the programme aims to meet the diverse needs of migrants at reasonable cost. On the other hand, it has been an important focus for a variety of experiments in autonomous learning. Opening a conference on self-directed learning and self-access in Australia in 1985, the Minister for Immigration and Ethnic Affairs, the Hon. S.J. West, summed up the way in which economic and pedagogical goals are often interwoven in his observation that 'a "one course for all" approach is not only educationally unsound but also extremely inefficient' (cited in Mason, 1985: vii).

---

the time. In higher education, the notion of 'student power' was current (Cockburn and Blackburn, 1970) and radically student-centred educational reforms were proposed by Freire (1970), Illich (1971), Rogers (1969) and others. Gremmo and Riley (1995) suggest that the rise of autonomy in language learning corresponded to an ideological shift away from consumerism and materialism towards an emphasis on the meaning and value of personal experience, quality of life, personal freedom and minority rights. It could well be argued that the ideological values surrounding the idea of autonomy are especially appealing to language educators today. Breen and Mann (1997: 140) argue:

> A common experience among many teachers in western democratic societies in recent time is the growing sense that the locus of control over their work is shifting away from themselves and their immediate institutions to centralized bureaucracies . . . Might it be possible that the current interest by teachers in the autonomy of learners is an expression of a growing personal uncertainty and a feeling of powerlessness so that many teachers are beginning to question the culture of 'authority' as it manifests itself towards the end of the century, including that which they themselves represent as teachers?

As new technologies and commercial imperatives lead to what many perceive as the 'dumbing down' of education and the undermining of the intellectual authority of the teacher, it may be that autonomy serves as a focal point for educators to reconceptualise their roles from more humanistic perspectives.

At the same time, the basic ideas of autonomy have also come into harmony with major innovations in language teaching theory and methodology over the last 30 years. At the root of these innovations lies an intellectual shift away from the behaviourist assumptions underlying innovations such as audiolingualism and the language laboratory in the 1960s and 1970s. The growth of fields of inquiry such as discourse analysis, pragmatics and sociolinguistics and the development of functional approaches to grammar have supported a shift towards more communicative approaches to language teaching oriented towards communication in context rather than the acquisition of decontextual-ised knowledge about the target language (Breen and Candlin, 1980; Littlewood, 1981). The idea that language learning should be a process of learning how to communicate also underpins the notion of learner-centredness, which holds that the learner rather than the teacher should stand at the centre of the process of teaching and learning (Nunan, 1988; Tarone and Yule, 1989).

Communicative teaching, learner-centredness and autonomy share a focus on the learner as the key agent in the learning process, and several prominent researchers in the fields of communicative language teaching and learner-centred practice have incorporated the idea of autonomy into their work (see, for example, Breen and Mann, 1997; Littlewood, 1996, 1997; Nunan, 1996, 1997). For Breen and Mann (1997: 133), in aiming at the goal of autonomy, we may well be engaging in a degree of self-delusion, but:

> The professional energy which we may devote to aiming towards auto-nomous language learning will almost certainly uncover and achieve an unanticipated range of new possibilities in language pedagogy.

In this sense, the current value of the concept of autonomy to language educators may well lie in its usefulness as an organising principle for the broader possibilities contained within a framework of communicat-ive and learner-centred pedagogies.

However, if the concept of autonomy can serve as a rallying point for resistance to bureaucratic, technocratic and commercial pressures within language education, it must also be recognised that there are elements within the concept and its associated practices that make it attractive to funding authorities with less radical agendas.

The so-called 'information explosion' has both increased the quantity of learning that is expected of students and altered its quality. At university level, especially, packed timetables mean that institutions are willing to experiment with modes of instruction that reduce teacher contact time. At the same time, there is a growing awareness of the educational implications of the rapid obsolescence of task-specific skills and factual knowledge leading to an emphasis on transferable learning skills.

The rapid increase in the number of people attending educational institutions and the growth of adult education have forced educational authorities to search for alternative means of providing education to individuals with diverse needs, opportunities and preferences. Open learning and distance learning have grown rapidly and traditional institutions now accommodate a greater diversity of students than ever before.

The commercialisation of public education has had a particular effect on language teaching, which is increasingly taking on a 'service' role within educational institutions. Private sector language-teaching institutions experience student needs in the form of consumer demand and pressure to provide a wide range of learning options and have for some time been at the forefront of developments in innovations associated with autonomy such as self-access learning and learner training. Public institutions are understandably more inclined to accept such innovations if they have proved themselves to be cost-effective in the private sector.

The growth of technology in education, driven largely by the boom in personal consumer electronics (audio, video and computer) and the Internet, has freed students in many parts of the world from the need to attend classes at predetermined times and locations. Language-teaching institutions have long been enthusiastic consumers of new educational technologies and the self-access boom has been largely technology driven. Important technological developments have also taken place in educational publishing, leading to the production of ever more sophisticated self-instructional multimedia materials.

The information explosion, growing student numbers, the commercialisation of education and developments in educational technology have had a particular impact on language teaching. Not only has the number of students in educational institutions increased rapidly, but the importance of language within the education sector has also increased with the growth of international travel. Migration, tourism and the internationalisation of business and education are three important factors in the world-wide expansion of language teaching. The information economy is also fundamentally a communication economy, meaning that individuals who have contact with speakers of other languages are likely to have far more diverse and complex communication needs than at any other time in the past.

Changes within education systems and the practice of language teaching are indicative of more fundamental changes in the functions of knowledge in social and economic life and in the ways in which knowledge is constructed and exchanged. In the light of these changes, the successful learner is increasingly seen as a person who is able to construct knowledge directly from experience of the world, rather than one who responds well to instruction. Socio-economic and ideological changes are rapidly bringing the notion of the autonomous learner into harmony with dominant ideologies of what it means to be a fully functioning member of a modern society. One indication of this harmony is the parallel that can be drawn between constructs belonging to autonomy in learning and constructs belonging to progressive models of management, such as total quality management and transferable skills (Little, 1995b; Marshall, 1996).

1.7   The two faces of autonomy

While many of the economic and social developments favourable to the idea of autonomy in language learning are welcomed by its advocates, they also pose contradictions. Autonomy now increasingly appears among the broad goals of education as they are formulated by educational authorities, but as Boud (1988: 20) observes, 'as long as autonomy remains an abstract concept divorced from any particular situation it can be an ideal to which we can aspire but it is not something that we realistically expect to emerge from any given course'. In particular, educational change is often implemented in climates that are both economically and politically unfavourable to the fundamental idea of autonomy as a shift in the balance of power in learning towards the learner. Changes designed to give more control to learners are implemented in order to achieve reductions in unit costs and are accompanied by measures that ensure that little real power is actually transferred.

Arguably, the current trend is for education providers to see language education as a service to a global economy in which language skills represent a form of economic capital. As language educators respond to this trend, there is clearly a risk that autonomy will be viewed simply as a matter of consumer choice. There is equally a risk that the concept of autonomy will become assimilated to consumerist approaches to learning through a shift in focus from the goals and purposes of language learning to the skills and strategies employed by the 'autonomous learner' (Quote 1.4).

> **Quote 1.4** Pennycook on the 'psychologisation' of autonomy
>
> The idea of autonomy has therefore moved rapidly from a more marginal and politically engaged concept to one in which questions are less and less commonly asked about the larger social or educational aims of autonomy. Broader political concerns about autonomy are increasingly replaced by concerns about how to develop strategies for learner autonomy. The political has become the psychological.
>
> Pennycook (1997: 41)

As the importance of the idea of autonomy grows in the field of language teaching, it is therefore important that we examine its development critically. Aside from the possibility that autonomy will simply become the latest fad in language-teaching methodology, there is the risk that it will be used for politically ambiguous ends. Placing the responsibility for learning onto the learner should not become a matter of shifting the economic burden of education from the state to the individual. Learning to learn should not become a matter of shifting the burden of ongoing retraining from those who demand it to those who need it in order to keep their jobs. Meeting individual needs should not become a matter of dispersing learning communities and privileging those who possess 'learning capital' over those who do not.

Addressing these concerns, I would argue, does not necessarily imply an explicitly political approach to language teaching. On the other hand, it does imply that political concerns about the goals of learning should not be divorced from the practice of teaching. The fostering of autonomy requires, above all, a focus on the learner's perspective in regard to the goals and processes of learning. As Holec (1985a: 182) argues:

> Providing yourself with the means to undertake your own learning programme presupposes that, at the very least, you think it is possible to be both 'producer' and 'consumer' of such a programme. This runs counter to the usual attitudes of members of our modern consumer society; indeed for the individual it means withdrawing from it to some extent,

since the usual procedure for acquiring 'goods' (in this case competence in a foreign language) is not a creative one.

Although the idea of autonomy currently appears to be in harmony with the need for skilled language learners within a global economy, it does not arise from these needs, nor is it dependent upon them. Autonomy is fundamentally concerned with the interests of learners, rather than the interests of those who require their skills.

Chapter 2

Autonomy beyond the field of language education

The concept of autonomy in language learning (Figure 2.1) has influenced, and has been influenced by, a variety of approaches within the field of language learning. It is not, however, originally or primarily a language-learning concept. Galileo, like many other great thinkers throughout the ages, evidently believed in autonomous learning (Quote 2.1), while the term itself has been widely used in connection with educational reform, adult education, the psychology of learning and political philosophy in the twentieth century. One of the characteristics of research

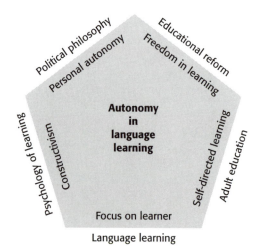

Figure 2.1   Major influences on the theory of autonomy in language learning

> **Quote 2.1** Galileo on teaching and learning
>
> You cannot teach a man anything; you can only help him find it within himself.
>
> Galileo Galilei (1564–1642)

on autonomy in language learning has been its willingness to look at sources beyond the field of language education for insights and intellectual guidance. Before proceeding to a more detailed discussion of definitions of autonomy in language learning, we will look briefly at some of the more important of these sources.

2.1   Educational reform

2.1.1   Jean-Jacques Rousseau

In *Emile*, Rousseau described the ideal of a 'natural education' as it is experienced by a boy brought up on a country estate away from the corrupting influence of social conventions and institutions. Rousseau's ideas on education were grounded in a philosophical view of the human subject as intrinsically good, in contrast to the dominant doctrine of the time, which held that human beings had fallen from grace through sin. He also believed that the source of corruption in human affairs lay

> **Biography 2.1**   Jean-Jacques Rousseau
>
> Jean-Jacques Rousseau (1712–78) was born in Geneva and later moved to France. He received no formal education, but became known for his work on political philosophy and 'natural' education. On its publication in 1762, copies of Rousseau's classic work on education, *Emile*, were burned for religious heresy and Rousseau was forced to leave France. For an excellent review of Rousseau's contribution to educational thought and links to Rousseau on the web, see Mark K. Smith's *Informal Education Homepage* <http://www.infed.org/thinkers/et-rous.htm>.

in verbal abstraction and social institutions, both of which distanced humanity from nature. The idea of the human subject as intrinsically good tied in with the idea that social order was maintained through a social contract in which individual wills are integrated with the general will. As the individual will is part of the general will, each individual is his or her own authority.

Emile proposed a model of education that followed the child's natural impulses and inclinations (Quote 2.2). Rather than master preordained subject matter, children should learn what they want to learn when they want to learn it. Moreover, they should learn primarily through direct contact with nature rather than through the transmission of abstract ideas in verbal form. In Rousseau's model the teacher is a permissive individual who supports learners and learns with them. Learners are responsible for their own actions and learn by enjoying or suffering their consequences. Under the influence of a natural education, children develop naturally into individuals subject to their own authority rather than the authority of others.

Quote 2.2 **Rousseau on teaching and learning**

Make your pupil attend to the phenomena of nature, and you will soon arouse his curiosity. But to nourish this curiosity, be in no hurry to satisfy it. Suggest problems but leave the solving of them to him. Whatever he knows, he should know not because you have told him, but because he has grasped it himself. Do not teach him science: let him discover it. If ever you substitute authority for reason in his mind, he will stop reasoning, and become the victim of other people's opinions...

If he goes wrong, do not correct his errors. Say nothing till he sees them and corrects them himself; or at most, arrange some practical situation which will make him realise things personally. If he never made mistakes he would never learn properly. In any case, the important thing is not that he should know the topography of the country, but that he should be able to get this information for himself.

Boyd (1956: 73–6)

Although Rousseau is seldom cited as a source, the germs of the modern idea of autonomy in learning are to be found within his thought. For modern educational theorists the problem with Rousseau's model lies in his romantic view of human nature. However, his emphasis on the learner's responsibility for learning is a key idea of autonomy. Many advocates of autonomy in language learning would also share

Rousseau's view that the capacity for autonomy is innate but suppressed by institutional learning. Similarly Rousseau's idea that learning proceeds better through direct contact with nature re-emerges in the emphasis on direct contact with authentic samples of the target language that is often found in the literature on autonomy in language learning. Rousseau's influence is indirect, however, and comes principally through later progressive educators such as John Dewey and William Kilpatrick, whose influence on the theory and practice of autonomy has been profound.

2.1.2 John Dewey

Dewey was a philosopher of the Pragmatist school, for whom education was a vital philosophical issue. Pragmatism held that truth consists of tentative conclusions drawn from experience and that philosophy should be oriented towards solving problems of everyday life. Dewey rejected the romantic premises of Rousseau's thought as part of a more general rejection of philosophical dualism, which contrasts the imperfection of reality with an ideal realm of truth. Nevertheless, Dewey's educational ideas reflected many of Rousseau's concerns and grounded them within a project of social reform. His contribution to the idea of autonomy lies mainly in three areas: the relationship between education and social participation, education as problem solving, and classroom organisation.

Dewey's philosophy of education rested upon the belief that individuals have a moral responsibility to engage in the betterment and reform of the societies in which they live. The aims of education in a democratic society thus go beyond the mastery of subject matter to preparation for participation in social and political life. In this respect, Dewey's view of education is a precursor of the view that informed the early Council of Europe work on autonomy in language learning.

Biography 2.2 John Dewey

John Dewey (1859–1952) was both a philosopher and educator who has exercised a wide-ranging influence on western educational practice. A prolific writer on education, the best introduction to his thought is perhaps *Democracy and Education*, first published in 1916. The Center for Dewey Studies web site at Southern Illinois University at Carbondale is an excellent place to begin an exploration of Dewey's work
<http://www.siu.edu/~deweyctr/>.

Dewey also held the view that schooling should not be a preparation for situations that students would face later in life. Instead, it should be concerned with the solution of current problems (Quote 2.3). He therefore argued that educational activities should begin from the immediate personal and social experience of the learners. Dewey saw learning as an adaptive process, in which interaction with the environment generates problems that must be solved in order for individuals to satisfy their needs. This view of learning as an adaptive process is also at the root of constructivist approaches to learning that are currently highly influential in the theory of autonomy in language learning and has been proposed as a theoretical basis for autonomy in language learning by Esch (1996).

In Dewey's problem-solving method, the school and the classroom were seen as microcosms of the community, in which learners worked together to solve shared problems. It was through collaborative work that learning contributed to the development of community. At the same time, the problem-solving method implied the deconstruction of the authority of the teacher as learners acquired internal discipline based on the need to solve the problems with which they were faced. In order for learners to acquire this internal discipline, however, Dewey emphasised that the starting point of activities must be the learners' own felt needs so that the educational aims were those of the learners rather than those of the teachers. The teacher's role was not to direct the process of learning, but to act as a resource or guide for the learners' own self-directed efforts. Many of the principles of classroom and curriculum organisation

---

Quote 2.3 John Dewey on problem solving

While we may speak, without error, of the method of thought, the important thing is that thinking is the method of an educative experience. The essentials of method are therefore identical with the essentials of reflection. They are first that the pupil have a genuine situation of experience – that there be a continuous activity in which he is interested for its own sake; secondly, that a genuine problem develops within this situation as a stimulus to thought; third, that he possess the information and make the observations needed to deal with it; fourth, that suggested solutions occur to him which he shall be responsible for developing in an orderly way; fifth, that he have opportunity and occasion to test his ideas by application, to make their meaning clear and to discover for himself their validity.

Dewey (1916/1966: 163)

advanced by Dewey are evident in the work of Dam (1995) and others whose efforts to promote autonomy are focused on the classroom.

2.1.3 William Kilpatrick

> **Biography 2.3** William Kilpatrick
>
> William Heard Kilpatrick (1871–1965) was a follower of the early twentieth-century North American progressive education movement, which shared many of the philosophical assumptions of Rousseau, including the belief that people were essentially good. Kilpatrick began his career as a mathematics teacher in elementary school, where he abolished report cards and grades and encouraged children to work cooperatively. He was especially critical of textbooks, which, in his view, led to mechanistic learning and favoured memorisation over understanding.

Kilpatrick's distinctive contribution to the idea of autonomy was the 'project method'. In the project method, students plan and execute their own learning projects, which may be of four kinds (Kilpatrick, 1921): *construction projects* involve the development of a theoretical plan and its execution (e.g. writing and performing a drama); *enjoyment projects* are activities such as reading a novel or seeing a film; *problem projects* require the students to resolve an intellectual or social problem; and, lastly, *specific learning projects* involve learning a skill such as swimming or writing. Like Dewey, Kilpatrick believed that his methods lent themselves to group work, through which students might acquire skills and attitudes needed for democratic social participation. Legutke and Thomas (1991: 270) acknowledge Kilpatrick as a source for their work on project learning and argue that project work provides a principled and practicable route towards autonomy.

2.1.4 Paolo Freire

Freire's early educational work in literacy programmes in Brazil combined educational and political goals. He believed that authoritarian political systems rested upon the depoliticising influence of mass education and could be challenged through radical educational reform. Freire's (1974: 3) conception of learning was also based on a distinctive view of the human condition:

> **Biography 2.4** Paolo Freire
>
> Born in 1921, Paolo Freire (1921–77) was exiled from Brazil following the 1964 military coup for his educational work among the Brazilian poor. He taught at Harvard University before returning to Brazil under a political amnesty to be appointed as Minister for Education in Sao Paolo. His best-known work, *Pedagogy of the Oppressed*, was published in English in 1970. A short critical review of Freire's contribution to educational thought, with a bibliography and web links can be found on Mark K. Smith's *Informal Education Homepage* <http://www.infed.org/thinkers/et-freir.htm>.

To be human is to engage in relationships with others and with the world. It is to experience that world as an objective reality, independent of oneself, capable of being known.

Individuals thus realise their humanity by engaging with others in the social process of knowing the world. For Freire, this should be a process of 'integration' with, rather than 'adaptation' to, the world since it is the exercise of our critical capacity to make choices and transform reality that makes us truly human (Quote 2.4). Adaptation, according to Freire, is a characteristic of the animal world and a symptom of dehumanisation when exhibited by people. Quoting Simone Weil (1952), Freire (1974: 16) argues that responsibility is a fundamental human need, and:

For this need to be satisfied it is necessary that a man should often have to take decisions in matters great or small affecting interests that are distinct from his own, but in regard to which he feels a personal concern.

> **Quote 2.4** Freire on transformative learning
>
> *Integration* with one's context, as distinguished from *adaptation*, is a distinctively human activity. Integration results from the capacity to adapt oneself to reality *plus* the critical capacity to make choices and to transform that reality. To the extent that man loses his ability to make choices and is subjected to the choices of others, to the extent that his decisions are no longer his own because they result from external prescriptions, he is no longer integrated. Rather, he has adapted.
>
> Freire (1974: 4)

This responsibility is acquired through reflection on experience and the transformation of social reality. The idea of deep learning as the transformation of individuals and the social realities in which they live has been developed in the context of adult self-directed learning by Mezirow (1991) and is particularly relevant to approaches to autonomy in language learning which emphasise the purposes to which second language learning is put (e.g. Kenny, 1993; Pennycook, 1997; Ramadevi, 1992).

Freire's methods aimed not at the acquisition of abilities that would later enable the individual to become an autonomous member of society, but at critical social participation within the process of education itself. They centre on the identification and discussion of learning material based on everyday social and political issues facing the learners. The contribution of Freirean education theory to the theory of autonomy, however, lies mainly in its emphasis on the need to address issues of power and control in the classroom within broader social and political contexts.

According to Freire (1970), the 'banking model' of teaching and learning, in which knowledge is transmitted from teacher to learner, presupposes that knowledge is neutral or objective. The goal of this model is the assimilation of the learners into the logic of the dominant system, or their 'domestication'. Freire argues that education ceases to be domesticating when it begins to address the learner's role in the social order. The role of the teacher in Freirean pedagogy is thus to present knowledge in the form of problems that engage students in dialogue and reflection, leading to the analysis of their social realities for the purpose of transforming them.

Although Freire is often cited as a source for autonomy in language learning, his ideas on the political character of education have exercised a greater influence on critical language pedagogy (see, for example, Auerbach, 1995). Some current writers on autonomy have, however, argued for the continuing relevance of Freire's ideas and for greater interaction between autonomy and critical language pedagogy (e.g. Benson, 1996, 1997a, 2000; Lamb, 2000; Littlejohn, 1997).

2.1.5   Ivan Illich

In his work on deschooling, Illich (1971) argued that schooling was not only unnecessary and economically misguided, but also 'anti-educational'. As an alternative to schools, he discussed 'the possible use of technology to create institutions which serve personal, creative, and autonomous interaction and the emergence of values which cannot be substantially controlled by technocrats' (p. 2). Although Illich saw the value of direct

Biography 2.5   Ivan Illich

Ivan Illich (1926–) was born in Vienna and moved to the USA in 1951. He was co-founder of the Center for Intercultural Documentation in Cuernavaca, Mexico, a centre for radical thought on technology and education in the 1970s. His best-known work is *Deschooling Society*, published in 1971. More information on Illich, including links to his major works can be found at the *Ivan Illich Studies* web site, maintained by the Department of Philosophy at Pennsylvania State University
<http://www.la.psu.edu/philo/illich/>.

instruction in certain circumstances, he argued that the belief that learning necessarily involved teaching was misguided and only served to justify the existence of schools. Illich (1971: 12–13) cited second language learning as an example of 'casual' learning:

> Most learning happens casually, and even most intentional learning is not the result of programmed instruction. Normal children learn their first language casually, although faster if their parents pay attention to them. Most people who learn a second language well do so as a result of odd circumstances and not of sequential teaching. They go to live with their grandparents, they travel, or they fall in love with a foreigner.

Illich believed that schooling reduces learning to acquisition of the prefabricated products of subject matters and ultimately deprived students of the opportunity to learn (Quote 2.5). His main concern was to find alternatives to schools rather than alternative methods of organising schooling. While many researchers on autonomy in language learning would agree that institutionalised learning inhibits the development of autonomy, they would also argue that it can be organised in ways that foster autonomy. Nevertheless, they would largely accept Illich's critique of schooling, which has been an important influence on the theory of autonomy.

Illich's proposals for informal learning are often highly practical and reflected in current educational practice. One proposal with particular relevance to the late 1990s is the idea of 'learning webs', or networks that facilitate self-motivated learning outside the school system. Illich proposed four kinds of network that would help learners define and achieve their own goals: (1) reference services to educational objects, tools and resources; (2) directories of individuals willing to share skills; (3) peer matching, or communication networks for students to find

> **Quote 2.5** Illich on the effects of schooling
>
> School pretends to break learning up into subject 'matters', to build into the pupil a curriculum made of these prefabricated blocks, and to gauge the result on an international scale. People who submit to the standard of others for the measure of their own personal growth soon apply the same ruler to themselves. They no longer have to be put in their place, but put themselves into their assigned slots, squeeze themselves into the very niche which they have been taught to seek, and, in the very process, put their fellows into their places too, until everybody and everything fits.
>
> People who have been schooled down to size let unmeasured experience slip out of their hands. To them, what cannot be measured becomes secondary, threatening. They do not have to be robbed of their creativity. Under instruction, they have unlearned to 'do' their thing or 'be' themselves, and value only what has been made or could be made.
>
> Illich (1971: 40)

partners for similar learning projects; and (4) reference services to 'educators-at-large', or experts willing to provide assistance or instruction. These proposals take on a modern form in the use of the Internet to network learners across classrooms, which Warschauer et al. (1996) argue, empowers learners and enhances autonomy.

2.1.6   Carl Rogers

Rogers's (1969, 1983) ideas on teaching and learning derived from his work in the field of humanistic psychology, which adopts Rousseau's view that people are basically good and focuses on what it means for normal and healthy individuals to be fully human. Humanistic psychology conceives of people as 'self-actualizing' beings striving for health,

> **Biography 2.6**   Carl Rogers
>
> Carl Rogers (1902–87) was born in Illinois and is best known as a psychologist and founder of 'client-centred' therapy. In *Freedom to Learn* (1969) Rogers reworked therapeutic notions of learning in the context of education. His ideas on person-centred learning and teaching and the concept of teaching as facilitation have had a major influence in spite of criticisms of the individualism implicit in Rogers's educational thought.

individual identity and integrity, and autonomy. Rogers also believed that people have a natural tendency towards exploration, growth and higher achievement.

For Rogers, effective learning arises from the uniquely individual experiences of the learner and leads to a change in behaviour. The optimal relationship in teaching is therefore one in which the teacher adopts a non-judgemental, facilitating role in helping the learner achieve self-actualisation and intervenes as little as possible in the natural development of the person (Quote 2.6). Humanistic psychology was especially influential in shaping thinking on self-direction in North American adult education in the 1970s. Although its major impact on language education has been in the field of humanistic language teaching (Stevick, 1990), it has also influenced the theory of autonomy in language learning (see, for example, Little, 1991; Broady and Kenning, 1996). The emphasis on the uniqueness of individual learning in humanistic psychology has also led to criticism, however. Candy (1991: 42), for example, describes humanistic psychology as being concerned with the 'essential aloneness of the individual' and argues that,

> The corollary of this in the field of self-direction has been that many adult educators have lost sight of the interdependent and socially determined nature of much adult learning.

Quote 2.6   Rogers on facilitation

Suppose I had a magic wand that could produce only one change in our educational systems. What would that change be?

I finally decided that my imaginary wand, with one sweep, would cause every teacher at every level to forget that he or she is a teacher. You would all develop a complete amnesia for the teaching skills you have painstakingly acquired over the years. You would find that you were absolutely unable to teach....

Traditional teaching, no matter how disguised, is based essentially on the mug-and-jug theory. The teacher asks himself, 'How can I make the mug hold still while I fill it from the jug with these facts which the curriculum planners and I regard as valuable?' The attitude of the facilitator has almost entirely to do with climate, 'How can I create a psychological climate in which the child will feel free to be curious, will feel free to make mistakes, will feel free to learn from the environment, from fellow students, from me, from experience? How can I help him recapture the excitement of learning that was natural in infancy?'

Rogers (1983: 135–6)

Outside the field of self-directed learning, however, Rogers's major contribution lies in his reconceptualisation of the role of the teacher. His notion of the teacher as facilitator is central to classroom-based approaches to autonomy in language learning.

2.2 Adult education

Further reading

Candy, P.C. (1991) *Self-direction for Lifelong Learning*. San Francisco: Jossey-Bass.

The most immediate influence on the early theory and practice of autonomy in language learning came from research and practice in the field of adult self-directed learning. Candy (1991) traces interest in self-directed learning to nineteenth-century concerns with self-improvement and self-education. For many involved in the field, modern adult education emerges from this tradition, and self-directed learning is its characteristic form. In the early 1960s, adult educators began to study the learning habits of individuals engaged in informal self-instruction and in the 1970s and 1980s numerous studies were published on the nature of self-directed learning.

The focus in the literature on adult self-directed learning tends to fall on the processes involved in learning outside the context of formal education. Thus Knowles (1975: 18), a leading figure in adult education, defines self-directed learning as follows:

> In its broadest meaning, 'self-directed learning' describes a process in which individuals take the initiative, with or without the help of others, in diagnosing their learning needs, formulating learning goals, identifying human and material resources for learning, choosing and implementing appropriate learning strategies, and evaluating learning outcomes.

In the more recent literature, however, researchers have begun to consider self-directed learning as an umbrella concept embracing both self-instructional processes and the psychological characteristics of the learner that support them. Brockett and Hiemstra (1991: 24), for example, refer to 'learner self-direction' as a dimension of self-directed learning that centres on 'a learner's desire or preference for assuming responsibility for learning'. Similarly, Candy (1991: 22–3) states that:

... the term *self-direction* actually embraces dimensions of process and product, and . . . refers to four distinct (but related) phenomena: 'self-direction' as a personal attribute (personal autonomy); 'self-direction' as the willingness and capacity to conduct one's own education (self-management); 'self-direction' as a mode of organizing instruction in formal settings (learner-control); and 'self-direction' as the individual, noninstitutional pursuit of learning opportunities in the 'natural societal setting' (autodidaxy).

Candy's multidimensional view of self-direction has much in common with the idea of autonomy as it has developed within the field of language education (Concept 2.1).

Much of the research on adult self-directed learning has focused on the ways in which institutionalised adult education can support self-directed learners and enhance their self-direction. Ideas from the field of adult self-directed learning have thus exercised a strong influence on approaches to autonomy in language learning in contexts where adult learners are studying languages largely of their own volition. The

---

Concept 2.1   Autonomy and self-directed learning

The distinction between autonomy and self-directed learning is often the object of some confusion arising from differences in the use of these terms in the fields of adult education and language learning.

In North American adult education, *self-directed learning* defines a broad field of inquiry into the processes of non-institutional learning. *Self-direction* tends to refer to the learner's global capacity to carry out such learning effectively, while *autonomy* often refers to the particular personal or moral qualities associated with this capacity.

In the field of language learning, it is autonomy that defines both the broad field of inquiry and the global capacity to exercise control over one's learning. Self-directed learning tends to refer simply to learning that is carried out under the learner's own direction, rather than under the direction of others.

Perhaps the most important distinction to be made in the field of language learning is between autonomy as an attribute of the learner and self-directed learning as a particular mode of learning in which the learner makes the important decisions about content, methods and evaluation. Autonomy can be considered as a capacity that learners possess to various degrees. Self-directed learning can be considered as something that learners are able to do more or less effectively, according to the degree that they possess this capacity.

idea of the self-access language-learning centre, for example, originally developed as a resource for adult and university level learners who were not enrolled on classroom-based courses. Ideas from the field of adult learning can be problematic, however, when applied to contexts in which students study foreign languages as part of a formal course of learning, especially if they lack the strong motivation to learn that is often assumed to be characteristic of adult self-directed learners. As the idea of fostering autonomy has spread within the field of language education, therefore, the influence of ideas from the field of adult education has tended to become weaker.

The practice of institutionalised adult self-directed learning has been subject to criticism from within the field itself. According to Brookfield (1993: 228), a leading advocate of self-directed learning in the 1980s, an 'alternative form of practice that began as a challenge to institutional adult educational provision has become technocratic and accommodative'. Where theories of self-directed learning are closely associated with Rogerian humanistic psychology, there has been a particular concern with their advocacy of individualism in learning. Critical approaches to self-directed learning have also been developed, which emphasise collaboration and learner control over resources and institutional contexts of learning (e.g. Brookfield, 1993; Garrison, 1992; Hammond and Collins, 1991; Mezirow et al., 1990). To date these appear to have little influence on the theory and practice of autonomy in language learning (Benson, 1996).

2.3 The psychology of learning

2.3.1 Constructivist theories of learning

Candy (1991: 252) describes constructivism as a cluster of approaches which hold that 'knowledge cannot be taught but must be constructed by the learner'. This belief is implicit in the thought of Rousseau, Dewey, Kilpatrick, Freire, Illich and Rogers and has been developed systematically in the literature on the psychology of learning (Concept 2.2). Recent research in the field of autonomy in language learning has drawn freely on research in the constructivist tradition, within which the work of Kelly, Barnes, Kolb and Vygotsky has been especially influential.

George Kelly's (1963) personal construct theory, developed within the field of psychology, was an important early influence on the theory

---

Concept 2.2   Constructivist theories of learning

The term constructivism has been applied to a variety of theoretical approaches to the psychology of learning that share the underlying assumption that knowledge is produced through socially conditioned processes of interpretation. Paris and Byrnes (1989: 170) distinguish constructivist approaches from both structuralist and empiricist approaches. Structuralist approaches emphasise 'innate categories of knowing and concepts that are imposed by individuals on the world'. Empiricist approaches emphasise 'how experiences imprint the structure of the world into the minds of individuals'. In contrast, constructivist approaches 'describe how people transform and organise reality according to common intellectual principles as a result of interactions with the environment'.

Constructivist approaches to the psychology of learning provide strong support for the contention that effective learning begins from the learner's active participation in the processes of learning. If knowledge is constructed uniquely within each individual through processes of social interaction, it follows that learning will be most effective when learners are fully involved in decisions about the content and processes of learning.

---

of autonomy. Kelly's psychology views human thought as a process of hypothesis testing and theory building involving the continual development and revision of constructs, or meanings attached to objects or events, in the light of new experience (Quote 2.7). Personal constructs are derived from shared assumptions and values, but systems of constructs are unique to the individual since they are shaped through attempts to make sense of experiences that are uniquely one's own. Personal construct systems are also developed over long periods of

Quote 2.7   Kelly on personal constructs

People look at their world through transparent templets which they create and then attempt to fit over the realities of which the world is composed. The fit is not always very good. Yet without such patterns, the world appears to be such an undifferentiated homogeneity that people are unable to make any sense out of it. Even a poor fit is more helpful than nothing at all.

Kelly (1955: 8–9)

time and lead us to function in terms of plans based on expectations of future events.

Applied to learning, personal construct theory holds that individual learners bring their own systems of constructs to bear on learning tasks. When learning is a matter of adding information to an existing construct, it is likely to be relatively unproblematic. When new knowledge contradicts existing construct systems, learning is likely to be more difficult and resistance may be encountered. Both in therapy and in education, resistance is overcome by helping individuals to become more aware of their existing personal construct systems and gradually to assume control of their psychological processes. In education, this means helping learners to become more aware of their assumptions about learning and to assume control of their own learning processes. It is acknowledged that these processes can be arduous and disorienting for the learner, both cognitively and emotionally, and that they are not easily implemented where learners are not fully motivated to change.

Little (1991) argues that the value of personal construct theory to the theory of autonomy in learning is twofold. First, it provides a justification for the promotion of autonomy in terms of the operation of normal psychological processes. Second, it highlights, rather than conceals, the difficulties involved in the process of fostering autonomy. Little (1991: 21) argues that:

> . . . it is a common experience that attempts to make learners conscious of the demands of a learning task and the techniques with which they might approach it, lead in the first instance to disorientation and a sense that learning has become less rather than more purposeful and efficient. However, when the process is successful, it brings rich rewards.

He also argues that in the process of assisting learners to become more autonomous in their learning, teachers must pay attention to their own personal constructs, or 'the assumptions, values and prejudices which determine their classroom behaviour' (p. 22).

Douglas Barnes's (1976) critique of the school curriculum is often quoted in the literature on autonomy in language learning. His distinction between 'school knowledge' and 'action knowledge' entails a hypothesis about the value of different kinds of learning. School knowledge, or knowledge presented and retained in abstract decontextualised form, remains someone else's knowledge and is easily forgotten. Action knowledge, or knowledge that is integrated into the learner's view of the world, becomes the learner's own knowledge and forms the basis of the learner's actions and way of living. The distinction also

> **Quote 2.8** Barnes on school knowledge and action knowledge
>
> School knowledge is the knowledge which someone else presents to us. We partly grasp it, enough to answer the teacher's questions, to do exercises, or to answer examination questions, but it remains someone else's knowledge, not ours. If we never use this knowledge we probably forget it. In so far as we use knowledge for our own purposes, however, we begin to incorporate it into our view of the world, and to use parts of it to cope with the exigencies of living. Once the knowledge becomes incorporated into that view of the world on which our actions are based I would say that it has become 'action knowledge'.
>
> Barnes (1976: 81)

entails a hypothesis about teaching and learning. Action knowledge cannot be transmitted from teachers to learners. It can only be acquired through active involvement in learning. In Barnes's model, teaching is therefore more a matter of communication than of instruction.

Kolb (1984) has developed a model of learning, known as experiential learning, based on the work of Dewey, Kelly, Rogers and others, which has influenced the theory of autonomy in language learning primarily through Kohonen's (1992, 2000) work. In experiential learning, the learner's immediate experience is taken as the focus of learning, giving 'life, texture, and subjective personal meaning to abstract concepts and at the same time providing a concrete reference point for testing the implications and validity of ideas created during the learning process' (Kolb, 1984: 21). Especially important in experiential learning is the notion of learning as a cyclical process that integrates immediate experience, reflection, abstract conceptualisation and action. Within this cycle, reflection is viewed as the bridge between experience and theoretical conceptualisation. The experiential model thus proposes a methodology to help learners to integrate knowledge into their own systems of meaning and take control of their own learning. The methodology emphasises the importance of reflection and is both collaborative and transformative.

In his work on developmental psychology, Vygotsky assumed that learning begins from the starting point of the child's existing knowledge and experience and develops through social interaction. This assumption was made explicit in Vygotsky's (1978: 86) idea of the 'Zone of Proximal Development', which he defined as:

... the distance between the actual development level as determined by independent problem solving and the level of potential development as determined through problem solving under adult guidance or in collaboration with more capable peers.

According to Vygotsky, under guidance from adults or more experienced peers, children internalise meanings acquired through linguistic interaction as the directive communicative speech of others is transformed into self-directive inner speech. Vygotsky's view of learning is distinguished from that of others within the constructivist tradition mainly by its emphasis on the importance of social interaction. His influence on the theory of autonomy in language learning is relatively recent, and lies mainly in the support it offers to the idea of collaboration as a key factor in the development of autonomy (Quote 2.9).

Quote 2.9 Little on Vygotsky, group work and autonomy

The chief argument in favour of group work as a means of developing learner autonomy is Vygotskyan in origin: collaboration between two or more learners on a constructive task can only be achieved by externalizing, and thus making explicit, processes of analysis, planning and synthesis that remain largely internal, and perhaps also largely implicit, when the task is performed by a learner working alone.

Little (1996: 214)

Biography 2.7 Lev Vygotsky

Lev Vygotsky (1896–1934) is best known for his attempts to elaborate a Marxist psychology in collaboration with Leontiev and Luria. Following his death from tuberculosis at an early age, Vygotsky's theories were repudiated in Stalinist Russia and his major works were not translated into English until the 1960s. Vygotskyan theories of developmental psychology have recently acquired renewed importance in the fields of educational psychology and first and second language acquisition.

An element within Vygotsky's thought that has yet to be fully explored in the context of autonomy in language learning is the notion of self-directive inner speech. According to Rohrkemper (1989: 145–6):

After repeated exposure to word meanings by *other persons* in their social/ instructional environments, children subsequently become able to expose

> *themselves* to word meanings and thereby direct their own behaviour. . . . The developmental sequence of the two functions of language, communication with others and self-direction, is from social or *inter*personal to self-directive or *intra*personal. The implications of this progression are critical. Not only does language acquire two distinct functions, but the source of self-directive inner speech is the social environment.

From a Vygotskyan perspective, therefore, self-direction is a function of inner speech, which is both social in origin and mediated through language. The notion of inner speech may therefore help us to understand how reflection functions as a bridge between social interaction in learning and self-direction.

It should be acknowledged that in its early development, the theory of autonomy in language learning lacked strong support from within the psychology of learning for the efficacy of its claims concerning the value of self-directed learning. The influence of constructivist theory has been relatively recent and has entered the field of autonomy primarily through the work of David Little. The key idea that autonomy in language learning has borrowed from constructivism is the idea that effective learning is 'active' learning. According to Wang and Peverly (1986: 353):

> Effective learners are characterised in the research literature as being cognitively and affectively active in the learning process. They are seen as being capable of learning independently and deliberately through identification, formulation and restructuring of goals; use of strategy planning; development and execution of plans; and engagement of self-monitoring.

If learning is a matter of the construction of knowledge, effective learners must be cognitively capable of performing actions that enable them to take control of their learning. Similarly, the capacity to manage one's own learning activities must be grounded in certain cognitive capacities intrinsic to the process of learning. The importance of this hypothesis to the theory of autonomy is evidenced in Little's (1994b: 431) claim that 'all genuinely successful learning is in the end autonomous'.

2.3.2 Self-regulated learning

Self-regulation is a term used by a loosely affiliated group of North American educational psychologists whose work has been published in several collections by Dale Schunk and Barry Zimmerman (Schunk and Zimmerman, 1994, 1998; Zimmerman and Schunk, 1989). These

> **Quote 2.10** Zimmerman on self-regulation
>
> There are many biographies of inspiring figures, such as Benjamin Franklin, Abraham Lincoln, and George Washington Carver, who despite humble origins and limited access to high-quality instruction, educated themselves through reading, studying, and self-disciplined practice. Contemporary accounts of less famous but similarly dedicated learners continue to reveal the benefits of academic self-regulation, such as recent immigrant groups from Indochina... These Asian youngsters have succeeded academically despite many disadvantages, such as a lack of fluency in English, poorly educated parents, and attending inner city schools with few resources and large numbers of low-achieving classmates. Self-regulated learners, whether historic or contemporary, are distinguished by their view of academic learning as something they do for themselves rather than as something that is done to or for them.
>
> Zimmerman (1998: 1)

researchers are particularly interested in the social, psychological and behavourial characteristics that contribute to academic success, especially among socially and educationally disadvantaged students (Quote 2.10). Zimmerman (1998) defines self-regulation as 'the self-directive process through which learners transform their mental abilities into academic skills'. Research on self-regulated learning has been conducted from a range of perspectives within the constructivist tradition, with a particular emphasis on cognitive aspects of school learning.

Zimmerman (1998) has identified processes associated with self-regulation within learning cycles consisting of three phases: forethought, performance or volitional control and self-reflection. He argues that all learners try to self-regulate their learning, but some are more successful than others. He also observes that self-regulation is unlikely to be the outcome of formal instruction and that the two most important factors in its development appear to be the influence of adults and peers and rehearsal and practice. Optimal self-regulatory development, according to Zimmerman, 'appears to take root in socially supportive environments that provide extensive opportunities for self-directed practice' (p. 11).

The concept of self-regulation is somewhat narrower than the concept of autonomy and it has exercised a stronger influence on North American research on learning strategies than it has on the theory of autonomy. However, the literature on self-regulation is a potentially rich source of insights into the cognitive aspects of control over learning which deserves to be explored more fully in the literature on autonomy in language learning. It is also a source of interesting insights on the role of family, teacher and peer support in the development of autonomy (Strage, 1998).

2.3.3   Self-organised Learning

Strongly influenced by the work of George Kelly, psychologists Sheila Harri-Augstein and Laurie Thomas (1991) have developed an approach to the development of self-organised learning known as the 'learning conversation'. Their methodology depends upon a battery of training instruments and techniques that have been used in numerous workshops in the professional and educational fields. Among those acknowledged for their participation in these workshops is Philip Riley of CRAPEL for his 'keen interest in "Learning Conversations" as a method for adults learning a foreign language'.

Harri-Augstein and Thomas (1991: 27) define self-organised learning as 'the conversational construction, reconstruction and exchange of personally significant, relevant and viable meanings with awareness and controlled purposiveness'. The learning conversation is essentially a structured approach to training built around reflection on learning experiences (Quote 2.11). It is designed to enable learners to work out their own theories about themselves as learners and act as their own 'personal scientists' in testing and revising them. According to Harri-

---

Quote 2.11   Harri-Augstein and Thomas on learning conversations

Personally significant and valued learning through experience is not imposed by Skinnerian conditioning, nor is it achieved by inventing any reality we choose. It is achieved by exercising the *freedom to learn in 'conversational encounters' which are valued by using criteria which arise from within the experience itself.* Thus, we do not necessarily learn from life's experiences, only through awareness, reflection and review of such encounters from within a conscious system of personal beliefs, values, needs and purposes. This is a highly skilled activity. Each of our clients, including ourselves, came to value these learning experiences more fully after being 'talked back' through the experience and then systematically helped to reflect upon it.

Harri-Augstein and Thomas (1991: 9)

Augstein and Thomas, the learning conversation 'enables the learner to challenge his or her personal myths about themselves as learner and to convert these into a viable, systematically validated set of myths that warrant the title "personal theory"' (p. 27).

Perhaps the most important contribution of the learning conversation approach to the theory of autonomy in language learning has been a recognition that the cognitive and affective processes by which learners move towards autonomy are both complex and difficult. Citing Thomas and Harri-Augstein (1990), Little (1991: 21) notes that 'the crucial trigger to total self-organization in learning' occurs at a stage of reflection at which the focus of attention shifts to the process of learning itself. Thomas and Harri-Augstein observe that most learners find it difficult to attain this stage on their own without professional assistance. This suggests that autonomy in language learning is unlikely to develop simply through the practice of self-directed learning in the absence of dialogue and the skilled assistance of teachers.

2.4 Political philosophy

The idea of autonomy is not confined to the field of education or learning. It can be traced back to ideas of personal autonomy in contemporary western political philosophy and it could be argued that our present understanding of the importance of autonomy in language learning is ultimately grounded in the belief that personal autonomy is somehow important to our existence as social beings (Quote 2.12 overleaf). As Crabbe (1993: 443) argues, the ideological argument for autonomy in language learning is simply that 'the individual has the right to be free to exercise his or her own choices, in learning as in other areas, and not become a victim (even an unwitting one) of choices made by social institutions'.

The concept of personal autonomy derives from the political sense of the word, which originally described the condition of cities in Ancient Greece in which citizens were governed according to their own laws rather than those of a conquering power. By analogy, the term came to be applied to individuals who were in command of themselves and not subject to the authority of others. The educational philosopher Gibbs (1979) distinguishes between approaches to autonomy that emphasise its intellectual dimensions and those that emphasise its moral dimensions. From an intellectual perspective, autonomy is equated with critical

> **Quote 2.12** Raz on personal autonomy
>
> Autonomy is not the natural state that individuals are in when left to exercise free choice. The ideal of individual autonomy is actually a strong theory of the good – that the good life is one in which individuals are the authors of their own lives. Autonomy is socially defined in that the goals, preferences, and values of individuals, in sum the meanings of individual activities, are derived from the shared social matrix. Meaningful autonomy requires the existence of various social goods which the State has the duty to provide and which the citizens have duties to provide to one another.
>
> Raz (1986: 83)

intelligence, independence of thought and judgement, discernment and readiness to think things out for oneself. From a moral perspective, autonomy involves self-mastery and self-discipline. Crittenden (1978: 108) also identifies a third dimension, emotional autonomy, which 'implies not simply that a person would exercise self-mastery in the face of strong emotional involvement, but that he or she would remain emotionally detached in relationships with other persons and things'.

Within contemporary liberal-humanist philosophy, personal autonomy tends to be valued for its intrinsic worth. According to Raz (1986: 369), autonomy 'transcends the conceptual point that personal well-being is partly determined by success in willingly endorsed pursuits and holds the free choice of goals and relations as an essential ingredient of individual well-being'. People value personal autonomy for its own sake and, for this reason, it is not simply instrumental in the achievement of well-being, but an aspect of well-being deserving of protection in its own right. Similarly, according to Young (1986: 81), 'in exercising autonomy, we shape our own lives, an engagement valuable in itself'. Without autonomy our lives are less than human. For many philosophers, the protection of personal autonomy is the fundamental basis of human rights.

Much of the philosophical debate over the concept of personal autonomy concerns the nature of legitimate constraints upon freedom of action. According to Young (1986: 1), the political sense of autonomy is relevant to its personal sense:

The autonomous person (like the autonomous state) must not be subject to external interference or control but must, rather, freely direct the course of his or her own life.

From a libertarian point of view, personal autonomy consists purely in the absence of constraints since individuals are held to know best where their own and others' best interests lie. However, from the liberal-humanist point of view, constraints on freedom of action are justified when the exercise of one person's freedom inhibits the exercise of another's.

Constraints on freedom of action may also be justified in the individual's own interests because, according to Young (1986: 8):

> ... it is necessary to distinguish the *occurrent* sense of autonomy, the sense intended when we talk of people acting autonomously in particular situations, from a further deployment of the term to which we resort when we wish to make a more comprehensive or *dispositional* claim about the overall course of a person's life.

Short-term freedom of choice may therefore justifiably be constrained by paternalist intervention if it can be shown that it will inhibit the individual's personal autonomy in the longer-term:

> To maximise autonomy over the course of a lifetime, dispositional autonomy must be preserved. If it is this conception of autonomy which we would seek to foster, then strong paternalist interventions will sometimes be needed. The strong paternalist may thereby be required to violate occurrent autonomy . . . [and] he will think such forfeitures worthwhile because they succour dispositional autonomy. (p. 76)

In its liberal-humanist form, the concept of autonomy is thus one that is grounded both in the freedom of the individual and in the necessity for legitimate constraints on that freedom.

From a critical philosophical perspective, most notably represented in the field of education in the work of Freire, this conception of autonomy can, however, be challenged on the grounds that it involves a philosophical dualism in which individuals are counterposed to the communities of which they are members. In the liberal-humanist view, personal autonomy is a matter of concern to the individual rather than the community as a whole and the community charged with the task of imposing constraints on personal autonomy is conceptualised independently of the individuals of which it is composed. The problem of autonomy is thus reduced to a problem of determining the *degree* of freedom allowable to individuals within the overall constraints demanded by a liberal society. A critical view of personal autonomy and its constraints, on the other hand, would view the individual as a social being whose participation in the collective decisions affecting his or her life is legitimately constrained only by the conditions of the decision-making process itself. In other words, autonomy is to be understood not only as the authoring of the individual's life, but also as the authoring of the social realities that constitute our collective lives.

Philosophical debates on the nature of personal autonomy are highly relevant to the theory of autonomy in learning in several ways. To the extent that we must learn to be autonomous, it could well be argued that autonomy in learning is the foundation of personal autonomy. Similarly, to the extent that personal autonomy is the foundation of human rights, it could be argued that educators have a responsibility to provide learners with educational experiences that help them to develop their autonomy. It is also evident, however, that autonomy in learning does not imply absolute freedom in learning. Indeed, liberal-humanist conceptions of personal autonomy offer relatively weak support to the argument for freedom in learning, if it is allowed that educational systems may legitimately constrain individuals to acquire socially needed knowledge and skills or that freedom in learning may be constrained on the grounds that learners are incompetent to determine their own long-term interests. Stronger support for freedom in learning is found in the critical conception of personal autonomy as the right to participate in the decisions that affect one's life and to transform the social realities in which those decisions are made.

In the context of language education, the more convincing arguments for autonomy are likely to be pedagogical rather than philosophical or political. Yet we should also recognise that pedagogical decisions in respect to autonomy are often based upon underlying philosophical and political assumptions. We may, for example, be more prepared to allow freedom of choice to adult learners than to young learners, even when we are convinced that both are equally likely to exercise that freedom 'irresponsibly'. Our decisions in each case are likely to be influenced less by pedagogical considerations than by our understanding of the relative status of adults and young people as human beings and the rights that are naturally accorded to them. In attempting to foster the exercise of autonomy on a day-to-day basis, we will often find ourselves constrained to violate it. As we do so, it may be that our decisions will be more satisfactory to ourselves and to our learners if the philosophical and political grounds on which they are based are made explicit.

Chapter 3

Defining and describing autonomy

Autonomy is usually defined as the capacity to take charge of, or responsibility for, one's own learning. If we wish to describe autonomy in language learning in more detail, therefore, we will need to say exactly what 'taking charge' or 'taking responsibility' means in the context of learning. In this book, I prefer to define autonomy as the capacity to take control of one's own learning, largely because the construct of 'control' appears to be more open to investigation than the constructs of 'charge' or 'responsibility'. It is assumed that it is neither necessary nor desirable to *define* autonomy more precisely than this, because control over learning may take a variety of forms in relation to different levels of the learning process. In other words, it is accepted that autonomy is a multidimensional capacity that will take different forms for different individuals, and even for the same individual in different contexts or at different times.

Little (1990: 7) argues that autonomy is not 'a single, easily describable behaviour' (Quote 3.1 overleaf). Nevertheless, it is important that we attempt to describe it for two reasons. Firstly, construct validity is an important precondition for effective research. In order for a construct such as autonomy to be researchable, it must be describable in terms of observable behaviours. Secondly, programmes or innovations designed to foster autonomy are likely to be more effective if they are based on a clear understanding of the behavioural changes they aim to foster. Put simply, whether we are concerned with research or with practice, it is important that we know and are able to state what we mean when we talk about autonomy. This is not to say, however, that we all should necessarily mean exactly the same thing. Autonomy may be recognised

> **Quote 3.1** Little on what autonomy is *not*
>
> - Autonomy is **not** a synonym for self-instruction; in other words, autonomy is **not** limited to learning without a teacher.
> - In the classroom context, autonomy does **not** entail an abdication of responsibility on the part of the teacher; it is **not** a matter of letting the learners get on with things as best they can.
> - On the other hand, autonomy is **not** something that teachers do to learners; that is, it is **not** another teaching method.
> - Autonomy is **not** a single, easily described behaviour.
> - Autonomy is **not** a steady state achieved by learners.
>
> Little (1990: 7)

in a variety of forms, but it is important that we are able to identify the form in which we choose to recognise it in the contexts of our own research and practice.

3.1   Levels of control

One of the earliest and most frequently cited definitions of autonomy is found in Holec's (1981: 3) report to the Council of Europe, where autonomy is described as 'the ability to take charge of one's own learning'. Holec elaborates on this basic definition as follows:

> *To take charge of one's own learning* is to have, and to hold, the responsibility for all the decisions concerning all aspects of this learning, i.e.:
>
> - determining the objectives;
> - defining the contents and progressions;
> - selecting methods and techniques to be used;
> - monitoring the procedure of acquisition properly speaking (rhythm, time, place, etc.)
> - evaluating what has been acquired.
>
> The autonomous learner is himself capable of making all these decisions concerning the learning with which he is or wishes to be involved.

In this definition, taking charge of one's own learning is described in terms of the capacity to make decisions at successive stages of the learning process. The autonomous learner is able to direct the course of his own learning by making all the significant decisions concerning its management and organisation.

Holec's definition adequately covers the main areas of the learning process in which one might expect the autonomous learner to exercise control. The definition is problematic, however, in that it describes the decision-making abilities involved in autonomous learning in largely technical terms, leaving open the nature of the cognitive capacities underlying effective self-management of learning. Although it is clear that Holec is aware of cognitive factors involved in the development of autonomy (e.g. Holec, 1985a), his definition does not make them explicit. In contrast, Little (1991: 3) argues that 'autonomy is not exclusively or even primarily a matter of how learning is organized':

> Essentially, autonomy is a *capacity* – for detachment, critical reflection, decision-making, and independent action. It presupposes, but also entails, that the learner will develop a particular kind of psychological relation to the process and content of his learning. The capacity for autonomy will be displayed both in the way the learner learns and in the way he or she transfers what has been learned to wider contexts.
>
> (Little, 1991: 4)

In this definition, the capacity to take responsibility for one's own learning is described more in terms of control over the cognitive processes involved in effective self-management of learning. Little's definition is complementary to Holec's, but adds a vital psychological dimension that is often absent in definitions of autonomy.

Holec's and Little's definitions cover two aspects of the nature of autonomy as an individual capacity, but both tend to underplay a third vital element in autonomous learning: that the content of learning should be freely determined by the learners. Control over learning content has a situational aspect. Autonomous learners should, in principle, have the freedom to determine their own goals and purposes if the learning is to be genuinely self-directed. It also has a social aspect, which may involve control over learning situations and call for particular capacities concerned with the learner's ability to interact with others in the learning process. In an earlier paper (Benson, 1996: 33), I argued that control over learning necessarily involves actions that have social consequences:

> Greater learner control over the learning process, resources and language cannot be achieved by each individual acting alone according to his or her own preferences. Control is a question of collective decision-making rather than individual choice.

In approaching learner control in this way, I was concerned to emphasise the essentially political and transformative character of autonomy (evident, for example, in the writings of Dewey, Freire and Illich), which is often absent from definitions of autonomy in language learning focused on the individual capacities of the learner.

It should be emphasised that any *definition* of autonomy that attempts to cover every potential aspect of control over learning risks becoming too long for practical use. Indeed, we might well accept a simple definition of autonomy as the capacity to take control of one's learning as one that establishes a space in which differences of emphasis can co-exist. However, it can also be argued that an adequate *description* of autonomy in language learning should at least recognise the importance of three levels at which learner control may be exercised: learning management, cognitive processes and learning content (Figure 3.1).

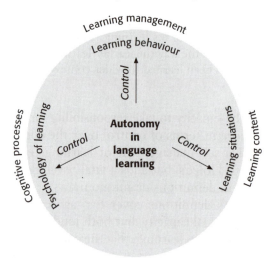

Figure 3.1   **Defining autonomy: the capacity to take control over learning**

These three levels of control are clearly interdependent. Effective learning management depends upon control of the cognitive processes involved in learning, while control of cognitive processes necessarily has consequences for the self-management of learning. Autonomy also implies that self-management and control over cognitive processes should involve decisions concerning the content of learning. As we will see throughout this book, however, researchers and practitioners often attach more importance to one level of control than others, and for this reason it can be helpful to consider each dimension separately.

3.2 Measuring autonomy

If we are able to define autonomy and describe it in terms of various aspects of control over learning, we should also in principle be able to measure the extent to which learners are autonomous. As Nunan (1997: 92) suggests, autonomy is not an 'all-or-nothing concept' but a matter of degree, and throughout the literature on autonomy we find writers referring to learners 'acquiring autonomy' or 'becoming more autonomous'. For the purposes of research and the evaluation of practice, it would indeed be convenient if we had a reliable method of measuring degrees of autonomy. Such a measure might also allow us to identify developmental processes in the acquisition of autonomy. In practice, however, the measurement of autonomy is problematic for a number of reasons.

Perhaps the most important factor influencing the possibility of measuring degrees of autonomy is the fact that autonomy is clearly a multidimensional construct. Although we may be able to identify and list behaviours that demonstrate control over learning and hypothesise certain relationships among them, we have little evidence to suggest that autonomy consists of any particular combination of these behaviours. On the contrary, it appears that autonomy can be recognised in a variety of forms. As Little (1991: 4) argues:

> It is true, of course, that we recognize autonomous learners by their behaviour; but that can take numerous different forms, depending on their age, how far they have progressed with their learning, what they perceive their immediate learning needs to be, and so on. Autonomy, in other words, can manifest itself in very different ways.

In general, we may well be able to observe whether learners display a greater degree of control in particular aspects of their learning. For example, we may be able to say that they are more able to self-assess their learning, to reflect upon the value of their learning activities or to design their own learning programmes. We could also hypothesise that learners who are able to control more of these aspects of their learning, more systematically and more effectively in terms of their personal goals, are more autonomous. However, in doing so it is important that we take account of the learning context and its influence on the possibility and relevance of control.

A second problem in the measurement of autonomy, however, concerns the nature of the construct itself. According to Holec, autonomy is a capacity and the possession of a capacity does not necessarily imply

> **Quote 3.2** Holec on autonomy as a capacity
>
> To say of a learner that he is autonomous is therefore to say that he is capable of taking charge of his own learning and nothing more: all the practical decisions he is going to make regarding his learning can be related to this capacity he possesses but must be distinguished from it.
>
> Holec (1981: 3)

that it will be exercised (Quote 3.2). Autonomous learners know how to direct their own learning, but this does not necessarily mean that they will put this knowledge into practice:

> Knowing how to learn in this way naturally confers the POWER to carry out learning under conditions of total responsibility and total independence; it is indeed a vital pre-condition for this. But it does not automatically entail this type of learning: just as the ability to drive a motor vehicle does not necessarily mean that whenever one gets into a car one is obliged to take the wheel, similarly the autonomous learner is not automatically obliged to self-direct his learning either totally or even partially. The learner will make use of his ability to do this only if he so *wishes* and if he is *permitted* to do so by the material, social and psychological constraints to which he is subjected.
>
> (Holec, 1988: 8)

In applied linguistic research more generally, ability is measured indirectly through performance. For example, learners' ability to write in a foreign language will be measured through their performance in a writing task. Although the relationship between ability and performance is always problematic, it will usually be assumed that the learners will demonstrate their ability in task performance. In the case of autonomy, however, it is hardly reasonable to give the learners a 'test'. As Breen and Mann (1997: 141) point out:

> Learners will generally seek to please me as the teacher. If I ask them to manifest behaviours that they think I perceive as the exercise of autonomy, they will gradually discover what these behaviours are and will subsequently reveal them back to me. Put simply, learners will give up their autonomy to put on the mask of autonomous behaviour.

Put somewhat differently, the essence of genuinely autonomous behaviour is that it is self-initiated rather than generated in response to a task in which the observed behaviours are either explicitly or implicitly required.

An alternative method of assessing abilities in applied linguistic research is to observe performance in natural contexts of learning. Although this is perhaps the best way to observe and measure degrees of control over various aspects of learning, again problems arise due to the importance of factors of willingness and opportunity. In contrast to Holec, Littlewood (1996: 428) argues that autonomy as a capacity involves two components, ability and willingness. Willingness 'depends on having both the *motivation* and the *confidence* to take responsibility for the choices required'. In this sense, willingness and ability are interdependent since 'the more knowledge and skills the students possess, the more confident they are likely to feel when asked to perform independently; the more confident they feel, the more they are likely to be able to mobilise their knowledge and skills in order to perform effectively; and so on'. Similarly willingness cannot be considered independently of opportunity. If the institutional context of learning or the immediate demands of the learning task do not value or reward autonomous behaviour, it is likely that the learners will be reluctant to exercise whatever capacities for autonomy they have. In general, therefore, we might say that the exercise of control in natural contexts of learning is likely to constitute positive evidence of autonomy. On the other hand, the absence of autonomous behaviour can rarely be taken as reliable evidence for the absence of autonomy as a capacity.

A third factor affecting our ability to measure degrees of autonomy concerns the nature of the acquisition of autonomy as a developmental process. At present, we know very little about the stages that learners go through in developing their autonomy in different contexts of learning other than that the process is highly variable and uneven. As Little (1991: 5) argues:

> The fact is that autonomy is likely to be hard-won and its permanence cannot be guaranteed; and the learner who displays a high degree of autonomy in one area may be non-autonomous in another.

In particular, we know that that the capacity to control an aspect of learning in one domain of learning is not readily transferred to others. Since the exercise of control over certain aspects of learning appears to be influenced by subject matter competence, lack of competence in a new domain may be one factor influencing transfer. In this context it is worth noting that almost all language learners have experience of learning to speak their own first language, a task that requires a considerable degree of autonomy. Many learners will also have exercised autonomy in non-institutional learning tasks such as learning to use a computer, learning to play the guitar or learning to cook. The problem of developing autonomy in the context of second language acquisition, therefore, is often one of transferring abilities that students have already acquired in other domains.

We also know that the acquisition of autonomy in institutional contexts is rarely a smooth process. Little (1991: 21) observes:

> Indeed, it is a common experience that attempts to make learners conscious of the demands of a learning task and the techniques with which they might approach it, lead in the first instance to disorientation and a sense that learning has become less rather than more purposeful and efficient. However, when the process is successful, it brings rich rewards.

Similarly, Breen and Mann (1997: 143) comment that in situations where learners have been socialised into relations of dependency, autonomy may initially manifest itself in 'individualistic and non-co-operative or competitive ways of being'. This may, however, be a necessary intervening step towards the fuller realisation of autonomy. Because autonomy calls for a fundamental reconceptualisation of the learner's role in the learning process, a smooth developmental process is not to be expected. It may therefore be that any developmental model for the acquisition of autonomy, if such a model is possible, should take account of the need for phases of uncertainty or confusion and for reversals as well as sudden leaps forward. If this is the case, a snapshot of the learner's performance at any given moment in time may give a misleading picture of his true abilities.

Much that has been said about the measurement of autonomy here applies equally to the measurement of other constructs in applied linguistic research, and the fact that measurement of autonomy is problematic does not necessarily mean that we should not attempt to measure it. If we aim to help learners to become more autonomous, we should at least have some way of judging whether we have been successful or not. At the same time we need to be aware of potential pitfalls. In Sections I and II of this book, which deal with the effectiveness of various methods of fostering autonomy and with the possibilities for action research, I will again refer to problems in the measurement of autonomy. For the moment it will be noted that the description of specific levels of control over learning is a far easier task than the description or measurement of autonomy in general. Consequently, it is important that research and practice in the field are grounded in an adequate description of the potential behaviours involved in autonomous learning.

3.3 Autonomy and culture

Quote 3.3 Riley's questions on autonomy and culture

- Are the principles and practice on which 'autonomous' and 'self-directed' learning schemes are based *ethnocentric*?
- Are there any ethnic or social groups whose cultural background pre-disposes them for or against such approaches?

Riley (1988: 13)

If we accept that autonomy takes different forms for different individuals, and even for the same individual in different contexts of learning, we may also need to accept that its manifestations will vary according to cultural context. However, the argument concerning autonomy and culture goes somewhat deeper than this to the point where we may also wish to consider whether a concept that is largely grounded in European discourses on philosophy, psychology and education is relevant to non-European contexts at all. Although the idea of autonomy is often located at the margins of these discourses, the basic idea behind it – that individuals have the right to author and control their own lives – may be one that has greater resonance in western than in non-western cultures. Similarly, narrower definitions of autonomy and the practices associated with it that have grown up in European educational institutions may be entirely inappropriate elsewhere in the world.

Concerns about the cultural appropriateness of the idea of autonomy in language learning were first raised by Riley (1988) at a time when discussion of the concept was largely confined to Europe (Quote 3.3). Riley's concerns were directed at the fate of non-European students in European educational institutions that adopted autonomy among their goals. In the 1990s, these concerns have gained a renewed importance as the idea of autonomy has spread around the world with much of the more recent discussion focusing on its relevance to Asian students. Jones (1995: 229), for example, has argued in the context of a self-access project in Cambodia, that 'to make autonomy an undiluted educational objective in a culture where it has no traditional place is to be guilty at least of cultural insensitivity'. Similarly, Ho and Crookall (1995: 237) have argued:

> Being autonomous often requires that students work independently of the teacher and this may entail shared decision making, as well as

presenting opinions that differ from those of the teacher. It is, thus, easy to see why Chinese students would not find autonomy very comfortable.

Doubts about the cultural appropriateness of the goal of autonomy for Asian students have been mainly based on a view of Asian cultures as collectivist and accepting of relations of power and authority (Littlewood, 1999). Littlewood is sceptical of the validity of these cultural stereotypes, but if the concept of autonomy enshrines values that are inimical to non-European cultures, its promotion in non-European settings could be regarded as a form of cultural imperialism.

One of the strongest arguments against this view states that the fundamental ideas of autonomy are in fact shared by diverse cultures. Kirtikara (1997), for example, argues that traditional rural learning in Thailand was autonomous and that some of the most noted Thai scholars were largely self-educated. It was only with the introduction of western-style education in urban centres a century ago that the tradition of autonomous learning began to disappear. Similarly, Pierson (1996) has shown that ideas of autonomy and self-education have a strong tradition within Chinese scholarship (Quote 3.4). He points out that research has painted a picture of the typical Hong Kong learner as one who is 'passive, reticent and reluctant to openly challenge authority' (p. 51). But these characteristics are, he argues, as much a product of 'the structure of the present colonial education system with its excessive workloads, centralized

---

Quote 3.4 Sung Dynasty advocates of autonomy

Pierson (1996) argues that learning attitudes in Hong Kong favouring teacher authority and rote learning are as much a legacy of colonial education policies as they are of Chinese cultural values. He cites two Sung Dynasty scholars in support of the contention that the idea of autonomy in learning has roots in Chinese thought:

The youth who is bright and memorizes a large amount of information is not to be admired; but he who thinks carefully and searches for truth diligently is to be admired.

Lu Tung-lai (1137–81)

If you are in doubt, think it out by yourself. Do not depend on others for explanations. Suppose there was no one you could ask, should you stop learning? If you could get rid of the habit of being dependent on others, you will make your advancement in your study.

Chu Hsi (1130–1200)

curricula, didactic and expository teaching styles, concentration on knowledge acquisition, examinations emphasizing reproductive know-ledge over genuine thinking, overcrowded classrooms, and inadequately trained teachers' as they are a product of Chinese culture (p. 55).

The notion that autonomy is inimical to Asian learning cultures is also called into question by the reported success of several programmes designed to promote it. To take one example, Yang (1998: 133), who has run a programme designed to promote autonomy among students at a Taiwanese university for four years, reports that 'the course raised students' awareness of language-learning strategies, improved students' use of strategies, taught students how to assess their own language proficiency, set goals, and evaluate progress, and enabled students to experience greater overall autonomy in learning'. Although programmes designed to foster autonomy vary in their effectiveness, there is no empir-ical evidence to suggest that non-European programmes are any less successful than their European counterparts or that the cultural back-ground of the learners is a significant factor in their effectiveness.

A third argument relates to the nature of culture itself. As Aoki and Smith (1999: 23) point out, 'arguments against the aspirations of people and/or for the political status quo in a particular context can easily be masked by stereotyping or arguments against cultural imperialism'. In both European and non-European settings, the idea of autonomy represents a challenge to cultural and educational tradition. The notion that cultural traits are fixed is itself inimical to the idea of autonomy, which implies that learning should be a process in which individuals contribute to the transformation of culture. Aoki and Smith (1999: 21) argue that,

> It is important to recognize that autonomy is not an approach enforcing a particular way of learning. It is, rather, an educational goal, as Holec (1981) explicitly states. Objections to autonomy based on students' cur-rent incapacity to learn in a wholly self-directed manner therefore lack validity in any context.

To the extent that education contributes to the development of culture, the promotion of autonomy can be seen as a culturally legitimate goal in the sense that autonomous learners are likely to be the most able to contribute to cultural development and transformation.

Lastly, the framing of the debate on culturally appropriate pedagogies in terms of national or ethnic stereotypes has been called into ques-tion by a number of writers, especially Holliday (1999). Holliday dis-tinguishes between 'large' and 'small' cultures and urges a 'small culture approach', which 'attempts to liberate "culture" from notions of ethnicity and nation and from the perceptual dangers they carry with them' (p. 237). For Holliday a small culture can be any cohesive social group- ing and the small culture paradigm serves as a framework within which to investigate the specific behaviours of the group, which have no neces- sary subordination to larger cultural patterns or stereotypes. Press (1996), in her study of cultural influences on student responses to autonomy, also stresses the importance of assessing the degree of students' attach- ment to their broader cultural identities (see 16.1, case study). In the field of autonomy, the small cultures paradigm has a parallel in Crabbe's (1993: 444) focus on the issue of whether 'minute-by-minute classroom practice *fosters* or discourages autonomy'. A culturally appropriate approach to autonomy might well be one that focuses less on the 'grand theory' of autonomy and more on the negotiation of practice among teachers, administrators and learners within the specific situation of each educational institution.

In spite of these arguments the fact remains that the concept of autonomy in language learning has been articulated largely within the framework of European cultural discourses. It would be an oversim- plification, however, to suggest that the spread of the idea of autonomy in language learning represents just one more example of culturally inappropriate pedagogy. Often autonomy serves as a convenient start- ing point for local educators concerned to reform education systems that they perceive to be authoritarian and outdated. At the same time, the extent to which the spread of the concept of autonomy has been encouraged by western educators working in non-western contexts may need to be acknowledged. In broad terms, autonomy in learning and in life may well be a universal aspiration. The risk of cultural inappropriateness arises, however, when this aspiration is articulated in terms of discourses that are specific to a particular culture, such that in order to 'buy in' to the idea of autonomy, one also has to buy in to associated values that are perhaps alien to one's own.

Those who are committed to autonomy as an educational goal are naturally inclined to promote it as a goal that others should follow. But if the goal of autonomy and the practices associated with it are too rigidly defined, cultural insensitivity may be the consequence. As in the case of the measurement of autonomy, it is important that researchers and practitioners are aware of the specific behavioural changes aimed at in the fostering of autonomy and the specific contexts of learning in which they are to be applied. Again, this underlines the importance of an adequate description of the potential behavioural components of autonomous learning.

Chapter 4

Control as a natural attribute of learning

For many of its advocates, autonomy is a natural attribute of the learning process. Thomson (1996), for example, argues that we are born self-directed learners. As young children, we take control over the learning of our mother tongue, but as learning becomes more complex and is channelled through the institution of the school, we appear to give up much of our autonomy. When we learn foreign languages as teenagers or adults, we seem to find self-directed learning difficult and even show a preference for direction by teachers and learning materials. The idea that autonomy is the natural state of learning, suppressed by institutionalised education, is characteristic of thinkers such as Rousseau and Illich. Many researchers on autonomy would argue, however, that the learning tasks prescribed by modern education systems (literacy in particular) require a higher degree of autonomy that must be acquired in the course of institutionalised learning. Nevertheless, there is considerable evidence that learners exercise control over their learning even in relation to these more complex tasks within the context of learning institutions.

Evidence that learners have a natural tendency to take control of various aspects of their learning in both non-institutional and institutional contexts is important to the theory of autonomy for two main reasons. Firstly, the validity of the concept of autonomy depends in part on the fact that it is grounded in observable behaviours. In other words, if autonomy is not to be an abstract ideal, it must be built upon generalisation of capacities that learners can and do exercise. Secondly, if autonomy is not to be a goal available only to exceptional learners, we need to be able to show that the behaviours on which it is grounded are natural behaviours observable in ordinary contexts of learning. In short, evidence of control in the normal course of learning suggests that autonomy can be developed on the basis of capacities that most, if not all, learners already possess and exercise to some degree.

The kinds of evidence that we are concerned with can be found in research concerned with three hypotheses:

- Learners routinely initiate and manage their own learning both outside and within the context of formal instruction.
- Learners receiving formal instruction tend to follow their own learning agendas rather than those of their teachers.
- Learners tend to exercise control over psychological factors influencing their learning, especially those concerned with motivation, affective state and beliefs or preferences.

The evidence found in these areas of research often reveals that learner control is 'episodic', 'private' to the learner and possibly 'ineffective' in terms of the learner's goals (Dickinson, 1997). Evidence of such behaviour does not, therefore, constitute evidence that learners are naturally autonomous, if autonomy is understood as a systematic capacity for effective control over learning. It does, however, suggest that the seeds of autonomy can be found in behaviours that are independent of any formal efforts by teachers to encourage them.

4.1 Self-management in learning

Research on self-directed learning began in the early 1960s with empirical studies of the ways in which adults go about learning in their everyday lives. In the best known of these studies, Tough (1971) interviewed 66 adults about their 'learning projects' and found that, although the number of projects varied according to the subject's occupation, the typical adult reported being involved in around eight different learning projects in the year leading up to the interview. Of these projects, 68% were planned by the individuals themselves. Tough also found that adults often studied in self-organized 'autonomous learning groups' (Quote 4.1). The finding that adults regularly initiate and plan their own learning projects has been confirmed by numerous replication studies conducted in North America and elsewhere in the world. These studies provide us with basic evidence that individuals from a wide range

> **Quote 4.1** Tough on autonomous learning groups
>
> In some small and medium-sized groups that meet frequently, the members themselves plan the group learning sessions. The entire group, or a small committee or even a single member selected by the group, is responsible for planning each session. Instead of relying on an outsider or a set of materials to guide its learning, the group itself accepts the responsibility for planning.... The range and diversity of autonomous learning groups is surprising. Many bible study groups, investment clubs, current affairs groups, Alcoholics Anonymous chapters, book review clubs, local consumer associations, literary and philosophical groups, local historical societies, science clubs, conservation and nature groups, and rock-collecting clubs could be included. Groups are also formed to learn about cross-country motor-cycle riding, collecting buttons, and casting soldiers.... Autonomous learning groups exist for almost all ages. In our exploratory interviewing in Toronto, for example, we found a naturalist club of 12-year-old boys in which each boy had an area of specialty (birds, astronomy, or whatever). At the other end of the age scale was an 85-year-old woman responsible for a weekly meeting of about 10 women to hear speakers on the United Nations and other international topics.
>
> Tough (1971: 143–5)

of social and cultural backgrounds can and do initiate and direct their own learning as part of the normal course of their lives.

Although learning foreign languages does not appear among the learning projects identified in Tough's (1971) survey we know that adults often do learn foreign languages under their own direction, with varying degrees of success. Jones (1998), for example, identified 70 self-instructed learners registered at a foreign language study lab at the University of Newcastle in the United Kingdom. His study suggested that self-instruction from beginner level was associated with high drop-out rates and low proficiency. Nevertheless, the fact that adults frequently attempt to teach themselves foreign languages is evidence that they are prepared to initiate and direct their own language learning.

In contrast to many of the learning projects identified in adult-learning studies, acquiring proficiency in a foreign language is a relatively complex long-term achievement that is unlikely to be realised through self-instruction alone. However, there is some evidence that most language-learning careers include phases of self-instruction. Many language learners also create naturalistic learning situations for

---

Concept 4.1   Self-instruction, self-directed naturalistic learning and out-of-class learning

Jones (1998: 378) defines *self-instruction* as 'a deliberate long-term learning project instigated, planned, and carried out by the learner alone, without teacher intervention'. In this strong sense, self-instruction often implies that the learner studies alone, with little or no contact with teachers or speakers of the target language.

Self-instruction can also be understood as any deliberate effort by the learner to acquire or master language content or skills. In this weaker sense, self-instruction is episodic, and may take place inside or outside the classroom (Dickinson, 1987: 5). When researchers argue that autonomy is not a synonym of self-instruction (e.g. Little, 1990; Riley, 1986), they are generally referring to the stronger sense of the term: long-term self-initiated learning in isolation from teachers and other learners. Autonomy does, however, imply the ability to engage in self-instruction in the weaker, episodic sense.

Naturalistic language learning occurs through direct communication with users of the target language. The term is usually used for situations where the learner is living with members of the target language community and learns mainly through spoken interaction, although it could also be extended to situations in which learning takes place mainly through interaction with target language texts. The difference between naturalistic learning and self-instruction is the degree of deliberate intention to acquire language content or skills at the time of the learning event itself. Learners may also create naturalistic learning situations for themselves with the advance intention of learning the language, although at the time of the learning event, the focus of attention is on communication or on learning something other than the language itself. For situations of this kind, I use the term *self-directed naturalistic learning*.

Out-of-class learning refers to any kind of learning that takes place outside the classroom and involves self-instruction, naturalistic learning or self-directed naturalistic learning. Most language learning research to date has focused on the classroom and the study of out-of-class learning is a relatively new area of research with considerable implications for the theory of autonomy.

---

themselves and reflect upon them as language-learning experiences – a process that can be called 'self-directed naturalistic learning' (Concept 4.1). Often these phases run concurrently with classroom learning. Schmidt and Frota's (1986) longitudinal study of Schmidt's learning of Portuguese, for example, illustrates how these three modes of learning interacted during the subject's residence in Brazil. Many language-learning programmes, especially those that include periods of residence abroad, also assume that self-directed learning is essential to the development of proficiency (Coleman, 1997). Proficient adult language learners may also display self-directive attitudes towards formal instruction. For learners such as Schmidt, choosing to follow a course of formal instruction appears to be less a sign of dependency than a rational decision made within a plan of learning that is self-directed overall.

Language learners also appear to engage in self-instruction and self-directed naturalistic learning even when their learning is primarily classroom-based. Littlewood and Liu (1996), for example, surveyed Hong Kong secondary school and university students and found that they used a variety of out-of-class strategies to supplement their classroom learning. In a similar study of Hong Kong secondary students, Yap (1998) also found that students engaged in out-of-class learning irrespective of their proficiency levels and encouragement by their teachers (see 16.2, case study). In a study of 44 learners who had developed high levels of foreign language competence, Nunan (1989, 1991) found that virtually all the learners attributed their success in part to the activation of their language outside the classroom. Pickard's (1995) descriptive study used retrospective interviews and questionnaires to find out how proficient German learners of English studying at the University of Humberside used out-of-class learning in their schooldays. He found that the students generally had a wide repertoire of out-of-class strategies, that reading newspapers and novels and listening to the radio figured prominently among them, and that these out-of-class activities 'stem from the learners' own volition rather than from a teacher' (p. 37).

Studies of the role of formal instruction in second language acquisition also offer some evidence for the importance of self-direction in the acquisition of proficiency. Long (1983) reviewed 11 studies on the effectiveness of formal instruction and found that only six demonstrated that instruction was beneficial. Nunan (1995b) reviewed 13 studies and found that the evidence was inconclusive, while de Graaff (1997: 250) found that out of 20 studies published in the late 1980s and early 1990s, only nine showed 'a clear positive effect of some kind of explicit instruction'. One of the problems of drawing general conclusions from such studies, however, is that they often focus on learning under highly controlled conditions. De Graaff's own study, for example, claims to confirm the hypothesis that explicit instruction facilitates the acquisition of L2 grammar on the basis of tests conducted on students following a computer-controlled self-study course in an artificial language. As Nunan (1995b: 251) points out, the research instruments used in many of the studies on the effectiveness of instruction are 'relatively blunt' and leave open crucial questions about the nature of the instruction.

The idea that foreign language acquisition proceeds best through naturalistic learning is supported by the theoretical work of Krashen (1982), who argues that languages are acquired in order to be used only through exposure to comprehensible input under non-threatening conditions. Krashen also argues that speech emerges as a consequence of exposure and that production practice and formal instruction in the rules of the language do not help acquisition. Prabhu (1987: 1) argues similarly that 'the development of competence in a second language requires not systematisation of language inputs or maximisation of planned practice, but rather the creation of conditions in which learners engage in an effort to cope with communication'. Ellis (1994: 216), however, suggests that the empirical evidence for a strong version of the natural hypothesis is weak. In particular, longitudinal studies of migrants show that although learners can and do learn foreign languages without the benefit of instruction, they often fail to achieve a level of proficiency beyond that needed for their immediate communicative needs. The extent to which naturalistic language learning succeeds is, however, clearly influenced by factors such as the goals of the learners, their social status and the degree to which they are accepted by the target language community. Success is also likely to be influenced by the learner's capacity to create and take advantage of naturalistic learning situations.

In his review of research on the effectiveness of formal instruction, Ellis (1994: 617) observes that the most likely hypothesis is that foreign language acquisition proceeds most rapidly through a combination of instruction and exposure to the target language. The benefits of formal instruction appear to lie principally in increased accuracy and accelerated progress through natural developmental sequences. According to Ellis (1994: 657), however, research suggests that there is 'little, if any, support for the claim that classroom learners must have formal instruction in order to learn the L2' and 'that much of the language learning that takes place in the classroom takes place "naturally" as a result of learners processing input to which they are exposed'.

Research evidence from the field of adult learning suggests that learners routinely initiate and self-manage learning projects outside the context of formal education both individually and collaboratively. Learning in general is thus in no sense dependent on the management structures provided by educational institutions. Research from the field of language learning suggests that self-instruction is not an effective method of learning a language by itself. Perhaps this is because entirely self-instructed learners lack opportunities for collaboration and communication that are essential to second language acquisition. On the other hand, there is no strong evidence that formal instruction is either necessary or effective in language learning. Although the research evidence is by no means conclusive, it seems reasonable to conclude that most learners who achieve proficiency in a foreign language do so by employing a variety of modes of learning within which self-management of learning plays an important role. Even in the classroom, self-instructional processes appear to be at work. Irrespective of the evidence for the effectiveness of self-instruction, it is clear that learners who achieve proficiency in foreign languages tend to take some degree of control over the overall direction of their learning. Moreover, if high levels of proficiency cannot be achieved through formal instruction alone, it seems likely that they are to some extent dependent upon the capacity to initiate and manage one's own learning.

4.2   Learner agendas in the classroom

Further evidence for learner control as a natural attribute of learning comes from research on the relationship between learning and instruction in classroom settings, which suggests that even in the classroom, learners tend to follow their own agendas rather than those of their teachers (Quote 4.2). According to Block (1996), the idea of a mismatch between learning and instruction dates back to Corder (1967)

Quote 4.2 Nunan on learner agendas

I should like to argue that the principal reason for the mismatch between teachers and learners, which gives rise to a disparity between what is taught and what is learned, is that there is a mismatch between the pedagogical agenda of the teacher and that of the learner. While the teacher is busily teaching one thing, the learner is very often focusing on something else.

Nunan (1995b: 135)

and Dakin (1973: 16), who wrote of an 'inbuilt syllabus' and argued that 'though the teacher may control the experiences the learner is exposed to, it is the learner who selects what is learnt from them'. The idea that teachers should take account of learners' autonomous behaviour in the classroom was reiterated by Allwright (1984, 1988) and has been pursued by Breen (1987b) and Nunan (1995b). Empirical evidence of mismatches between learning and instruction in language classrooms is reported by Barkhuizen (1998), Block (1996), Breen (1991) and Slimani (1992).

In Breen's (1991) study, 106 graduate applied linguistics students were assigned roles of teacher, observer and learners in artificially constructed language lessons. At the end of each lesson the participants wrote about what had happened in the class. Breen found that there were considerable differences among participants' reports on the techniques used by the teacher to help learners with the new language. Slimani's (1992) study investigated what a group of 13 Algerian EFL learners claimed to have learned within an authentic programme of study. Focusing on 'uptake', or what learners claimed to have learned at the end of a lesson, Slimani asked participants to write down what they had learned after each of six lessons that she observed and recorded. She found that the learners were more likely to claim to have learned items initiated by themselves than items initiated by the teacher. She also found that they were more likely to claim to have learned items initiated by other learners than those initiated by themselves.

Block (1996) asked six MBA students and their teacher to keep oral diaries in their native languages during a series of English classes. The learners were asked in their diaries to respond to questions on the activities that stood out in class and their purpose, on what they had learned and on how the teacher had helped them to learn. Again, Block observed considerable variation among the accounts. He concluded that the rich data furnished by the oral diaries provided 'ample evidence that learners are constantly attempting to make sense out of classroom instruction' (p. 192). Barkhuizen (1998) also found significant differences between ESL learners' and teachers' perceptions of classroom activities in a South African high school and concluded that learners should play a greater part in the classroom decision-making process.

Studies of learners' and teachers' reports of classroom events provide evidence that learners tend not to respond directly to classroom instruction, but rather treat it as an experience to be interpreted. As such they furnish evidence of 'autonomy of learner thought' (Block, 1996:

168). Even when subject to direct instruction in classroom settings, therefore, learners appear to take some degree of control over their learning. The conclusion is likely to be related to Ellis's (1994: 657) hypothesis that much of the language learning that takes place in the classroom takes place 'naturally' as a result of learners processing input to which they are exposed. Although the teacher may provide much of the input, it is ultimately the learners who decide what is processed and learned.

To date, however, research does not clearly indicate how learner agendas work in the longer term, or how they relate the overall direction of learning. It appears that learner control of the cognitive processes involved in language learning is a crucial factor in what is learned. But it may be that the natural exercise of control of these processes is neither goal-oriented nor effective. Nevertheless, the research on learner agendas suggests that control over cognitive processes is a pervasive and perhaps universal attribute of the language-learning process. This hypothesis will be discussed further in 5.2.1, where the capacity to control attention is proposed as one of the basic psychological components of autonomy.

4.3   Control of psychological factors influencing learning

The ways in which individuals learn languages and the outcomes of their learning efforts are influenced by a variety of individual psychological variables (Concept 4.2 overleaf). Some of these variables, such as aptitude and personality, describe relatively stable conditions that are not readily amenable to change. This is also true of learning style, to the extent that it refers to factors such as a predisposition towards visual, auditory, kinaesthetic or tactile learning modalities (Reid, 1987) or field-dependence/independence (Chapelle and Green, 1992) rather than more general learning preferences. Other variables, such as motivation, affective state and beliefs, describe conditions that are dependent on context or experience and therefore more amenable to change. Although the research evidence is limited, there is good reason to believe that language learners can and do exercise some degree of control over these variables in attempting to overcome obstacles to their learning.

Concept 4.2   Individual learner differences

Ellis (1994: 469) makes a distinction between social factors influencing learning (such as class, sex and ethnicity) and individual learner differences, or 'factors that affect learners as *individuals* and that are psychological in nature'. Researchers are yet to agree on the classification of individual learner differences and there is often a degree of vagueness in the definition of terms. Nevertheless, there is general agreement that factors of aptitude, personality, learning style, motivation, affective state and belief are influential in learning.

Individual learner differences can be approached from two directions in the context of the theory and practice of autonomy. On the one hand, they can be treated as evidence that learners are *individuals* with different needs and preferences. Since learners are different, they should be allowed the freedom to learn in the ways that suit them best. On the other hand, they can be treated as factors that are open to change through reflection and training. Evidence that learners are able to recognise the disabling or enabling influence of certain individual variables and exercise control over them may be treated as further evidence for learner control as a natural attribute of learning.

Whether learners are able to exercise control over these variables depends in part on whether they are intrinsically stable or mutable. Ellis (1994: 472–3) suggests that individual variables form a continuum according to how mutable they are:

> For example, language aptitude is generally considered a stable factor, not readily influenced by the environment, . . . while certain types of motivation are likely to change as a result of the learner's learning experiences . . . The general factors also vary according to the extent of the learner's control over them. For example, learners can do nothing about their age, but they may be able to change their learning style.

To date, however, research does not provide conclusive evidence on the mutability of individual variables in learning, their interrelationships, or the role of experience, training and self-control in change. Learner control over individual variables in language learning is therefore an important research area for the theory of autonomy.

4.3.1   Controlling motivation

Further reading

Dörnyei, Z. (2000) *Teaching and Researching Motivation* (ALIA series).
Ushioda, E. (1996) *Learner Autonomy 5: The Role of Motivation*. Dublin: Authentik.

Research on motivation in language learning was for many years dominated by the integrative/instrumental paradigm established by Gardner and Lambert (1972), which argues that language learning motivation differs from general learning motivation in that it crucially involves attitudes towards the ethnolinguistic community associated with the target language. More recent research has drawn on cognitive theories of motivation in general learning. According to Dörnyei (1998: 118), cognitive approaches to motivation focus on 'the individual's thoughts and beliefs (and recently also emotions) that are transformed into action' rather than inner forces such as instinct, volition, will and physical energy. Within the cognitive approach to motivation, self-determination theory and attribution theory have been seen as particularly relevant to learner control.

Self-determination theory is based upon a distinction between intrinsic and extrinsic motivation. Learners who are intrinsically motivated carry out learning activities for the pleasure of learning, for the satisfaction of achievement or to experience stimulation (Vallerand, 1997). Extrinsically motivated learners carry out activities either for reasons other than interest in the activity or in learning in general (e.g. for external reward) or because they are subject to external or internalised pressures. In recent research, extrinsic motivation has also been viewed as a continuum from self-determined to controlled (Deci et al., 1991). It is argued that intrinsic motivation leads to more effective learning and that it is promoted by structures and events that are 'informational' rather than 'controlling' and by situations in which the learner is self-determined and the locus of control lies with the learner. According to Deci (1978: 198), 'intrinsic motivation implies self-direction'. By taking control over their learning, learners develop motivational patterns that lead to more effective learning.

Attribution theory is concerned with learners' perceptions of the reasons for success and failure in learning. Research designed to elicit learners' opinions on the reasons for success and failure in learning has revealed four major perceived causes: ability, task difficulty, effort and luck (Dickinson, 1995). The crucial factor in motivation is identified as the 'stability' of attributions for success or failure. Thus, according to Weiner (1984: 25):

> Success at academic tests and tasks attributed to stable factors such as high ability results in higher future expectancies than does success ascribed to unstable factors such as luck. In a similar manner, failure attributed to stable factors such as low aptitude results in lower future expectancies than does failure ascribed to unstable factors such as low effort.

There is also evidence that learners who attribute success to stable factors and failure to unstable causes are more likely to take on challenging tasks, to be positively motivated by success and to view intelligence as mutable (Dickinson, 1995). Weiner also reports research suggesting that learners' attributions for failure can be modified through informational feedback that suggests, for example, that failure may be due more to lack of effort or inappropriate strategies than to lack of ability. Dickinson (1995: 172) argues that attribution theory,

> . . . provides evidence to show that learners who believe that they have control over their learning – that by accepting new challenges they can increase their ability to perform learning tasks and so increase their intelligence – tend to be more successful than others.

Like self-determination theory, attribution theory makes a direct link between learner control and motivational thinking.

In the context of language learning, Ushioda (1996: 54) argues that, in the face of negative affective experiences, learners 'who know how to limit the motivational damage and take self-motivational initiatives will be at a considerable advantage'. Crookes and Schmidt (1991: 495) also argue that 'a number of strategies can be used to manipulate motivation, including the selection of appropriate goals and their periodic reevaluation, periodic review of learning situations, and so on'. Although the nature of these strategies and their relationship to motivation remain to be explored systematically, there is a good deal of anecdotal evidence in the literature that shows how language learners attempt to motivate themselves (see Quote 4.3).

The relationship between autonomy and motivation is a relatively new area of interest and the research to date is mainly theoretical. Self-determination theory and attribution theory appear to be the most likely frameworks within which this relationship will be developed. However, neither theory offers a comprehensive account of motivation in language learning, which is increasingly seen as a complex and multi-dimensional construct (Dörnyei, 1998; Williams and Burden, 1997). Moreover, research on motivation has been criticised for failing to take account of the social dimensions of language learning. Pierce (1995: 17), for example, prefers the term 'investment' to 'motivation' arguing that, 'if learners invest in a second language, they do so with the understanding that they will acquire a wider range of symbolic and material resources, which will in turn increase the value of their cultural capital'. The return on investment must be seen as commensurate with the effort expended on learning the second language. If this is the case, control

Quote 4.3 Ushioda on motivational thinking

Ushioda's study of autonomy and motivation includes a number of examples of students describing how they raise their motivation. The following example is from a student of French:

'I'm not always permanently well-motivated. I think when I feel that I just can't be bothered doing it, I just leave it. And then after that, it doesn't take very long for me to get involved again, because all I'd have to do would be watch the French news and listen to it. And really just start thinking about why I'm doing it and how much I like it. And say – oh well, you know, I really should go back to it and keep it up.'

Data of this kind, drawn from interviews or learner journals, can tell us a great deal about the ways in which learners go about influencing their motivation to learn.

Ushioda (1996: 54)

over motivation may crucially involve control over the content of language learning and the purposes to which it is put.

4.3.2   Controlling anxiety

Much of the research on language learning and affective state has focused on anxiety, which has been recognised as a key factor in successful language learning (Horwitz and Young, 1991; MacIntyre and Gardner, 1991). In a review of the literature, MacIntyre and Gardner (1991: 96) argue that 'studies have consistently shown that anxiety is one of the best predictors of success in the second language'. They also observe that the intimate relationship between self-concept and self-expression makes foreign language anxiety distinct from other anxieties and that students tend to report greater anxiety in foreign language classrooms than in other subjects. Horwitz et al. (1986) have proposed that foreign language anxiety should be considered a distinct process particular to second language acquisition and have divided it into three components: communication apprehension, test anxiety and fear of negative evaluation.

Research on foreign language anxiety has tended to focus on the classification of its forms and the effects of classroom environments, rather than on learners' own attempts to control their anxieties (Concept 4.3 overleaf). Research on learning strategies provides some evidence that

---

Concept 4.3   **Controlling anxiety**

In her PhD thesis on foreign language anxiety in Hong Kong secondary schools, Walker (1997) observes that anxieties connected with speaking English in the classroom tend to increase rather than diminish during students' secondary careers. High anxiety is associated with the students' feeling that they should speak accurately according to the requirements of the teacher rather than their own learning needs. In interviews, students reported a number of strategies for controlling their anxiety, including:

- telling oneself not to mind classmates laughter
- imagining oneself having a friendly chat with the class
- standing up slowly to signal that you need help
- telling a classmate that you feel afraid
- telling yourself that 'it won't take long'
- looking for support in the teacher's eye. (p. 124)

Environmental factors within the classroom may reduce the effectiveness of such strategies, however, and Walker's main conclusion is that teachers should provide environmental, emotional and linguistic support. Interview data can be an important source of data on strategies for controlling anxiety, a relatively unexplored area in research, but Walker's study also shows that data on strategies must be interpreted in the context of environmental factors influencing their effectiveness.

---

successful language learners do take measures to control their anxieties (e.g. Naiman et al., 1978) and, in her research on learner beliefs, Wenden (1986b) has shown that learners can and do analyse their own feelings and attitudes about their language learning. Oxford (1990: 140) has argued that 'good language learners are often those who know how to control their emotions and attitudes about learning' by using affective strategies such as lowering anxiety, encouraging themselves and 'taking their emotional temperatures'. As in the case of motivation, there is considerable anecdotal evidence in the literature that learners do employ such strategies, but the empirical research base on learner control of affective factors influencing their learning is not strong. In particular, there remains much to be learned about the ways in which learners go about dealing with foreign language anxiety in everyday contexts of learning.

4.3.3   Controlling beliefs and preferences

Further reading

Wenden, A. (ed.) (1999) Special issue on metacognitive knowledge and beliefs in language learning. *System* 27: 4.

Studies in the area of learner beliefs have shown that learners hold a wide variety of beliefs about language and language learning and that these may influence learning attitudes and behaviour. It has also been hypothesised that certain beliefs may be disabling (Horwitz, 1987, 1988). In an early study, Wenden (1986b, 1987) interviewed 25 adults of various nationalities studying ESL at an American university and found that they held a variety of beliefs related to the importance of using the language, learning about the language and personal or affective factors. Wenden also found that, although the interviewees varied greatly in the beliefs they expressed, each appeared to have a preferred set of beliefs within one of the three categories she identified.

Little and Singleton (1990) observed that attitudes towards language learning among a random sample of foreign language students at Trinity College, Dublin, were shaped by previous experiences of education and language learning. Analysing statements made in interviews by first-year Arts students at the University of Hong Kong, Benson and Lor (1998) also found that beliefs were related to previous learning experiences, but not necessarily conditioned by them. They also observed that the learners in their study expressed a qualitatively different range of beliefs to the range recorded in Wenden's studies. They hypothesised that the beliefs of individuals are likely to be constrained by the range of beliefs available to the groups to which they belong and that they may be amenable to change through reflection on the experiences and beliefs of themselves and others within the groups.

A number of studies have investigated learner preferences in a more general way. Willing (1987) investigated the learning styles of 517 adult immigrant ESL learners in Australia using a 30-item questionnaire analysed by means of factor analysis and identified four learning styles, which he described as concrete, analytical, communicative and authority-oriented. He also found that the learners were able to articulate views on the learning process and that their preferences were individual rather than related to biographical variables such as ethnic background, age or level of education. Learners are also reported to disagree with their teachers on matters of preference in language learning. Nunan (1987 – reported in Nunan, 1996: 16) made a comparative study of the preferences of teachers and students in the Australian Adult Migrant Education Program and found dramatic mismatches between the two. Teachers and students disagreed on error correction, teacher explanations, the use of games and video, the use of cassettes and pair work and agreed on little more than the importance of conversation practice. Widdows and Voller (1991) surveyed 86 students learning English at four Japanese universities and report that their most important finding was 'the dichotomy between what students want to learn and experience in university English classes and what they are actually taught there' (p. 134).

Research in the area of learner beliefs and preferences tends to assume that changes in learning behaviour are likely to be deeper and more effective if they are accompanied by higher order changes in the learners' cognitive representations of the learning process. Benson and Lor (1999) have also argued that learners' reported beliefs and preferences are likely to be conditioned both by a higher order of conceptions concerned with the nature of language and language learning and by practical responses to immediate contexts of learning. Researchers also tend to assume that beliefs and preferences can be changed. Wenden (1986a: 9) reports on a course designed to help learners think about their beliefs, arguing that:

> The value of activities in which younger and older adults reflect upon their beliefs about language learning lies in the fact that such activities can surface for examination, evaluation, and possible change and/or modification of the expectations that adult learners bring to their language learning.

Little and Singleton (1990) also argue that it is possible to help learners to explore their own preferences and styles and shape them to the learning task. Learners may change their beliefs and preferences in response to new information or changes in their learning environments that cause them to see that their existing beliefs are untenable. In both cases, however, the change will also be dependent on reflection. As in the case of motivation and affective state, there is considerable anecdotal evidence in the literature that learners are capable of reflecting on their learning experiences and changing their beliefs or preferences in ways that are beneficial to their learning.

4.4   The seeds of autonomy

The research evidence suggests that there is good reason to believe that the notion of control over learning, on which the concept of autonomy is based, is one that can be validated through observation of the normal process of language learning. In a wide variety of learning situations, learners initiate and manage their own learning, set their own priorities and agendas and attempt to control psychological factors that influence their learning.

This is not to say that these learners are necessarily autonomous, however, as the research also shows that learners' independent efforts to control their learning are often episodic and ineffective. Autonomy implies not only that learners *attempt* to take control of their own learning from time to time, but that they possess the capacity to do so systematically. Similarly, fostering autonomy does not imply that we simply leave learners to their own devices, but that we actively encourage and assist them to take control of their learning in ways that will be effective in terms of goals that they have determined for themselves.

We have good reason to believe that autonomy can grow from the seeds of control that we are able to observe in the everyday activity of language learning. At the same time, it has been argued that autonomy implies systematic and effective control over learning. In order to recognise the various forms that autonomy may take, we therefore need to explore in more detail the behaviours associated with control over learning and the ways in which they are interrelated. In 3.1, I suggested that these behaviours can be divided into three levels of control – learning management, cognitive processes and learning content – and in the remainder of this section I will follow this division. In discussing each level of control, I will be particularly concerned with the possibility of describing the potential components of autonomy and their interrelationships on the basis of research evidence.

Chapter 5

Levels of control

5.1 Control over learning management

In 3.1, learning management was identified as one level at which control can be exercised over learning. Control over learning management can be described in terms of the behaviours that learners employ in order to manage the planning, organisation and evaluation of their learning. A number of studies, notably in the literature on adult self-directed learning and learning strategies, provide us with a basis on which we might attempt to identify and classify these behaviours. It is at the level of learning management that control over learning is most directly observable. However, it is also clear that most profiles of the autonomous learner go beyond this level to incorporate attitudinal factors underlying the capacity for self-management in learning.

5.1.1 The adult self-directed learner

Further reading

Candy, P.C. (1991) *Self-direction for Lifelong Learning*. San Francisco: Jossey-Bass, ch. 5.

A large proportion of the published research on adult self-directed learning is concerned with the ways in which self-directed learners go about the management of their learning. In an often cited but yet to be replicated study, Gibbons et al. (1980) examined the biographies of 20 public or historical figures (including Walt Disney, Frank Lloyd Wright, Pablo Picasso and Harry Houdini) who became experts in their fields without formal training. They concluded that: (1) self-educated experts possess a much greater diversity of skills than are generally found in formal schooling; (2) their expertise grows out of extra-curricular activity and school plays a minimal or negative role; (3) they focus on their area of expertise rather than develop less in-depth knowledge in a variety of areas; (4) they have an active, experiential orientation to learning; and (5) they are able to pursue their learning in spite of great odds, failure and public disapproval.

Brookfield (1981) also investigated the learning of individuals who had become acknowledged experts in their fields without formal training, using semistructured interviews rather than biographies as a source. Areas of expertise included fields as diverse as organic gardening, chess, philosophy and pigeon racing. Brookfield identified three shared attitudes among the interviewees: (1) they viewed their learning as ongoing with no identified end point; (2) (in contrast to the findings of Gibbons et al., 1980) they did not limit their learning to their area of expertise; and (3) they believed that they were part of a larger 'fellowship of learning'. Brookfield also found that the experts in his study held both cooperative and competitive attitudes towards learning. They were willing to share their knowledge and skills with peers, but at the same time they valued awards and other indicators of competitive success.

Interesting as they are, studies of experts are problematic in that the subjects studied are, of necessity, extraordinary individuals. Whether the characteristics of these extraordinary learners are relevant to those of less expert learners is unclear. Spear and Mocker's (1984) investigation of preplanning of learning projects, based on an analysis of interviews with 78 adults who had not completed high school, is unusual in its focus on non-expert learners. In this study, Spear and Mocker found that preplanning was not the norm. Instead they found four different characteristic organising circumstances for self-directed learning: (1) learners enter the learning situation with little knowledge of what needs to be learned or how to learn and assume that the means for learning will be available to them within the situation itself; (2) learners carry out learning tasks on a frequent and regular basis but do not necessarily view themselves as being engaged in a learning process; (3) learning consists of a non-deliberate series of events which appear to represent a progression, but the logic of the progression is not foreseen in advance; and (4) learning consists of a much longer series of unrelated learning experiences which are later seen as coherent by the learner. Spear and Mocker (1984: 9) conclude:

> Because self-directed learning occurs in a natural environment domin-ated by chance elements and is in contrast to the artificial and controlled elements which characterize formal instructional environments, it seems useful to investigate the possibly differing effects of the natural environ-ment on the learning process. This is opposed to seeking to understand self-directed learning by imposing what is known about formal learning upon it.

Spear and Mocker's findings are of interest because they call into ques-tion the assumption that autonomous learning is necessarily *planned* learning. Their study suggests that autonomy may also consist in the capacity to construe unplanned and unconnected learning experiences as ordered and connected.

Researchers in the field of self-directed learning have also devised a number of scales designed to measure the capacity for autonomous learning (Brockett and Hiemstra, 1991; Candy, 1991), of which the best known is the Self-directed Learning Readiness Scale (SDLRS), a questionnaire developed by Lucy M. Guglielmino in 1977. The ques-tionnaire, which was designed to assess the extent to which individuals report that they possess skills and attitudes associated with self-directed learning, has been used extensively in research on adult learning in North America. It has also been the subject of some controversy in the literature (Bonham, 1991; Field, 1989; Guglielmino, 1989).

The SDLRS was designed through a three-round Delphi survey involving 14 individuals considered to be experts on self-directed learn-ing, including Malcolm Knowles and Allen Tough. The Delphi survey process is designed to elicit expert opinion and move in the direction of consensus by allowing participants to see the results of earlier survey rounds and change their opinions if they wish. The version of the questionnaire most often used in subsequent research consisted of 58 items on a 5-point Likert scale. Guglielmino's (1977) study of 307 adult learners identified eight factors underlying readiness for self-directed learning: openness to learning opportunities, self-concept as an effective learner, initiative and independence in learning, informed acceptance of responsibility for one's learning, love of learning, creativity, future orientation, and ability to use basic study and problem-solving skills (Candy, 1991: 150). The SDLRS has subsequently been used in two main ways: to investigate relationships between readiness for self-directed learning and other variables, and as a diagnostic tool for measuring learners' perceptions of their readiness for self-directed learning.

The SDLRS represents one way of identifying the attitudes and skills associated with autonomy: survey expert opinion, devise a research instrument based on the results and test the reliability of the instrument on various populations. Many studies have found the SDLRS to be reliable, but some researchers have questioned the validity of the construct it measures. For Field (1989), who considered that the SDLRS was so problematic that it should no longer be used, the basic problem lay in the fact that neither readiness nor self-directed learning had been adequately defined at the outset. According to Field, given the degree of conceptual confusion over the concept of self-directed learning, use of the Delphi survey technique 'may do no more than transfer this confusion into a set of items' (p. 129). Bonham (1991: 92) also argues that high scores on the SDLRS 'seem to represent a positive attitude toward learning in general and not specifically toward the kind of learning called self-directed'. The opposite of the eight factors identified by Guglielmino may therefore be a dislike of learning rather than other-directedness.

The difficulty of measuring autonomy as a capacity to exercise control over learning was discussed in 3.2. The debate on the SDLRS also suggests that the process is fraught with theoretical and methodological difficulties. In particular, the SDLRS recognises that readiness for self-management in learning involves attitudinal factors, but it fails to specify these factors in terms of readily observable cognitive processes. An interesting attempt to design a survey in the context of language learning that performs a similar function has been made by Cotterall (1995b). Cotterall defines autonomy as 'the extent to which learners demonstrate the ability to use a set of tactics for taking control of their learning' (p. 195) – a definition couched in terms of learning management skills. She also recognises, however, that learners' readiness to use these tactics is influenced by their beliefs about language learning. Cotterall's survey therefore uses learner beliefs as the basis for measuring readiness for autonomy, and in the first application of the questionnaire, six underlying factors were identified. In subsequent studies, however, Cotterall (1999) reported difficulties in replicating the clusters of beliefs on which these factors were based. Her research suggests that we are still some distance from being able to identify the factors of attitude or belief on which successful self-management in learning are based.

5.1.2   Learning strategies

Further reading

Oxford, R.L. (forthcoming) *Teaching and Researching Learning Strategies* (ALIA series).

Quote 5.1 Cohen on learning strategies

In an earlier volume on language learning, I defined *learning strategies* as 'learning processes which are consciously selected by the learner'. The element of **choice** is important here because this is what gives a strategy its special character. These are also moves which the learner is at least partially aware of, even if full attention is not being given to them . . . It still seems appropriate to me to link the notion of consciousness to the definition of strategies, though as we will see below, this is a controversial issue. In my view, the element of consciousness is what distinguishes *strategies* from those processes that are not strategic.

Cohen (1998: 4)

Research on the behaviours involved in autonomous language learning has to a large extent drawn upon research on learning strategies, defined by Cohen (1998), one of the leading researchers in the field, as 'learning processes which are consciously selected by the learner'. Research on language learning strategies has taken three main directions: (1) identification and classification of strategies, (2) correlation of strategy use with learning outcomes, and (3) investigation of the possibility of training learners in strategy use. At this point, we will be concerned only with the first of these directions. The effectiveness of strategy use and strategy training will be discussed in more detail in Chapter 10. Since the conscious use of learning strategies implies control over learning management, taxonomies of strategies may be a logical place from which to begin a description of the behaviours involved in autonomous learning. On the basis of strategy research, control over learning could be described partly in terms of the capacity to make use of some or all of the strategies associated with the idea of control.

In an early schema, Wenden (1983) classified the strategies used by adult foreign language learners to direct their own learning into three categories: (1) knowing what language and language learning involves, (2) planning the content and methods of learning, and (3) self-evaluation of progress and the learning experience. She also found that adult learners pose questions to themselves in regard to each category and make decisions on the basis of the answers they give themselves. This observation is of lasting value because it suggests that all strategy use is, in a sense, founded upon reflection on the learning process.

Based on systematic research within the theoretical framework of information processing theory, O'Malley and Chamot (1990) proposed a more detailed schema based on three major categories: cognitive, metacognitive and social/affective strategies. Cognitive strategies are operations carried out directly on the material to be learned whereas metacognitive strategies make use of knowledge of cognitive processes to regulate the learning process. Social/affective strategies involve the ways in which learners interact with others and control themselves in order to enhance their learning. In the most extensive taxonomy to date, Oxford (1990) divides strategies into direct strategies, which involve mental processing of the target language, and indirect strategies, which support learning through 'focusing, planning, evaluating, seeking opportunities, controlling anxiety, increasing cooperation and empathy and other means' (p. 151). Indirect strategies are subdivided into three categories: metacognitive, social and affective.

Both O'Malley and Chamot (1990) and Oxford (1990) include systematic taxonomies of language-learning strategies in their books. Since cognitive/direct strategies involve direct operations on the language to be learned, they appear to have less to do with autonomy than metacognitive, social and affective strategies.

According to O'Malley and Chamot (1990: 137), metacognitive strategies involve 'thinking about the learning process, planning for learning, monitoring the learning task, and evaluating how well one has learned', behaviours that have been closely associated with autonomy in the literature (Concept 5.1 overleaf). Based on a longitudinal study of American students of Spanish and Russian using a think-aloud methodology, Chamot et al. (1988) came up with an extensive list of metacognitive strategies, which could be described as a taxonomy of the operations involved in the self-management of learning. It is worth noting that their description of metacognitive strategies points to the cognitive basis of behavioural aspects of self-management. Managing one's own learning effectively calls for certain cognitive capacities. However, in the literature on learning strategies, these cognitive capacities tend to be listed and described as correlates of particular observable behaviours.

Concept 5.1   **Metacognitive strategies**

Metacognitive strategies describe mental operations used by learners in the self-management of their learning. O'Malley and Chamot (1990: 138) organise these into seven major groups:

1. *Planning*: Previewing the organizing concept or principle of an anti-cipated learning task (*advance organization*); proposing strategies for handling an upcoming task; generating a plan for the parts, sequence, main ideas, or language functions to be used in handling a task (*organizational planning*).

2. *Directed attention*: Deciding in advance to attend in general to a learn-ing task and to ignore irrelevant distractors; maintaining attention during task execution.

3. *Selective attention*: Deciding in advance to attend to specific aspects of language input or situational details that assist in performance of a task; attending to specific aspects of language input during task execution.

4. *Self-management*: Understanding the conditions that help one success-fully accomplish language tasks and arranging for the presence of those conditions; controlling one's language performance to maximize use of what is already known.

5. *Self-monitoring*: Checking, verifying, or correcting one's comprehen-sion or performance in the course of a language task.

6. *Problem identification*: Explicitly identifying the central point needing resolution in a task or identifying an aspect of the task that hinders its successful completion.

7. *Self-evaluation*: Checking the outcomes of one's own language per-formance against an internal measure of completeness and accuracy; checking one's language repertoire, strategy use, or ability to perform the task at hand.

The relationship of social and affective strategies to control over learning is more complex. Chamot et al. (1988) identified only two of each type, while Oxford (1990) provides a more extensive taxonomy (Concept 5.2). Social strategies represent actions taken in relation to others, while affective strategies represent actions taken in relation to self. Many of the items in Oxford's list also represent actions taken by learners to assume greater control over content and psychological aspects of language learning. It is clear, however, that the performance of these actions depends to a large extent on the learner's attitudes

Concept 5.2   **Social and affective strategies**

Social and affective strategies describe actions taken by the learner to control aspects of the learning situation related to others and to self. Social and affective strategies are also related to the learner's attitudes towards language as an object of learning. Oxford (1990: 21) lists the following strategies:

Social strategies

A. Asking questions:
    1. Asking for clarification or verification
    2. Asking for correction
B. Cooperating with others:
    1. Cooperating with peers
    2. Cooperating with proficient users of the new language
C. Empathising with others:
    1. Developing cultural understanding
    2. Becoming aware of others' thoughts and feelings

Affective strategies

A. Lowering your anxiety:
    1. Using progressive relaxation, deep breathing, or meditation
    2. Using music
    3. Using laughter
B. Encouraging yourself:
    1. Making positive statements
    2. Taking risks wisely
    3. Rewarding yourself
C. Taking your emotional temperature:
    1. Listening to your body
    2. Using a checklist
    3. Writing a language learning diary
    4. Discussing your feelings with someone else

towards the role of self and others in the learning process and towards their own capabilities. Thus, according to Wenden (1991: 55), unless plans to help learners to become more autonomous 'take into account learner attitudes about role and capability, attempts to induce strategy use will be limited in success'. As in the case of metacognitive strategies, the application of social and affective strategies implies certain cognitive capacities not fully accounted for in taxonomies of observable learning management behaviours.

A number of questionnaire instruments designed to assess strategy use have been reported in the literature. But according to Oxford and Burry-Stock (1995), many of these instruments lack published reliability and validity data and do not systematically cover all the kinds of strategies viewed as important to language learning. The most widely used instrument to date is the Strategy Inventory for Language Learning (SILL), published as an appendix to Oxford (1990). Versions exist for speakers of English learning a new language (80 items) and for speakers of other languages learning English (50 items). Oxford and Burry-Stock (1995) report that the SILL had at that time been used in 40 to 50 major studies. The SILL includes sections designed to elicit subjects' use of memory, cognitive, compensation, metacognitive, affective and social strategies. In principle, the last three sections of the SILL (comprising 21 questions in the EFL/ESL version) might be used to assess the degree to which students report that they take control of elements of their own learning. Oxford and Burry-Stock (1995) make strong claims for the reliability and validity of the SILL and, in contrast to the case of the SDLRS, no major critiques have been published.

5.1.3   Profiling the autonomous learner

Several researchers have attempted to profile the autonomous learner by building up lists of characteristics associated with autonomy in the literature. Candy (1991), for example, has compiled a list of more than 100 competencies linked with successful autonomous learning. In the context of language learning, Breen and Mann (1997: 134–6) suggest that autonomous learners:

* see their relationship to what is to be learned, to how they will learn and to the resources available as one in which they are in charge or in control;
* are in an authentic relationship to the language they are learning and have a genuine desire to learn that particular language;

Concept 5.3   **Profiling the autonomous learner**

Candy (1991: 459–66) has listed more than 100 competencies associated with autonomy in learning. These are grouped under 13 headings.
According to Candy, the learner capable of autonomous learning will
characteristically:

- be methodical and disciplined
- be logical and analytical
- be reflective and self-aware
- demonstrate curiosity, openness and motivation
- be flexible
- be interdependent and interpersonally competent
- be persistent and responsible
- be venturesome and creative
- show confidence and have a positive self-concept
- be independent and self-sufficient
- have developed information seeking and retrieval skills
- have knowledge about, and skill at, learning processes
- develop and use criteria for evaluating.

- have a robust sense of self that is unlikely to be undermined by any
  actual or assumed negative assessments of themselves or their work;
- are able to step back from what they are doing and reflect upon it
  in order to make decisions about what they next need to do and
  experience;
- are alert to change and able to change in an adaptable, resourceful
  and opportunistic way;
- have a capacity to learn that is independent of the educational processes in which they are engaged;
- are able to make use of the environment they find themselves in
  strategically;
- are able to negotiate between the strategic meeting of their own needs
  and responding to the needs and desires of other group members.

One observation that can be made about these checklists is that they do
not simply describe observable learning behaviours. Often the capacities described go beyond learning management and are concerned with

factors of personality and attitude. At the same time, these factors are often described in such a way that the autonomous learner appears to be a particular kind of person, rather than a person who possesses particular cognitive skills or abilities that can be acquired. Moreover, the longer the list, the less clear it is that we are dealing with a finite number of characteristics associated with autonomy and the closer we come to a description of the 'ideal learner'.

It is clear from the research evidence that although autonomy implies the capacity to manage the processes of one's own learning, the autonomous learner is not simply one who is capable of performing the actions associated with self-management. Studies concerned with the description of autonomous learning behaviour provide us with a good deal of evidence on what learners should be able to do in order to manage their learning effectively, but it has been less successful in describing the underlying cognitive capacities on which these behaviours are based. It is also clear that these capacities cannot be adequately described in terms of general attitudes towards learning or in the form of a list of the cognitive operations that necessarily precede each observable management behaviour. Instead, we must move to a second level of control concerned with the control of these cognitive operations themselves.

5.2 Control over cognitive processes

In 3.1, control over cognitive processes (Figure 5.1) was identified as a second aspect of autonomy. The discussion of control over learning

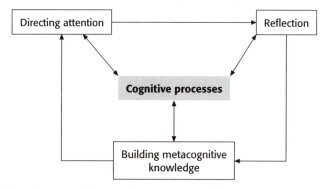

Figure 5.1 **The psychology of autonomous learning**

management in 5.1 also suggests that it may be the most fundamental level. Control over cognitive processes is understood as a matter of the psychology of learning, rather than directly observable learning behaviours, although it will generally be inferred from the observation of these behaviours. It is also less concerned with general attitudes towards learning than with particular mental processes associated with the idea of control. The hypothesis that I will develop in this section is that it may be possible to describe control over the cognitive processes involved in language learning in terms of a relatively small number of categories. The areas of research that currently hold most promise in this regard are concerned with attention, reflection and metacognitive knowledge. These are new areas of interest within the field of autonomy that are of considerable interest because they offer the possibility of a concise account of the psychological factors underpinning control over learning behaviour.

5.2.1   Attention

Cognitive approaches to second language acquisition, which broadly assume that acquisition is dependent on the learner's active mental engagement with linguistic input, offer a basis on which to begin an account of the fundamental psychological processes involved in autonomous learning (Quote 5.2). One of the most widely discussed among these approaches has been Schmidt's (1990) 'noticing hypothesis', which holds that learners must first demonstrate conscious apprehension and awareness of a particular linguistic form before any processing of it can take place. Schmidt has been criticised for a degree of looseness in his use of terms such as consciousness, awareness and

---

Quote 5.2 Tomlin and Villa on attention

Humans, like other cognizing organisms, are bombarded constantly with overwhelming amounts of sensory and cognitive information. It is the human attention systems that reduce and control that influx of information. Within the more narrowly defined problem of SLA, we find the learner also overwhelmed by incoming L2 input, and it is a virtual certainty that attention is employed to help sort out that input and to bring order to the chaos threatening to, and sometimes succeeding in, overwhelming the learner.

Tomlin and Villa (1994: 184)

attention and for the empirical evidence on which his work was based (principally the author's own diary study reported in Schmidt and Frota, 1986). Nevertheless, the general thrust of his argument has been accepted by subsequent researchers and at least two studies offer theoretical and empirical support for the hypothesis that awareness at the level of noticing is vital to second language acquisition (Robinson, 1995; Leow, 1997).

Developing Schmidt's hypothesis, Tomlin and Villa (1994) argue that the attentional system is crucial in 'sorting out' the chaos of L2 input. They object, however, to Schmidt's emphasis on the importance of noticing, which they argue 'may not be as critical a factor for SLA as other processes, specifically detection and orientation, attentional processes that can be dissociated from awareness' (p. 185). Orientation is defined as the direction of attentional resources to a type or class of sensory information at the expense of others, while detection is defined as the process that selects, or engages, a particular and specific bit of information within a type. According to Tomlin and Villa (1994: 189), the key functions in second language acquisition belong to the domain of attention rather than awareness, and are subject to control:

> At the neuroanatomical level, control of attention is exerted by the voluntary reactivation of areas that perform the task automatically. At the functional level, either by personal choice, or via instruction, or covert cues, people are able to regulate how much processing specific aspects of stimuli will receive.

Although contextual factors undoubtedly influence attention, language learners are in principle able to control what they attend to in linguistic input.

Bialystok (1994: 158), whose objective is to identify 'a minimum set of cognitive operations that are responsible for the acquisition and use of language', uses a somewhat different framework built around two cognitive processing components: analysis and control. Her framework assumes that 'an orderly mental world', consisting of representations and processes that constitute operations on representations, is fundamental to the long-term development of proficiency in a second language. According to Bialystok (1994: 159):

> The reason that thought evolves, or that language proficiency increases, is that mental representations develop. Analysis is the process by which mental representations that were loosely organized around meanings (knowledge of the world) become rearranged into explicit representations that are organized around formal structures.

The process of analysis also underlies the phenomenological experience by which implicit knowledge becomes explicit.

Control is 'the process of selective attention that is carried out in real time' and, Bialystok argues (p. 160):

> Because cognition originates in mental representations, then there must be a means of focusing attention on the specific representation, or aspect of a representation, relevant to a particular purpose.

Bialystok also considers consciousness and awareness to be concerned with attention, or the interaction between analysis and control (p. 165):

> Designated in this way, the problem of consciousness is redefined as the problem of awareness. Awareness is the result of the interaction between analysis and control. Analyzed representations can be attended to by means of control of processing in precise ways. More analyzed representations are more articulated, and they allow attention to be brought to more detailed and more precise specifications of those representations. Sometimes these details concern rules or structures and sometimes they concern processes or procedures. This process of focusing attention onto specific aspects of the representation gives rise to the subjective feeling of awareness that has been called consciousness.

Bialystok's view of the role of attention in second language acquisition is broader than that of other researchers, because it is concerned not simply with input but with analysed representations derived from input. It is also developmental, because it is the direction of attention towards mental representations that leads to the development of proficiency.

The idea that attention is a key process in second language acquisition is relatively recent. At present, research is characterised by a search for conceptual and terminological clarity and empirical evidence for hypotheses is often lacking. However, it is not essential for researchers on autonomy to take a position within current theoretical debates in order to recognise the importance of the hypothesis that control over attentional processes is central to second language acquisition. If attention is a precondition of acquisition, it follows that effective language learning may be dependent upon the learner taking cognitive responsibility for what is attended to in input. It may also be the case that several of the phenomena identified in 4.2 as evidence for control as a natural feature of language learning (i.e. self-directed phases of learning, learner agendas in the classroom, and control over psychological factors influencing learning) can be understood as symptoms of the necessity for control at the cognitive level.

It is important to note, however, that Bialystok and other second language acquisition researchers use the term *control* in a more specific sense than researchers in the field of autonomy. The notion of control in second language acquisition research is currently concerned with control over language input rather than control over the learning process, which as we will see in the following sections involves reflection on and knowledge of the learning process itself. However, if attentional processes are both central to second language acquisition and subject to learner control, there may be good reason to suppose that control over learning begins from their conscious direction by the learner.

5.2.2   Reflection

Further reading

Boud, D., Keough, R. and Walker, D. (eds) (1985) *Reflection: Turning Experience into Learning*. London: Kogan Page.

Quote 5.3   Little on reflection and autonomy

The growth and exercise of general behavioural autonomy may or may not entail processes of conscious reflection. In this regard human beings differ from one another as to their genetic endowment and the domestic, social and cultural environments in which they are born. But if we make the development of autonomy a central concern of formal learning, conscious reflection will necessarily play a central role from the beginning, for the simple reason that all formal learning is the result of deliberate intention.

Little (1997a: 94)

A number of researchers have described reflection as a key psychological component of autonomy, and for Little (1997a) conscious reflection on the learning process is a distinctive characteristic of autonomous learning. Reflection may also be a key cognitive process underlying self-management in learning if action is seen as its logical outcome. Reflection is a complex construct, however, and there has to date been relatively little research on its role in language learning.

Concern with the importance of reflection in learning dates back at least as far as Dewey (1933: 9), whose definition of reflection has been widely quoted:

> Active, persistent, and careful consideration of any belief or supposed
> form of knowledge in the light of the grounds that support it and the
> further conclusions to which it tends constitutes reflective thought . . . it
> includes a conscious and voluntary effort to establish belief upon a firm
> basis of evidence and rationality.

In retrospect, however, Dewey's definition seems somewhat idealised in
its emphasis on evidence and rationality and its failure to view reflection as 'socially conditioned and affective in nature' (Harris, 1990: 113).
Boud et al. (1985: 19) define reflection as 'a generic term for those
intellectual and affective activities in which individuals engage to
explore their experiences in order to lead to a new understanding and
appreciation', while Louden (1991: 149) defines it more broadly still as
'a mental process which takes place out of the stream of action, looking
forward or (usually) back to actions that have taken place'.

A number of researchers working in adult or professional learning contexts have attempted to identify different levels and forms of
reflection. Mezirow (1981), for example, has identified seven levels of
reflection: reflectivity, affective, discriminant, judgemental, conceptual,
psychic and theoretical. Louden (1991) discusses four forms:

- *Introspection*: deliberate contemplation of a past event at some distance
  from the stream of action.
- *Replay and rehearsal*: where events are reworked in our heads again
  and again.
- *Enquiry*: where there is a deliberate and explicit connection between
  thinking and doing.
- *Spontaneity*: tacit reflection, which takes place within the stream of
  experience.

Reflection has also been conceptualised as one phase within cyclical
processes of learning in which it plays a crucial role. Kohonen's (1992)
experiential language-learning model, for example, describes a cycle of
learning involving concrete experience, reflective observation, abstract
conceptualisation and active experimentation leading to further reflection on experience.

In emancipatory reflective learning models, reflection also implies
action. Smyth (1991), for example, represents the process of reflection
as a series of moments and questions:

- *Describe*:   What do I do?
- *Inform*:   What does this description mean?

- *Confront*:   How did I come to be like this?
- *Reconstruct*: How might I do things differently?

For the third moment, which is seen as the most problematic because it involves questioning the legitimacy of current practice, Smyth provides a series of questions:

- What do my practices say about my assumptions and beliefs?
- Where did these ideas come from?
- What social practices are expressed in these ideas?
- What is it that causes me to maintain my theories?
- What views of power do they embody?
- Whose interests seem to be served by my practices?
- What is it that constrains my views of what is possible?

Reflection leading to action can be understood as the cognitive basis for control over learning management, especially if it is carried out collectively for the purpose of change. It seems clear, however, that questioning fundamental beliefs is an exceptional form of reflection, which only occurs naturally at moments of crisis or change, as a result of a deliberate decision to expose assumptions to doubt or as a result of external intervention or prompting.

On the basis of research, we can say that we know several things about reflection:

- It is a mental process involving rational thought, emotion and judgement.
- It may be consciously initiated by the reflector or by others, or it may be prompted by a disturbance in the normal pattern of feelings or events.
- It is context-bound. We must reflect on something in some specific situation and under specific constraints.
- It is goal-oriented. Although the goals of reflection vary, they generally involve learning.
- It can be retrospective, introspective or prospective.
- It can be modelled as a cyclical process involving the deconstruction and reconstruction of assumptions or beliefs.
- It may or may not lead to action or deep change in the learner. Reflection leading to deep change is liable to be difficult and even painful.

The relationship between reflection and autonomy lies in the cognitive and behavioural processes by which individuals take control of the stream of experience they are subject to. According to Candy (1991: 389):

> If people are to develop a sense of personal control, they need to recognize a contingent relationship between the strategies they use and their learning outcomes, and this may well involve having learners maintain learning journals, analyzing their own approaches to learning, and discussing their beliefs and approaches to learning in groups or with a facilitator or counselor.

Reflection, defined by Candy as having both individual and social dimensions, can therefore be seen as a key internal mechanism for the development of control over learning. To date, reflection has been seen as particularly important in adult learning and professional education, where experience of practice can serve as a focal point of learning. Although there has been relatively little research on reflection in language learning, its relevance is clear if language learning is viewed as a practice that engages both intellect and feelings.

Reflection has been discussed in the context of autonomous language learning in three main ways: at the level of language, at the level of the learning process, and as a means of 'deconditioning'. According to Kohonen (1992: 17):

> Only experience that is reflected upon seriously will yield its full measure of learning, and reflection must in turn be followed by testing new hypotheses in order to obtain further experience. It can be argued, in fact, that theoretical concepts will not become part of the individual's frame of reference until they have been experienced meaningfully on a subjective emotional level. Reflection plays an important role in this process by providing a bridge, as it were, between experience and theoretical conceptualization. The process of learning is seen as the recycling of experience at deeper levels of understanding and interpretation. This view entails the idea of lifelong learning.

In this formulation, deep learning is seen as a process of hypothesis generation and testing within which reflection plays a crucial role. Applied to language learning, the experiential model implies 'learner reflection on language structure and explicit teaching of the systemic structure of the target language, aiming at control of the language' (ibid., p. 29). In this sense, reflection is oriented towards the content of language learning and principally contributes to the learner's autonomy as a language *user*.

At the same time, Kohonen argues that autonomous learners need to gain an understanding of the process of language learning (p. 24):

> Raising the awareness of one's own learning and gaining an understand-
> ing of the processes involved is thus an important key to the development
> of autonomous learning. Conscious reflection on learning experiences
> and the sharing of such reflections with other learners in cooperative
> groups makes it possible to increase one's awareness of learning.

In this sense, reflection is oriented towards the learning process and
contributes to the learner's autonomy as a language *learner*.

Reflection also plays an important role in Leni Dam's autonomous
language-learning classrooms in both of the senses discussed so far. Using
the term 'evaluation' in much the same way as others use the term conscious reflection, Dam (1995: 49) argues that:

> Evaluation plays a pivotal role in the development of learner autonomy.
> The function of evaluation is on the one hand to ensure that work
> undertaken is discussed and revised, and on the other to establish a basis
> of experience and awareness that can be used in planning further learn-
> ing. It is a recurrent activity between the teacher and individual learners,
> groups of learners, or the whole class. It can also be undertaken by the
> learners themselves.

Students are encouraged to bring examples of language noticed outside class into class for discussion, to write new language on posters,
in learning diaries, and so on. They are also asked to conduct short oral
evaluations at the end of each class and longer written evaluations at
the end of each term. Collective reflections on the learning process also
exercise an influence on the future organisation of the learning process
within the classroom.

Reflection has also been seen as a tool for 'deconditioning' learners
from learning habits or ways of thinking about learning that are inimical to autonomy. For some researchers, the fact that previous learning
experiences may predispose learners to resist autonomy means that
autonomy should not be imposed, but introduced gradually and at the
learners' own pace (see, for example, Nunan, 1997). One of the problems
with gradualist approaches to autonomy, however, is that we lack strong
empirical evidence that learners are, in fact, likely to accept the idea
of autonomy more readily if it is introduced gradually. The relationship
between the rate at which ideas of autonomy are introduced and their
uptake by learners is an issue that remains open to research.

For other researchers, the crucial issue is to help learners to confront
their ideas about learning that lead them to resist the idea of autonomy.
According to Candy (1991: 376), for example,

> . . . if, indeed, the disinclination or inability to accept responsibility is
> actually a learned phenomenon, akin to learned helplessness, then one

could argue that it would be possible, and perhaps even desirable, to jolt adult students out of their compliance and passivity. This may be achieved gradually, through the progressive devolution of control to the learners, or it may be sudden.

In both cases, the process of confrontation involves reflection on existing beliefs and practices. In the context of language learning, Holec (1980: 41) refers to the psychological level of learner training for autonomy as 'a gradual deconditioning of the learner', which can take place only if the learner (1) 'manages to re-examine all his prejudices and preconceptions about language learning and his role in it', and (2) 'is sufficiently well-informed concerning the new approach so that he can see for himself its advantages and disadvantages, but above all so that he will have a clearer idea of what his place and role in it will be, as well as what is to be expected of the other components of the system'. According to Holec, therefore, deep reflection on beliefs and practices interacts with the learner's expanding knowledge base in the development of autonomy.

It is clear that reflection is an important component of autonomous learning at a number of levels. It may even be legitimate to state that the autonomous learner is essentially one who is capable of reflection at appropriate moments in the learning process and of acting upon the results. However, to date we know very little about what language learners reflect upon and how they go about doing it (see 16.3, case study). Learner journal studies indicate that writing about language learning is a useful tool for reflection (e.g. Bailey, 1983; Lor, 1998; Matsumoto, 1989, 1996), but in view of what we have seen of the complexity of the concept of reflective learning, a great deal remains to be learned about the nature of reflection on language learning and its relationship to autonomy.

5.2.3   Metacognitive knowledge

> **Further reading**
>
> Wenden, A. (1998) 'Metacognitive knowledge and language learning'. *Applied Linguistics*, 19 (4): 515–37.

The notion of 'metacognitive knowledge', introduced into the literature on autonomy in language learning by Wenden (1995), adds a further dimension to our understanding of the cognitive level of

Quote 5.4 Wenden on metacognitive knowledge and autonomy

Teachers should also aim to help language learners develop a more reflective and self-directed approach to learning *their new language.* For the greater part, language instructors will view their goal as the provision of instruction that facilitates the development of linguistic autonomy. However, this research suggests that learners also need guidance in improving and expanding their knowledge about learning so that they may also become more autonomous in their approach to the learning of their new language. The following four procedures that define awareness raising activities for (metacognitive) knowledge acquisition may be used as a guide in devising tasks and materials for this purpose . . .

(1) *elicitation* of learners' metacognitive knowledge and beliefs

(2) *articulation* of what has come to awareness

(3) *confrontation* with alternative views

(4) *reflection* on the appropriateness of revising, expanding one's knowledge.

Wenden (1998: 531)

control (Quote 5.4). Wenden observes that planning, monitoring and evaluation are the three main strategies identified in the literature on autonomy in language learning and self-regulation in learning. Wenden's concern, however, is that the use of planning, monitoring and evaluation strategies does not in itself define autonomy. Citing Perkins and Salomon (1989), she argues that 'if they fail to make contact with a rich knowledge base, these three strategies are weak' (Wenden, 1995: 188). Wenden refers to this knowledge base as metacognitive knowledge, which she defines as 'the stable, statable and sometimes fallible knowledge learners acquire about themselves as learners and the learning process' (p. 185). Wenden describes three kinds of metacognitive knowledge: person, strategic and task knowledge. Of these, the most relevant to the idea of control over the learning process is task knowledge.

Wenden defines task knowledge as 'what learners need to know about (i) the purpose of a task, (ii) the task's demands, and (iii) implicit in these considerations, a determination of the kind of task it is' (p. 185). Task knowledge is thus understood as metacognitive knowledge contextualised within the task at hand, which is implicated in the decision to carry out a learning task, decisions about content, progression, pace, place and time of learning, the selection and use of cognitive strategies and the criteria selected for evaluation. Wenden (1995: 189) notes, for example, that expert learners construct mental representations of task demands in order to determine how best to go about completing them. These representations include task goals and subgoals, possible states through which the task will pass on its way to completion and the constraints under which the task is to be done. Decisions about planning, monitoring and evaluation of learning, therefore, always occur within some context of task and are dependent upon task knowledge, which is derived from experience. In the context of language learning, a task may be as broad as learning the target language in order to use it communicatively with others or as narrow as learning a new word. Whatever the task, the learner must draw on her knowledge of language and language learning in order to complete it.

If we link the notion of task knowledge to Bialystok's (1994) framework of analysis and control, it can be argued that the metacognitive knowledge that is brought to bear in the process of planning, monitoring and evaluating language learning is fundamentally metalinguistic and consists of analysed representations that are brought to consciousness and made available for further analysis through the direction of attentional resources. As Bialystok points out, these representations may concern rules and structures or processes and procedures (p. 165). In both cases, however, the representations are necessarily metalinguistic since they are derived from the experience of processing linguistic input. In other words, control over language learning appears ultimately to be dependent upon the mobilisation of the learner's metalinguistic knowledge base.

Little (1997a) develops a similar argument in relation to autonomy and language awareness based on Karmiloff-Smith's (1992) model of 'representational redescription', which describes the process of learning as a process of representation and re-representation of knowledge at varying levels of explicitness. Little notes that language awareness refers to two apparently distinct phenomena: (1) 'the "awareness" that learners have of language, *independently of conscious reflection on language*' (Nicholas, 1991: 78), which may be innate, and (2) the externally derived knowledge of language that learners acquire through formal or informal learning. Little argues that as we move from implicit knowledge to explicit knowledge, or the closer knowledge of language comes to verbalisable form, the greater the likelihood that it derives from external as well as internal sources (p. 97). In other words, the development of language awareness involves the interaction between implicit (internally derived) and explicit (externally derived) processes of learning. Little observes that the development of autonomy in language learning aims both 'to enable learners to maximise their potential for learning via critical reflection and self-evaluation, and to enable them to become independent and self-reliant users of their target language' (pp. 98–9). However, he also argues that learning-to-learn goals and language-learning goals are interrelated (p. 99):

> In practice these concerns are not easily separable; for the truly auto-nomous learner, each occasion of language use is an occasion of language learning, and *vice versa*. Proficiency in spontaneous use of the spoken language requires the gradual development of language awareness in the sense that knowledge about the target language provides the indispens-able basis for critical reflection and analysis.

In other words, the process of learning how to learn languages is inseparable from the process of learning languages. Both build upon awareness of language, or the development of the learner's implicit and explicit metalinguistic knowledge base.

5.2.4   The importance of control over cognitive processes

The importance of the level of control over cognitive processes in the description of autonomy lies in Little's (1991: 4) observation that auto-nomy presupposes that the learner 'will develop a particular kind of psychological relation to the process and content of his learning'. Learners who are asked to take greater control of their learning, or who are forced by circumstances to do so, may be capable of performing the actions involved in self-management of learning, but they will not necessarily possess the cognitive capacities that will make these actions systematic or effective. They may put on 'the mask of autonomy' (Breen and Mann, 1997: 141), but they will not necessarily be autonomous. The nature of the autonomous learner's psychological relation to the learn-ing process is often described in general attitudinal terms or in terms of a capacity for 'detachment', 'critical thinking', 'creativity', and so on. In this section I have argued that it may also be described more pre-cisely as a capacity to control cognitive processes that are both observ-able and central to the learning process. Current research suggests that attention, reflection and the development of metacognitive knowledge are among the more important processes on which further research is needed.

5.3   Control over learning content

> **Quote 5.5** Kenny on autonomy as the expression of self
>
> Autonomy is not just a matter of permitting choice in learning situations, or making pupils responsible for the activities they undertake, but of allowing and encouraging learners, through processes deliberately set up for the purpose, to begin to express who they are, what they think, and what they would like to do, in terms of work they initiate and define for themselves. This is holistic learning and it transcends the subject disciplines.
>
> Kenny (1993: 440)

In 3.1, the content of learning was identified as a third level of control relevant to the description of autonomy. Self-determination of learning content is, in fact, an aspect of self-management in learning, which like other aspects of learning management has its basis in control over cognitive processes. It is discussed separately, however, for two reasons. Firstly, there is good reason to believe that control over content is fundamental to autonomy. If learners are self-managing methodological aspects of the learning process, but not learning what they want to learn, their learning may not be authentically self-directed. Secondly, in institutional contexts, learner control of content has social and political dimensions. In short, the learners may have to learn how to exercise control over the collective situation of their learning, using capacities for social interaction that are distinct from those required in the management of individual learning.

Littlewood (1999: 75) distinguishes between proactive and reactive autonomy. Proactive autonomy is the kind of autonomy we find when learners determine objectives, select methods and techniques and evaluate what they have learned. It is the kind of autonomy 'which affirms their individuality and sets up directions in a world which they themselves have partially created'. Reactive autonomy is 'the kind which does not create its own directions but, once a direction has been initiated, enables learners to organize their resources autonomously in order to reach their goal'. It is the kind of autonomy that causes learners to learn vocabulary without being pushed, to take the initiative to do past examination papers or to organise study groups to complete an assignment. Littlewood argues that although for many writers 'proactive autonomy is the only kind that counts', reactive autonomy may be a step towards it or a goal in its own right. However, in terms of the three levels of control discussed so far, reactive autonomy might be described as control over method (at the management and cognitive levels) without control over content.

Setting goals and determining what will be learned come first within the logical sequence of self-management tasks. Although self-management also involves elements of planning, selection of resources, task design, progress monitoring and self-assessment, all these operations are performed in relation to specific goals and content. If the goals and content are self-determined, subsequent phases of the learning process become aspects of the solution of a learning problem that is authentic in the sense that it is the learner's own. It is the interplay between self-determined goals and self-determined methods that gives autonomy a dynamic and developmental character. If the goals and content are other-determined, self-direction at the level of method may be reduced to a choice of the most appropriate method of completing a task that lacks authenticity in terms of the learner's own perceived learning needs. The exercise of autonomy itself may be reduced to the routine application of tried and tested methods of completing prescribed tasks outside the classroom.

From a constructivist point of view (see 2.3), all effective learning begins from the learner's existing knowledge and develops through the interpretation of experience. Again, learning is more authentic and effective if it begins from a problem that the learner immediately faces, because new knowledge will be more effectively integrated with existing meaning systems. Self-determination of learning content also has motivational implications. Norton (1997), for example, considers that motivation is dependent on the development of a sense of 'ownership' of a second language, which is intimately bound up with the learner's identity as a second language user. If the language to be learned is ultimately to be the learner's own, it follows that the locus of control regarding linguistic content should lie with the learner rather than with the teacher, the textbook or the syllabus.

It is also often observed that language learners who successfully master the prescribed content of language-learning curricula are not necessarily the best users of the language in practical communicative contexts. Ramadevi (1992: 1), for example, observes that, when college level learners of English in India are unable to use the language with ease, they are 'deprived in a more serious way than merely being able to communicate, or use the language for academic purposes; this deprivation could be characterized as not being able to get out of language use, adequately, the services of an abstract tool of innovative thinking'. She suggests that autonomy is not simply a question of learners choosing from the linguistic core syllabus, but also a question of learners 'making active decisions about choices from areas of experience they would like to deal in and the particular meanings that they would like to explore' (p. 92). Pennycook (1997) has argued forcefully that autonomy means helping learners to acquire a 'voice' in the foreign language that corresponds to their own cultural and ideological standpoints. In this sense, autonomy is not simply a matter of knowing what has to be learned in order to be judged proficient by others and being able to learn it. Rather, it is a question of knowing what one wants to learn, or knowing what has be learned in order to interpret and convey meanings that are uniquely one's own.

For Kenny (1993), autonomy in the context of foreign language learning also implies that the learners must be able to define the overall nature of the language-learning task for themselves (Quote 1.27). Kenny argues that 'chaining a learner to some subject discipline is a restriction of that learner's autonomy, for it acts as a control on discovery, and on the production of knowledge' (p. 433). As long as the learning task is defined as the acquisition of a body of knowledge concerned with language, it does not particularly matter whether this knowledge is transmitted by a teacher or acquired independently by the learners. For Kenny, autonomy implies that the learners use language rather than study it and that 'the curriculum becomes a way of organizing what the learner wants to do, rather than a sequencing of knowledge' (p. 435). Kenny's argument is ultimately related to two specific characteristics of language learning as a process of learning to communicate: (1) that foreign languages are often learned as a means to learn something else; and (2) that using a foreign language can be a means of learning the language itself. Control over the content of language learning thus implies a capacity to evaluate one's broad learning purposes and their relationship to language acquisition. It is as much a matter of determining the contexts of experience within which learning will take place, as it is a matter of determining the linguistic content to be learned.

According to Little (1996: 204), autonomy 'facilitates target language use in the larger world that lies beyond the immediate learning environment' and 'allows the learner to take maximum advantage of the language-learning opportunities that continually arise in language use'. Thus, to the extent that control extends to the domain of content, autonomy in formal educational contexts projects learning beyond the curriculum towards more authentic contexts of language use. However, this may also entail a new set of problems for the learner, for, as Little again argues, 'learning can only proceed via interaction, so that the freedoms by which we recognize learner autonomy are always constrained by the learner's dependence on the support and cooperation of others'. Paradoxically, learners who succeed in taking control of the content of their language learning may be rewarded by academic failure if their own goals depart too far from those explicit or implicit within the curriculum. In research in progress, Benson and Nunan have even observed that successful learners of English in the Hong Kong system come to regard learning English autonomously and effectively outside the classroom as a process that is functionally distinct from studying English in the classroom in order to pass examinations.

Control over the content of learning, in contrast to control over methods, necessarily involves the learner in social interactions regarding the right to determine and implement their own learning goals. These interactions may take place with other learners in the collective negotiation of learning goals and tasks, or with teachers and higher authorities in the negotiation of the curriculum. Negotiations of the second type do not necessarily imply conflict, although in practice many formal education systems severely constrain the extent to which learners may self-determine the overall direction of their learning within the framework of the curriculum. In such situations, teachers often succeed in creating spaces in which control over content can be exercised (in projects, self-access, extra-curricular activities, and so on), but the effectiveness of their initiatives may be blunted if the curriculum itself is unresponsive to change. Control over the content of learning requires, more than any other aspect of autonomy, that teachers and education authorities create situational contexts in which freedom in learning is encouraged and rewarded. It also requires that learners develop their own capacity to participate in social interactions concerning their learning, to negotiate for the right to self-determine its broad direction and ultimately to participate in the transformation of educational structures.

The political dimension of autonomy is perhaps its most controversial aspect. Autonomy is in part rooted in proposals for radical educational reform in the work of Dewey, Freire, Illich and others. Yet Allwright (1988: 35) expresses a concern of many language teachers in writing that autonomy is 'associated with a radical restructuring of language pedagogy, a restructuring that involves the rejection of the traditional classroom and the introduction of wholly new ways of working'. Like

Allwright, other researchers and practitioners have sought to find ways of conceptualising and fostering autonomy independently of educational reform within the domains of individual learning management and the psychology of learning. The importance of control over the content of learning in autonomy, however, suggests that the controversy lies within the realm of learning theory rather than ideology. If autonomy without control over content is an inauthentic form of autonomy – the ability to apply methods rather than the ability to control the overall direction of one's learning – we may need to accept that autonomy necessarily involves the social and political domains of learning.

Chapter 6

Conclusion

Many language teachers would agree that autonomy is a good idea in theory, but somewhat idealistic as a goal of language teaching in practice. In this chapter I have explored the history of the concept of autonomy, its sources beyond the field of language education, its definitions and the nature of its component parts. On the basis of the evidence discussed, there are several things that we can say about autonomy that suggest that it is less idealistic than it may appear at first sight:

- Autonomy has a long and respected tradition in educational, psychological and philosophical thought. In particular, research within the psychology of learning provides strong grounds for believing that autonomy is essential to effective learning.

- The concept of autonomy in language learning is well researched at the level of theory and practice and has proved itself to be adaptable and responsive to change.

- The concept of autonomy is supported by evidence that learners naturally tend to exercise control over their learning both generally and in the field of language learning.

- Autonomy as a systematic capacity for effective control over various aspects and levels of the learning process is capable of description. Although we are yet to arrive at a non-controversial account of the nature of autonomy and the importance of various levels of control (and perhaps we never will), the potential forms of control that comprise it have been well-researched on the basis of observable behaviours, both within and beyond the field of autonomy.

> **Quote 6.1** Dickinson on the effectiveness of autonomous learning
>
> In recommending autonomy to learners, we are making the assumption that taking an active, independent attitude to learning and independently undertaking a learning task, is beneficial to learning; that somehow, personal involvement in decision making leads to more effective learning. This is not a universal view. Some teachers and researchers either articulate or demonstrate beliefs which are in conflict with those concerning learner autonomy. Thus the claims of the desirability and effectiveness of learner autonomy need to be justified through convincing arguments.
>
> Dickinson (1995: 165)

The assumption advanced by Dickinson (1995) that autonomy is beneficial to learning does, therefore, appear to be supported by convincing arguments (Quote 6.1).

The fact that we have gone some way towards demonstrating the validity and necessity of autonomy in effective language learning does not mean, however, that we have demonstrated the possibility of fostering it among learners in practice. For many teachers, the obstacles to autonomy lie less in the abilities or willingness of students than in the social and political problems involved in altering the structure of the teaching and learning process. In the course of its development, however, autonomy has been associated with a number of language-teaching practices that have been claimed to foster it. Evidence for the effectiveness of these practices, and the criteria by which they may be judged effective or not, will be the topic of Chapter 2.

|| Autonomy in practice

Chapter 7

Fostering autonomy

Chapters 7 to 14 in this section will...

- describe the main areas of practice that have been claimed to foster autonomy in language learning;
- discuss evidence for the effectiveness of each area of practice in terms of autonomy and better language learning;
- explain how practitioners and researchers can better demonstrate the effectiveness of their work in the field of autonomy.

In Section I, autonomy was defined as the capacity to take control over one's own learning and it was argued that the development of such a capacity is beneficial to learning. Many learners will be capable of developing autonomy independently of our efforts as teachers. If we speak of autonomy as a goal of language education, however, we imply that teachers and educational institutions should attempt to foster autonomy through practices that will allow learners to engage in modes of learning in which this capacity can be developed (Concept 7.1 over-leaf). The effectiveness of our efforts to foster autonomy is therefore a separate question from the effectiveness of autonomous learning itself.

Because the capacity for control over learning has various aspects, autonomy may take various forms. Fostering autonomy does not, therefore, imply any particular approach to practice. In principle, any practice that encourages and enables learners to take greater control of any aspect of their learning can be considered a means of promoting autonomy. In the field of language education, however, autonomy has

---

Concept 7.1   Autonomy and autonomous learning

Autonomy has been defined as the capacity to take control over one's own learning. However, the terms 'autonomy' and 'autonomous learning' are often used more loosely in the literature and in ways that can cause confusion when we ask questions about their effectiveness. In order to clarify the terminology, it is helpful to make a distinction between three aspects of autonomy: autonomy as an attribute of the learner, autonomous learning as a mode of learning, and educational practices designed to foster autonomy.

In this book, *autonomy* is treated as a capacity belonging to the learner. It is an attribute of the learner rather than the learning situation. Most researchers agree that autonomy cannot be 'taught' or 'learned'. In describing autonomy as a developmental process, I therefore use the term 'fostering autonomy' to refer to processes initiated by teachers or institutions and 'developing autonomy' to refer to processes within the learner.

Autonomous learning is learning in which the learner's capacity for autonomy is exercised and displayed. It is exhibited in various modes of learning, characterised by particular procedures and relationships between learners and teachers, which are more or less self-directed. Participation in self-directed modes of learning does not necessarily imply that the learner is autonomous, however. It is assumed that autonomy develops through participation in self-directed modes of learning, but not as a necessary consequence of it.

In this book, a *practice* refers to a particular way of organising the process of teaching and learning. In this sense, self-access and learner training are examples of practices that may involve different modes of learning depending on the ways in which they are implemented. In self-access, for example, the learners may be carrying out tasks set by a teacher from lesson to lesson or they may be working on a longer-term programme designed by themselves. It is often the modes of learning implied within the implementation of a practice and their interaction with other modes of learning in other practices that determines the effectiveness of our efforts to foster autonomy.

---

come to be closely identified with certain practices. In some cases, these practices have been developed specifically in order to support the goal of autonomy. In other cases, an established practice has been seen as having qualities that are intrinsically supportive of autonomy. In this section, these practices are discussed under six broad headings:

resource-based, technology-based, learner-based, classroom-based, curriculum-based and teacher-based approaches (Concept 7.2 and Figure 7.1).

The key question to ask of any practice that claims to foster autonomy is: 'How does this practice help learners take greater control over their learning?' Often this question can be divided into two parts:

- What *opportunities* do the modes of learning implied within the practice offer for learner control?

- How does the implementation of the practice *enable* learners take advantage of these opportunities?

A second, equally important question is: 'How does the practice improve language learning?' This question can also be divided into two parts:

- In what ways does the practice improve language *proficiency*?

- How does it help learners to become *more effective language learners*?

Concept 7.2   **Approaches to the development of autonomy**

Practices associated with the development of autonomy can be classified under six broad headings.

- *Resource-based approaches* emphasise independent interaction with learning materials.
- *Technology-based approaches* emphasise independent interaction with educational technologies.
- *Learner-based approaches* emphasise the direct production of behavioural and psychological changes in the learner.
- *Classroom-based approaches* emphasise learner control over the planning and evaluation of classroom learning.
- *Curriculum-based approaches* extend the idea of learner control to the curriculum as a whole.
- *Teacher-based approaches* emphasise the role of the teacher and teacher education in the practice of fostering autonomy among learners.

The distinctions made in this classification are largely a matter of focus. In practice, approaches are often combined, sometimes in eclectic ways. Although claims are often made for the particular effectiveness of one approach over others, most researchers and practitioners would accept that they are interdependent.

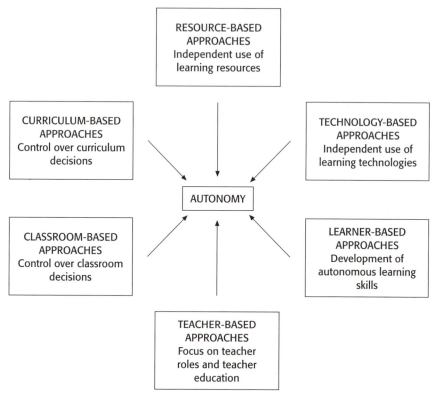

Figure 7.1 **Autonomy in language learning and related areas of practice**

As we saw in Section I, there are good theoretical reasons to suppose that autonomous language learners are better language learners. However, we will also see that research often fails to provide convincing empirical evidence that the practices associated with autonomy are effective either in helping learners to take greater control over their learning or in improving their language learning.

In this section, we will be particularly concerned with what research does and does not tell us about the effectiveness of practices associated with autonomy, debates within each field of practice and the research questions arising from them. We will also be concerned with the kinds of evidence that could demonstrate the effectiveness of our efforts to foster autonomy in practice.

Chapter 8

Resource-based approaches

In resource-based learning, the focus for the development of autonomy is placed upon the learner's independent interaction with learning resources. Resource-based learning offers learners the opportunity to exercise control over learning plans, the selection of learning materials and the evaluation of learning. Learners are expected to develop the skills associated with these activities through processes of experimentation and discovery, in which freedom of choice is a crucial factor. It is seldom assumed, however, that independent interaction with learning resources is sufficient in itself for the development of autonomy. The claims made for self-access as a means of fostering autonomy have been particularly strong. In the case of self-instruction and distance learning, the claims are weaker although it is often assumed that these modes of learning are in some sense associated with autonomy.

8.1 Self-access

Further reading

Gardner, D. and Miller, L. (1999) *Establishing Self-Access: From Theory to Practice.* Cambridge: Cambridge University Press.

Sheerin (1991: 143) defines self-access as 'a way of describing materials that are designed and organized in such a way that students can select

Quote 8.1 Gardner and Miller on self-access language learning

Self-access is probably the most widely used and recognised term for an approach to encouraging autonomy . . . Self-access language learning is an approach to learning language, not an approach to teaching language. There are misconceptions in the literature about self-access. It is sometimes seen as a collection of materials and sometimes as a system for organising resources. We see it as an integration of a number of elements which combine to provide a unique learning environment. Each learner interacts with the environment in a unique way.

Gardner and Miller (1999: 9–11)

and work on tasks on their own', while Gardner and Miller (1999) define it more broadly as an environment for learning involving resources, teachers, learners and the systems within which they are organized (Quote 8.1). At the core of the idea of self-access language learning is the self-access centre, which often functions as a quasi-independent unit with its own philosophy and routines for engaging learners in study outside the classroom.

Historically, self-access centres have occupied a central position in the practice of autonomy and many teachers have come to the idea of autonomy through their work in them. As a result, the effectiveness of self-access learning is often confused with the effectiveness of autonomous learning itself. However, self-access learning does not necessarily imply that learners possess or exercise the capacity to control their own learning. As Sheerin (1997: 55) points out, 'it is possible to have a marvellously well-stocked self-access centre and for student activity to be totally directed within that centre'. For many researchers, the crucial factor in the relationship between self-access learning and the development of autonomy are the goals of the self-access centre and the measures taken to achieve them.

A self-access centre can be broadly defined as any purpose-designed facility in which learning resources are made directly available to learners. These resources typically include audio, video and computer workstations, audiotapes, videotapes and computer software, and a variety of printed materials. Many self-access centres also contain areas for group work and a help desk and many provide counselling services or serve as a location for other services such as one-to-one writing support (Hayward, 1994) and language-learning exchanges (Voller and Pickard, 1996). Some self-access centres have their own web sites and offer some of their services and resources on-line. Many of the more recent self-access centres are generously financed and make use of the latest computer and communications technologies, while others make use of whatever resources are at hand.

Sheerin (1997) argues that self-access centres are set up for both pragmatic and ideological reasons. The pragmatic reasons are mainly concerned with individualisation of learning and 'are easily understood by, and have high face-validity for, learners, teachers and finance providers' (p. 54). The ideological reasons are concerned with the promotion of autonomy. For many teachers involved in self-access, language-learning goals are separate from, and have priority over, the goal of autonomy. Sturtridge (1997) observes, however, that unless self-access centres succeed in fostering autonomy, they are liable to fail in their language-learning goals. Much of the research on self-access therefore focuses on the ways in which self-access should be organised in order to foster autonomy.

Sturtridge (1997), based on her experience as a consultant to self-access projects in various parts of the world, has identified a number of factors contributing to the success or failure of self-access centres (Concept 8.1). It is widely accepted that effective self-access learning is dependent on some form of learner development or training, an area of practice that will be discussed in more detail in Chapter 10. I will therefore focus on two issues that are specific to the operation of self-access centres themselves: the management and use of self-access facilities and the design of materials for independent use.

Concept 8.1   **Key issues in the evaluation of self-access**

Sturtridge (1997) identifies a number of key factors in the effectiveness of self-access. These are presented below in the form of evaluation questions:

Management

- Is there adequate consultation between management and teachers in the planning and implementation of the centre?
- Are activities in the centre integrated into the curriculum and teaching timetable?
- Are learners involved in the planning and management of the centre? Are they aware of its functions and of its role in the curriculum?

Facilities

- Is the location of the centre easily accessible to its potential users?
- Is the centre appropriately resourced on an ongoing basis?
- Are available resources appropriately and imaginatively used and displayed?
- Does the access and retrieval system encourage the development of autonomy?

Staff training and development

- Is training available to all members of staff who have contact with the centre? Are all staff aware of its functions and role in the curriculum?
- Are staff involved in ongoing development programmes to encourage growth and change in the centre?
- Does the centre have adequate feedback mechanisms for staff comments and proposals?
- Are staff connected with the centre involved in research into its use?
- Does training cover the roles of teachers and learners in self-access learning?

Learner training and development

- Is training available to all learners who have contact with the centre?
- Is ongoing training available to regular users of the centre?
- Do training and development functions extend beyond practical aspects of using the centre to cover issues concerned with autonomous learning?

Learner culture

- Does the centre accommodate different learning styles and the strengths and weaknesses of the group of students who use it?

Materials

- Are the materials in the centre adapted for self-access use?
- Do the materials foster autonomous learning skills as well as language development?
- Are the materials appropriate to the functions of self-access learning in the curriculum?
- Does the range and arrangement of materials facilitate exploration and the exercise of choice?

8.1.1   Management and use of self-access centres

Appropriate technology

Further reading

Moore, C. (1992) *Self-access: Appropriate Technology*. Manchester: British Council.

Quote 8.2 Lonergan on self-access and technology

For many potential SALC (self-access learning centre) users, access to video and television, to computer-assisted learning programs, or to inter-active CD-ROM is a normal part of their learning experience in other disciplines. Not only do they welcome the use of technology, they in fact come to expect it, and question its absence in the modern curriculum.

Lonergan (1994: 122)

Self-access centres operate in a variety of cultural and educational settings and come in a variety of forms, including purpose-designed facilities within an institution, subsections of libraries and converted language or computer laboratories. The level of funding and the purposes for which funds are employed are key issues in the establishment of self-access. Self-access centres often appear to be the most logical place in which to experiment with and meet student demand for new learning technologies (Quote 8.2). It is therefore often assumed that one of the priorities in setting up self-access centres should be to secure the maximum amount of funding for high tech facilities. There is no research evidence, however, of any relationship between the level of funding of a self-access centre and its success in promoting autonomy or better language learning (Concept 8.2 overleaf).

The technological imperative in self-access is in part a matter of learner expectations, which are likely to vary from country to country. It is also clear that appropriate use of technology is in part an issue of the need to allocate funding for other purposes. Many self-access centres face the problem of having been set up in situations in which funding authorities see one-off capital expenditures on self-access as a viable alternative to more expensive ongoing expenditures on teacher salaries. But, as Gardner and Miller (1999: 31) point out, 'a key element

Concept 8.2   High tech and low tech self-access

The level of technology used in self-access centres varies greatly and appears to have little relationship to the effectiveness of self-access learning. Compare the facilities available in two centres in the United Kingdom and Nicaragua, both of which report success in achieving their goals.

University of Central Lancashire, England (Hurd, 1994)

- A large open-plan multi-activity room containing 12 video and 18 audio presenters, two Apple Mac computers loaded with Speakwrite, five BBC computers with a range of different software, an extensive shelving system containing worksheets in 12 languages, more shelves containing reference material, newspapers and magazines, a photo-copier and an area for private study.

- A satellite TV room with 24 presenters and access to a range of foreign TV channels.

- A computer room containing 17 networked computers carrying a range of CALL material.

- A Vektor room housing seven workstations with materials on laser disk in six languages and on CD-ROM in three. This room also contains material for the TELL consortium distributed free to all HE institutions during 1994.

- The technical and resources room containing, at the time of writing, in the region of 3,000 video cassettes, 700–800 audio cassettes and approximately 200–300 other resources including books, slides and OHP and CALL materials. This room also houses three technicians/resource assistants and the database.

- An office for another technician and technical equipment for satellite TV operation.

- A room for photocopying, storage and recording.

Universidad Nacional Autónoma de Nicaragua (Waite, 1994)

- Six listening booths and six other work spaces along two walls.
- A free-standing box with compartments for work cards.
- An adjoining table for audiocassettes.
- Ordinary cassette players secured by chains installed in the listening booths.
- Reference dictionaries secured to lecterns.
- Additional materials for language development, listening and reading, and a selection of course books.

in successful SALL (self-access language learning) is pedagogical input and this is relatively expensive'. If the development of autonomy through self-access learning depends on factors such as training, counselling and the management of the self-access system, an emphasis on high-tech facilities may be counterproductive.

Self-access systems

Further reading

Booton, P. and Benson, P. (1996) *Self-access: Classification and Retrieval.* Manchester: British Council.

Gardner and Miller (1999) have shown that self-access centres are distinguished both by the kinds of resources and services they provide and by the systems through which these are made available to the learners. Their typology of self-access systems uses metaphors such as 'fast-food restaurant', 'video-rental shop', 'supermarket' and 'cash-and-carry'. Self-access systems can also be described more broadly as 'information systems', or semiotic systems in which aspects of the organization of the centre and its resources convey messages to learners about the nature of language learning (Benson, 1994). For example, a centre that consists primarily of video, audio and computer booths arranged for individual use may convey the message that language learning is essentially a matter of individual study. A centre that contains open areas for group work and discussion is likely to convey the message that language learning is more a matter of communication and collaboration (Benson, 1995b).

Within a self-access system, the access and retrieval system represents the interface between the centre's learning resources and the learner (Quote 8.3 overleaf). The most typical models found in self-access centres are based on library access systems. However, as Riley (1986) points out, self-access centres differ from libraries in that their users are less likely to be interested in the authors, titles and topics of materials than in the kinds of learning activities they support. Among the factors that appear to be most important in fostering autonomy are the extent to which the system encourages and facilitates choice, the extent to which it is oriented towards the description of activities rather than materials and the transparency of the system to its users (Booton and Benson, 1996).

One approach to the design of access systems to support the development of autonomy is to examine how learners can best be supported

> **Quote 8.3** Sheerin on access and retrieval systems
>
> The other crucial aspect of planning which needs to be considered right at the outset is the question of how materials are to be classified and physically organised. Questions of classification and shelving may seem unimportant or uninteresting to those concerned with the higher ideals of autonomous learning, but the systems of access play a crucial role in ensuring that the learner has the freedom of choice that efficient information retrieval provides.
>
> Sheerin (1991: 147)

at each phase of the process of self-managed learning. Sheerin (1997), for example, identifies the following phases: analysing needs, setting objectives, planning a programme of work, choosing materials and activities, working unsupervised and evaluating progress. Research suggests that, in the more successful centres, a considerable portion of the resources belong to the self-access system and that these are often integrated with language-learning resources so that they are available to learners at appropriate phases of learning. Access system resources include catalogues, training documents or videos, documents describing the centre's resources and documents attached to learning materials to assist learners in their use. Some centres have also experimented with computerised cataloguing and indexing systems (Booton and Benson, 1996), 'pathways' to guide learners in constructing sequences of learning activities (Barnett and Jordan, 1991; Cooley, 1993), and self-assessment tasks inserted into learning materials (Gardner, 1996). Many centres also make use of documents for student use such as learning contracts, records of learning and learning logs to facilitate reflection and discussion with counsellors or teachers (Martyn, 1994).

Although it seems self-evident that self-access systems should be organised in ways that facilitate informed choices by the learner, we lack hard evidence on the effectiveness of particular innovations designed to meet this goal. At the University of Hong Kong, for example, a sophisticated computerised cataloguing system was developed in order to facilitate self-directed learning in the self-access centre, but it has been observed that students make little use of it unless they are encouraged to do so by counsellors (Booton and Benson, 1996). Martyn's (1994) study of the use of self-access logs showed that about half the students who used them found that they helped them to set realistic goals, while one third found them helpful in planning learning activities and keeping track of progress. However, the fact that the logs were used as a basis for negotiation of self-access work with a classroom was identified as an important factor in their effectiveness. It seems likely, therefore, that however innovative the self-access system, it is unlikely to be effective unless it is backed up by structures for counselling or classroom support in which learners have the opportunity to discuss and refine their goals and plans.

Teacher and learner involvement

> **Further reading**
>
> Sturtridge, G. (1992) *Self-access: Preparation and Training*. Manchester: British Council.

A third issue of importance in the effectiveness of self-access is the extent to which self-access centres succeed in involving teachers and learners in their development. A study by Littlejohn (1985: 259) suggested that the amount of work students put into self-access depended on the attitude of their teacher towards it and that effective use of the self-access centre 'depended principally on the extent to which each teacher viewed self-access work as valuable'. O'Dell (1992: 153) also observes that her experience at Eurocentre Cambridge in the United Kingdom 'has shown very clearly that most of the students who make full use of the learning centre's resources are in classes where the teacher is confident and well-informed as far as learning centre use is concerned'.

Sturtridge (1997: 70) argues that one reason for the failure of some self-access centres is lack of consultation between the managers of the centre and teaching staff:

> In some instances, the teaching staff, being inadequately briefed about the innovation, saw the introduction of a self-access centre as a threat to their jobs and therefore regarded it with animosity. In other cases, the teaching staff only saw the educational reason for the centre's existence, whereas the management saw it primarily in terms of good publicity for the institution and possibly as a way of saving salaries.

The attitudes of teachers towards self-access may in part be a question of the institution's attitudes towards their involvement in it. Sturtridge emphasises that all staff should be involved as stakeholders in the development of self-access facilities from the outset if they are to develop and grow.

Two research studies have documented teacher involvement in self-access. Martyn and Voller's (1993) two-year study of teachers involved in the introduction of self-access learning at the University of Hong Kong showed that teachers varied greatly in their awareness of theories of self-directed learning and autonomy and that both positive and negative attitudes towards self-access tended to be reinforced over the two years of the study. O'Dell (1997) found that teachers at Eurocentre Cambridge experienced four kinds of anxieties about self-access. These were related to students' reactions to self-access work, their own pedagogic skills, their familiarity with the resources of the centre and their ability to use learning technologies. She also found that worries about student reactions, pedagogic skills and technology tended to diminish with experience, while worries about familiarity with resources dramatically increased. This research suggests that in order for self-access to influence the development of autonomy, teachers must be well equipped to cope with the technicalities of self-access and with underlying assumptions about the relationship between self-access and autonomy.

Research on teacher roles in self-access has also focused on the specialised skills needed in one-to-one counselling for self-directed learning. Kelly (1996: 94) has developed a model of counselling for self-access based on the notion of a 'therapeutic dialogue that enables an individual to manage a problem'. For Riley (1997: 114), however, 'there are considerable problems involved in saying just what counselling *is* and how it differs from teaching or therapeutic discourse'. Evidently, learners come to self-access counsellors for advice, and not for teaching or for therapy, leading more recent researchers to focus on the nature of the advice given. In research conducted in Hong Kong, Voller et al. (1999) and Pemberton et al. (2001) have observed that self-access counsellors tend to be overly directive when giving advice and recommend action research focusing on the discourse of counselling sessions (distribution of turns, quantity of speech, speech acts, etc.) as a means of developing less directive styles.

Two studies have documented learner involvement in the planning and management of self-access centres. Aston (1993) reports on a language-learning project at the University of Ancona in Italy, in which eight learners investigated and evaluated the resources available in the university's self-access centre and produced leaflets and reports for other users and staff. Aston suggests that this type of involvement helps learners to take 'greater control not only of their own learning, but also of the institution whose task it is to make such learning and control possible' (p. 226). Jones (1995) describes how volunteer students were recruited to assist in the design and management of the self-access centre at the University of

Phnom Penh in Cambodia, a factor that contributed much to the cultural appropriateness of the centre's design. Proposals to involve learners in the life of self-access centres on a larger scale have also been made. Learners could, for example, be involved in selecting, cataloguing and describing materials and students' learning outcomes could be recycled as materials for other learners to use (Benson, 1994). However, as Aston (1993) points out, learner involvement in a self-access centre may only be possible if the number of students is not too great and their involvement lasts long enough for them to take full advantage of the centre.

Self-access and the curriculum

The extent to which teachers and learners are involved in the development of self-access is in part a question of the relationship of self-access work to the curriculum. If self-access is tightly integrated into the curriculum, the opportunities for teacher and learner involvement are likely to be greater. Similarly, the relationship of self-access work to the curriculum is likely to determine the way in which a self-access centre works. Sturtridge (1992) describes two kinds of centre: the 'practice centre' and the 'learning centre'. The 'practice centre' is typically oriented towards supplementary language practice for classroom-based courses. Self-access work is supplementary to the curriculum and the goal of autonomy is likely to be absent. The 'learning centre' is typically oriented towards exploration of resources and self-access work is closely integrated within a curriculum in which autonomy is a major goal. Although both types of centre are likely to be motivated by language-learning goals, Sturtridge (1997: 74) argues that 'it appears to be the centres which come into the learning centre category which not only survive, but grow'.

One approach to the integration of self-access work and classroom work is to allocate different functions to each mode of learning. Littlewood (1997: 91), for example, argues that self-access needs to be located within a theoretical framework that helps us to be 'aware not only of the strengths of self-access as a means for encouraging autonomy in learning and communication but also of its limitations'. He suggests that self-access is currently strong in the domain of receptive skills, pre-communicative work and communicative practice and weaker in the domain of authentic communication. According to Littlewood, this means that 'in the present state of the art, there are important aspects of the learning process which cannot be catered for by self-access alone'.

One solution to this problem lies in closer integration of self-access and classroom sessions. At Eurocentre Cambridge, O'Dell (1997) reports that students are taken to the self-access centre for lessons based on a theme, where they are provided with a choice of tasks using different media and focusing on different skills. This is followed up by a classroom activity in which the students share what they have done in the centre. Individual self-access work is the stimulus for communicative work in the classroom on the theme of independent learning. In a pre-sessional EAP course at the Victoria University of Wellington in New Zealand, Cotterall (1995a: 225) explains how the role of a self-access centre changed as it was integrated more closely into the course. Initially a focus for general language practice using a large bank of materials, the centre has become more of 'a laboratory where learners test out solutions to specific language problems'. One consequence of this changing role was a shift in the function of self-access counselling from a teacher located in the centre to the classroom teacher.

A great deal of the research on self-access is concerned with ways of making self-access work independently of other learning activities that students may be involved in. However, the elevation of 'self-access language learning' to a category of learning in its own right may be counterproductive. A more important question than the effectiveness of self-access in promoting autonomy may be the role that self-access plays within a curriculum that adopts autonomy as one of its goals.

8.1.2   Materials design

The selection and design of learning materials for self-study has been a key issue in research on self-access. Dickinson (1987: 68) lists three sources of materials for self-access: authentic texts, commercially produced courses and materials specifically designed for self-instruction. Strong arguments have been made for the value of authentic texts in fostering autonomy. Similarly, where self-access centres use commercial or teacher-produced materials, a strong case has been made that the materials need to be adapted in order to foster autonomy. Research has also begun to address the issue of the role of the learner in materials use and design.

Authentic texts

> ### Further reading
>
> McGarry, D. (1995) *Learner Autonomy 4: The Role of Authentic Texts*. Dublin: Authentik.

> **Quote 8.4** McGarry on autonomy and authentic texts
>
> There is now a general recognition of the valuable role which authentic texts can play in helping to create a language-rich environment in the classroom, and in providing students with bridges to the real world of the target language community. Used extensively and appropriately, however, activities around authentic texts have the potential to do much more than this – they can play a key role in enhancing positive attitudes to learning, in promoting the development of a wide range of skills, and in enabling students to work independently of the teacher. In other words, they can play a key role in the promotion of learner autonomy. That this is so becomes apparent when we examine the contribution authentic texts can make in two areas of major concern: (a) the matching of language learning opportunities to the needs and interests of individual students, and (b) the creation of the conditions under which students can most successfully exploit these opportunities.
>
> McGarry (1995: 3)

McGarry (1995) argues that the use of authentic materials in language learning helps foster autonomy by enabling learners to match learning opportunities to their needs (Quote 8.4). Little (1997b: 231) offers two further arguments: authentic texts draw language learners into the communicative world of the target language community and the development of autonomy entails interaction between language learning and language use. On the affective level, it is argued, learners who work with authentic materials from an early stage develop confidence when faced with authentic samples of the target language and do not worry that their comprehension may be incomplete. On the psychological level, authentic texts encourage the development of 'techniques of language learning that entail language use and techniques of language use that entail language learning'.

Effective use of authentic materials appears to depend on the learner's capacity to use them as learning materials. In consequence, authentic materials are often accompanied by tasks and training materials of various kinds. One example commonly used in self-access centres is the 'standard' worksheet designed to focus on a particular skill and genre, such as listening to the news or understanding a reading text (for examples, see Scott et al., 1984; Carvalho, 1993: 32–3). Originally conceived of as a means of economising on resource development, worksheets of this kind have the disadvantage that they cannot be accompanied by a

'standard' answer key (Carvalho, 1993). This may also be an advantage, however, if self-evaluation of performance is seen as an important
aspect of autonomous learning.

Authentic materials can also be placed within more complex structures
for learning. Little (1994a), for example, reports on experiments with
Autotutor, an interactive video system in which segments of authentic
video are embedded in a computer program designed to encourage
group interaction. He argues that programs of this kind can provide a
stimulus to the interaction of learner and user perspectives essential to
the development of autonomy (Little 1997b). Aston (1997) reports on a
course for students at the University of Bologna in Italy, where students
were provided with access to a concordancer and a corpus of authentic
English texts. The students were asked to work in small groups to isolate
a subcorpus of texts on a theme they had chosen and to look for regu-
larities in discourse patterns. Weekly discussion sessions were held and
final reports were circulated to the whole class. Aston reports that the
students claimed to have become more aware of recurrent patterning in
language and of its importance to 'native-like' performance. They also
claimed to have developed skills in acquiring encyclopaedic and linguistic
information by browsing through small collections of text. In other words,
through a structured programme of self-access work, they had acquired
awareness of the potential of authentic texts as learning resources.

Adapting and writing materials for self-study

> **Further reading**
>
> Carvalho, D. (1993) *Self-access: Appropriate Materials*. Manchester: British
>   Council.

Commercially produced materials appear to have less potential for
fostering autonomy than authentic materials and it is widely assumed that
most commercial textbooks are unsuitable for self-study without some
modification. Even when materials are produced in self-study versions,
this often means little more than the inclusion of an answer key with
little or no attention paid to task design. In particular, task instructions
and feedback are often insufficiently explicit for self-study, especially
those for group activities. In adapting commercial materials or writing
learning materials for self-instruction, Dickinson (1987: 77) suggests
that the important thing is 'to provide the learner with the kind of help,

---

Quote 8.5 Dickinson on self-instructional materials

Self-instructional materials should have all the features good language-teaching materials have – interest, variety, clarity and so on. However, in addition they should also contain the following:

- a clear statement of objectives;
- meaningful language input;
- exercise materials and activities;
- flexibility of materials;
- learning instructions;
- language learning advice;
- feedback and tests;
- advice about record keeping;
- reference materials;
- indexing;
- motivational factors;
- advice about progression.

Dickinson (1987: 80)

---

advice and encouragement given by a teacher using the same material in a classroom' (Quote 8.5). The factors that facilitate achievement of the language-learning goals of a self-instructional task, however, are not necessarily those that will best foster autonomy. Although well-designed self-instructional materials allow control at the micro-level of the completion of the learning task, they may discourage learners from making the kinds of decisions and choices that promote control over the macro-level tasks of planning, monitoring and evaluating learning.

In this context, Sheerin (1997) argues that feedback in learning materials can be antithetical to autonomy if the authority of the teacher is transferred to the materials in the form of 'right answers'. According to Sheerin, 'the less objective the feedback in self-access materials, the more prepared learners have to be to accept a degree of uncertainty'. By encouraging learners to accept uncertainty and to decide on appropriate responses to tasks for themselves, materials with more open-ended feedback may be more effective in fostering autonomy. Sheerin (1991: 150) provides a list of such material types:

- guided discovery tasks based on authentic data;
- questionnaires designed to help learners clarify or challenge their beliefs about language learning;

- study guides for language practice activities not based on didactic materials;
- fluency activities for pairs and groups together with checklists and guidelines for self- and peer evaluation;
- suggestions for different ways of using learning materials;
- student-generated materials;
- standard reading and listening exercises designed for a particular genre rather than a particular text.

The items in this list depart from the pedagogical model of transmission and testing of language content commonly underlying commercial materials. The list also suggests that the most effective materials for the development of autonomy may be those that help learners to exploit opportunities for learning that are external to the materials themselves.

An alternative approach to materials design for autonomy focuses on the incorporation of learning to learn goals into conventional language-learning textbooks. Responding to Johnston's (1985) concern that self-directed learning is based on the questionable assumption that 'the learner knows best', Nunan (1997: 194) argues that 'most learners, at the beginning of the learning process, do *not* know what is best'. The function of the materials enhancement Nunan describes is thus 'to develop skills and knowledge in learners which ultimately will leave them in a position where they do know what is best'. Nunan identifies five levels of autonomy that can be incorporated into different phases of a language-learning textbook (Table 8.1).

In Nunan's model, each level of autonomy is addressed by integrating learning-to-learn tasks with learning content tasks. Addressing Level 4 (learners create their own tasks), for example, Nunan suggests that a questionnaire type activity could be followed by these task instructions (p. 200):

- Create a questionnaire on a topic of your choice following the model provided.
- Interview five native-speakers using the questionnaire as a guide.
- Audio or video record the interviews.
- Create a worksheet based on the recording for use by other students in the self-access centre. The worksheet should contain the questionnaire, and should ask the viewer to identify the responses given by each of the speakers.

Table 8.1   Autonomy: levels of implementation (Nunan, 1997: 195)

LEVEL	LEARNER ACTION	CONTENT	PROCESS
1	Awareness	Learners are made aware of the pedagogical goals and content of the materials they are using	Learners identify strategy implications of pedagogical tasks and identify their own preferred learning styles/strategies
2	Involvement	Learners are involved in selecting their own goals from a range of alternatives on offer	Learners make choices among a range of options
3	Intervention	Learners are involved in modifying and adapting the goals and content of the learning programme	Learners modify/adapt tasks
4	Creation	Learners create their own goals and objectives	Learners create their own tasks
5	Transcendence	Learners go beyond the classroom and make links between the content of classroom learning and the world beyond	Learners become teachers and researchers

Nunan's model presupposes that autonomy develops alongside proficiency, which prompts the question of how materials writers can identify the appropriate proficiency levels at which to place learning-to-learn tasks. Nevertheless it is an elegant solution to the problem of enhancing commercial materials for autonomy, which has been adopted in Nunan's own *ATLAS* English language course (Nunan, 1995a) and Sinclair's (1996) *Activate Your English* course book for adult learners.

The role of the learner

Research has only recently begun to address the role of the learner in materials designed to promote autonomy. Focusing on the discourse roles implicit in materials used in self-access, Littlejohn (1997: 181) has argued that 'much self-access work places learners in a reactive, dis-empowered position by virtue of the tasks which they typically do' and suggests that 'self-access work may be redefined such that it engages learners in a wider range of responses and draws them more into decisions affecting their own work'. Using an analytical model designed to reveal underlying subject positions proposed for learners in language-learning tasks, Littlejohn poses three key questions:

1. What role in the discourse is proposed for the learner: initiate, respond or none?
2. What mental operation is to be engaged?
3. Where does the content for the task come from? From within the task itself, from the teacher or from the students?

In analysing discourse roles, Littlejohn uses 'none' to refer to tasks in which the learner simply attends to what is being presented, 'respond' for tasks in which learners are expected to express themselves in pre-defined language, and 'initiate' for tasks in which the learners can say what they want without any underlying 'script'.

Littlejohn argues that most of the language-learning tasks provided in self-access centres limit the learner to the 'respond' role, fail to engage the learner in higher level mental operations such as speculating, analysing, hypothesising, critiquing and reflecting and call upon the learner to work only with content supplied in the context of the task. According to Littlejohn, there is therefore an ideological tension between the ostensible aims of self-access materials and their realisation in practice (Quote 8.6).

One of the strengths of authentic texts as resources for the development of autonomy is that they place much of the responsibility for task design onto the learners themselves. Innovative resource books showing the potential of the involvement of learners in materials production

---

Quote 8.6 Littlejohn on self-access tasks and autonomy

The notions of personally appropriate language work, of personal control and self-direction *may* be involved at the level of the decision to enter into self-access work, but once this decision is taken the role which the learner then goes on to take is strongly suggested by the closed nature of the tasks which are provided and the existence of 'correct answers'. Thus, an intention on the part of many teachers for self-access work to 'liberate' the learner is accommodated into social reproduction, a process in which the student now becomes *individually* and, more immediately, engaged.

Littlejohn (1997: 188)

have been published by Deller (1990) and Campbell and Kryszewska (1992). Deller's materials were produced by learners, while Campbell and Kryszewska provide examples of tasks that require the learners to provide input from their own environment and resources. In both cases the products presented by the authors as resources are probably of less significance for autonomous learning than the processes by which they were produced. As Littlejohn (1997: 191) points out in relation to his own work with learner-generated materials, the important arguments are related to 'the construction of the learner as an *active* agent in the learning process, not simply the recipient of teaching'.

8.2   Self-instruction and distance learning

It is seldom claimed that self-instruction and distance learning are effective means of promoting autonomy. However, these modes of learning need to be mentioned for two reasons. First, self-instruction and distance learning are often described as 'autonomous' modes of learning because they require the learner to study independently of direct contact with teachers and, for some researchers, evidence of their ineffectiveness calls into question the value of the concept of autonomy (Quote 8.7). Second, some of the problems associated with these modes of learning bring the problems of self-access into starker relief.

As a mode of learning, self-instruction describes the situation in which learners study languages on their own, primarily with the aid of 'teach-yourself' materials. Although the self-instructional materials industry is a significant sector within the foreign language-teaching industry as a whole, little research on the effectiveness of self-instruction

| Quote 8.7 | Rosewell and Libben on self-instruction |

Most people (with the possible exception of those who market teach-yourself learning materials) know that learning in isolation is a poor way to acquire a language. In most of these attempts, learners flounder around in frustration, making little or no progress. However, some learners, presumably the most motivated and talented ones, do succeed in achieving at least some of their learning goals.

Rosewell and Libben (1994: 668–9)

has been carried out. Jones (1993: 453) even goes so far as to argue that academic opinion of teach-yourself courses is so disparaging as to render them 'unworthy of attention by the serious researcher'.

In the only major survey of self-instructed language learning to date, Fernández-Toro and Jones (1996) interviewed 70 adult learners about their experiences of self-instruction. On the basis of a factor analysis of their results, they observe that (p. 209):

> Self-instruction seems to raise proficiency, but only after a firm class-work grounding – in other words, it appears to 'kick in' at roughly inter-mediate level, i.e. once the learner is able to cope with real-life texts and interactions.

It also appears that self-instructed learners require a high degree of autonomy in order to succeed. Jones's (1994) study of his own learn-ing of Hungarian showed that he reached intermediate level only by switching to 'largely autonomous strategies once two related thresholds had been crossed: the ability to guess significant amounts of new lexis from the underlying building-blocks, and the ability to cope with authentic reading texts' (Jones, 1993: 466). Self-instructional materials, however, appear to do little to foster autonomy among their learners. In a survey of 40 teach-yourself packages, Jones (1993: 465) found that 'learner autonomy and strategy development rarely occurs' and that all the packages assumed that the user would follow a page-by-page route.

The evidence on self-instruction is not entirely negative, however. Rosewell and Libben (1994) observed a group of 30 university under-graduates learning a variety of foreign languages from beginner level using self-instructional methods alone. They found that at the end of six months the majority could be characterised as low achievers on the basis of their own self-assessments. Those students who judged them-selves to be more successful tended to have found real or imaginary ways of overcoming their communicative isolation. The fact that some learners find ways of overcoming the isolation implicit in self-instruction suggests that this mode of learning may prompt learners to develop strategies associated with autonomy. At the same time, it is clear that some degree of autonomy is a prerequisite for success in self-instruction. Learners who succeed in developing strategies to deal with their isolation may do so because they already possess a high degree of autonomy.

Like self-instructed learners, distance learners largely depend on packaged resources and are liable to be isolated from their peers. Unlike self-instruction, distance learning is an institutional form of learning involving teachers, although 'the teacher is not available to set up and oversee learning activities and to intervene when problems are struck' (White, 1995: 208). The literature on distance learning is vast, but there has been very little research on its effectiveness for language learning. Studies in Richards and Roe's (1994) volume on distance learning and ELT, for example, tend to be highly practical in their orientation with little concern for the issue of autonomy. In one important study, White (1995) compared strategy use among distance and classroom learners at a New Zealand university and found that the mode of study was the predominant influence on metacognitive dimensions of strategy use. In particular, the distance learners made greater use of self-management strategies. White suggests that distance learners may 'respond to the demands of a self-instruction mode of study by developing a knowledge of how they can manage the process of language learning for themselves' (p. 217). Again, however, it may be that learners who choose and persist with distance learning are those who already possess a sufficient degree of autonomy to allow them to develop such strategies on their own.

As in the case of self-instruction, distance learning materials rarely help learners to acquire the autonomous learning skills they need. The isolation of distance learners is often addressed in highly directive ways and some of the best-known general guides to writing distance materials emphasise the need to direct the learner explicitly. Rowntree (1990: 11), for example, states:

> The materials must carry out all the functions a teacher or trainer would carry out in the conventional situation – guiding, motivating, intriguing, expounding, explaining, provoking, reminding, asking questions, discussing alternative answers, appraising each learner's progress, giving appropriate remedial or enrichment help . . . and so on.

Although the concept of autonomy is clearly relevant to self-instruction and distance learning, it appears that those involved in promoting these modes of learning have given little attention to the ways in which procedures and materials can help learners take over the functions assigned to classroom teachers for themselves.

8.3   The effectiveness of resource-based learning

In principle, self-access, self-instruction and distance learning foster autonomy by providing learners with *opportunities* to direct their own learning. However, the research evidence suggests that the opportunity to direct one's own learning, does not in itself lead to greater autonomy or better language learning. Indeed, it seems likely that success in resource-based language learning presupposes that the learner already possesses some of the skills associated with autonomy. In self-instruction and distance learning, this problem tends to be addressed negatively by providing learners with explicit direction and feedback, so that the learner can survive without the requisite learning skills. In the field of self-access the problem has been addressed more positively by exploring ways in which the organisation of self-access can help learners develop these skills in the process of self-directed learning.

Gardner and Miller (1999: 231) observe that very little progress has been made in measuring the effectiveness of self-access either in terms of autonomy or language learning. Research suggests that the provision of self-access learning opportunities is insufficient in itself to foster autonomy, because learners may either founder without support or find sources of other-direction within the resources provided. It also suggests that unless self-access learners succeed in developing a degree of autonomy they are unlikely to be successful in their language-learning goals. Learner training and support mechanisms, appropriate use of technology, the design of access systems to support self-direction, teacher and learner involvement, and the integration of self-access with the curriculum have been identified as important factors contributing to the greater effectiveness of self-access. However, the complexity of self-access systems and the variety of contexts in which they are used means that much more empirical research on the outcomes of specific innovations for specific learner populations is needed before the importance of these factors can reliably be assessed.

A key issue in resource-based approaches to language learning is the provision of opportunities for authentic communication. If autonomy develops through communicative interaction, such opportunities are essential. The nature of resource-based approaches means that they are most effective in offering learners opportunities to develop greater control over their own *individual* learning. They are far less effective in offering opportunities for learners to make decisions concerned with the *collective* process of teaching and learning. Indeed, at the extreme, resource-based approaches may represent an approach to autonomy based on the withdrawal of the individual from the social process of learning. Group work, projects, the use of the self-access centre as a meeting place for learners and the use of new interactive technologies have been proposed as solutions to this problem, but there is as yet little research evidence on their effectiveness. One of the key questions in research and practice on self-access is, therefore, whether a mode of learning ideally suited to the individualisation of learning can support the kinds of collaborative decision-making that many researchers now see as vital to the development of autonomy.

Chapter 9

Technology-based approaches

Technology-based approaches to the development of autonomy are similar in many respects to other resource-based approaches, but differ from them in their focus on the technologies used to access resources. As Motteram (1997) points out, new learning technologies have a long association with autonomy (Quote 9.1). The first self-access centres at the University of Cambridge and CRAPEL, for example, were known as 'sound and video libraries' (Harding-Esch, 1982; Riley and Zoppis, 1985). In the recent literature, a number of interesting technology-based projects have been reported incorporating student-produced video (Gardner, 1994), computer-enhanced interactive video (Gardner and Blasco Garcia, 1996; Little, 1994a), electronic writing environments (Milton, 1997), concordancing (Aston, 1997), informational CD-ROMs (Guillot, 1996), hypermedia systems (Mayes, 1994), e-mail language advising (Makin, 1994), e-mail tandem learning (Lewis et al., 1996) and computer simulations (Mak, 1994). In many of these projects it is the interaction with the technology itself that is seen to be supportive of autonomy. In others, it is the potential of the technology to facilitate

> **Quote 9.1** Motteram on autonomy and educational technology
>
> There has always been a perceived relationship between educational technology and learner autonomy. This is taking educational technology in its broadest sense and taking learner autonomy as the superordinate term. This has become increasingly true for computers and self-access.
>
> Motteram (1997: 17)

interactions that would be difficult or impossible in the classroom that is at issue. Since much of the attention of educational technology now falls upon computers and the Internet, this chapter will be limited to a discussion of the claims made for computer-assisted language learning (CALL) in regard to autonomy.

9.1   Computer-assisted language learning

> **Further reading**
>
> Koebke, K. (forthcoming) *Teaching and Researching CALL* (ALIA series).

Warschauer and Healey (1998) divide the history of CALL into three phases: behaviouristic, communicative and integrative. The earliest CALL applications were designed to drill and test knowledge of vocabulary and grammatical structure either through multiple choice exercises or by matching learner input to pre-programmed answers. These applications encouraged a degree of control by offering a choice of materials and practice items, by allowing learners to choose instructional, practice or testing modes, and by encouraging them to 'try again' when a wrong answer was given. They were also designed to give learners individual control over the pace of learning. The elements within these applications that encouraged learner control, however, were overlaid by a model of the computer as tutor and behaviouristic assumptions about language learning as habit formation that were far less supportive of the development of autonomy (Fox, 1994).

In the 1980s, inspired by the work of Underwood (1984) and others, CALL entered a communicative phase in which applications were based explicitly on principles of communicative language teaching. Text reconstruction, game and simulation packages were designed to engage students in problem-solving activities that would stimulate cognitive involvement with the target language and spoken communication with other students engaged in the CALL task. Although these applications encouraged students to take some degree of control over the route taken towards the solution of a problem, they often retained the computer-as-tutor model established in behaviouristic CALL, especially when solutions to problems were pre-programmed into the software.

A second strand of communicative CALL focused on applications not specifically designed for language learning, such as word processors, desktop publishing packages, concordancers and databases. In this strand of CALL, the computer was either used as a tool to facilitate the linguistic processes involved in achieving non-linguistic goals (for example, in the use of a word-processor or desktop publishing programme to produce a class magazine), or as a tool to achieve linguistic goals that could not otherwise easily be achieved (for example, the use of a concordancer to identify regular patterns in text).

From the perspective of autonomy, the key characteristic of non-language-learning applications is their potential to facilitate creative manipulation of text. Control over text creation and interpretation promote the development of metacognitive skills and metalinguistic awareness. As Kenning (1996: 128) puts it, there is 'a prima facie case that by encouraging users to consider their text critically and try and make improvements, word processors are intrinsically supportive of cognitive and metacognitive autonomy'. Similarly, Stevens (1995: 2) argues of concordancing:

> First, it interjects authenticity (of text, purpose, and activity) into the learning process. Second, learners assume control of that process. And third, the predominant metaphor for learning becomes the research metaphor, as embodied in the concept of data-driven learning (DDL), which builds learners' competence by giving them access to the facts of linguistic performance.

The benefits to be derived from text manipulation applications may not, however, be equally available to all learners. Kenning (1996: 131) argues, for example, that evidence from the classroom suggests that 'self-directed interactive use of concordancers by learners must be seen as primarily suited to advanced students with a propensity for autonomy'. She also argues that, although IT in general offers opportunities for self-directed learning, 'the effective use of electronic tools and resources assumes certain prerequisites and that unless learners already have certain attitudes, skills and strategies, they are unlikely to derive much benefit' (pp. 132–3).

The integrative phase of CALL is characterised by the use of multimedia, hypermedia and interactive technologies to promote integration of skills. A large number of multimedia language-learning applications are now available on CD-ROM. The best of these applications support the development of autonomy by offering rich linguistic and non-linguistic input, by presenting new language through a variety of media, and by offering branching options. Such applications encourage exploratory learning and encourage learners to exercise control over the selection of materials and strategies of interpretation. However, even the best multimedia applications tend to restrict learner control to the process of text interpretation and do little to facilitate creative response to input. At worst, multimedia applications simply reproduce the behaviouristic assumptions of early CALL software with the addition of sound and images.

9.2 The Internet

Many of the conventional assumptions about CALL are currently being rethought in the context of the potential of computer-mediated communication tools and the Internet for language learning. According to Warschauer and Healey (1998), the Internet represents a way forward for integrative CALL as it runs into the limitations of the CD-ROM as a mode of delivery. Provided the learner has easy and inexpensive access (an assumption that cannot yet be made in many parts of the world), the Internet is also strongly supportive of two basic situational conditions for self-directed learning: learners can study whenever they want using a potentially unlimited range of authentic materials.

From the perspective of autonomy, the most significant Internet-based activities involve e-mail, on-line discussion and web authoring. A key characteristic of the Internet as a resource for self-directed learning is the opportunity it provides for collaborative learning. Internet technologies open up opportunities for interaction among learners, between learners and target language users, and between learners and teachers that could otherwise be difficult or impossible to achieve in the classroom or in self-access. The Internet also appears to facilitate learner control over interaction. Warschauer et al. (1996), for example, cite a number of studies suggesting that use of the computer-mediated communication tools in language learning leads to more student-initiated interactions, a social dynamic based on student–student collaboration, more student-centred discussion and a shift in authority from teacher to student.

The potential of the Internet in regard to autonomy may also lie in its capacity to facilitate important elements within larger projects. Warschauer (1996), for example, describes a project for students of English for Science and Technology in Mexico (reported in Bowers, 1995):

> First the students search the World Wide Web for articles in their exact area of specialty and then carefully read and study those specific articles.

Then they write their own drafts online; the teacher critiques the drafts online and creates electronic links to his own comments and to pages of appropriate linguistic and technical explanation, so that the students can find additional background help at the click of a mouse. Next, using this assistance, the students prepare and publish their own articles on the World Wide Web, together with reply forms to solicit opinions from readers. They advertise their web articles on appropriate internet sites (e.g., scientific newsgroups) so that interested scientists around the world will know about their articles and will be able to read and comment on them. When they receive their comments (by e-mail) they can take those into account in editing their articles for republication on the Web or for submission to scientific journals.

This project adopts a process approach to writing, which supports autonomy by placing control over learning content into the hands of the learners. The Internet adds a vital dimension of real-world publication and response to this approach. The Internet has also been used to facilitate self-access language learning as many centres have made learning resources available through the web (Benson, 1997b).

9.3 The effectiveness of technology-based approaches

The claim that technology-based approaches to language learning are supportive of autonomy rests in part on an assumption, shared with resource-based approaches, that they provide learners with opportunities to self-direct their own learning. In the case of CALL in particular, there is also an assumption that technology can provide learners with the kinds of support they need in order to develop skills associated with autonomy. This cannot be regarded as more than a potential, however, and a great deal depends on the ways in which technologies are made available to learners and the kinds of interaction that take place around them. In the case of CALL software, the degree of control offered to learners is often severely constrained by its structure and content. Text manipulation and computer-mediated communication applications offer greater opportunities for the development of control over learning content. They also offer opportunities for collaboration that are often lacking in other modes of self-access learning. But as in the case of self-access, it may be that learners require a degree of autonomy in advance in order to use new technologies effectively. Claims made for the potential of new technologies in regard to autonomy need to be evaluated against empirical evidence of the realisation of this potential in practice.

In spite of its long history, there has been very little empirical research on the effectiveness of CALL. Chapelle (1997: 22) argues that the evaluation of CALL from the perspective of second language acquisition should address two central questions:

1. What kinds of language does the learner engage in during a CALL activity?
2. How good is the language experience in CALL for L2 learning?

Chapelle's first question calls for a description of the language that the learners are exposed to and produce during a CALL activity, while the second calls for a description of the kinds of communicative exchanges in which they participate. Research on educational technology and autonomy will additionally be concerned with a description of the ways in which learners exercise control over their learning during CALL activities and of the ways in which the use of the technology enables them to do so. The key research questions in regard to technology-based approaches to autonomy are concerned less with the characteristics of new technologies than they are with the learning activities in which they play a role.

Chapter 10

<hr>

Learner-based approaches

Further reading

Oxford, R.L. (forthcoming) *Teaching and Researching Learning Strategies* (ALIA series).

In contrast to resource-based and technology-based approaches to autonomy which focus on providing opportunities for learner control, learner-based approaches focus directly on the production of behavioural and psychological changes that will enable learners to take greater control over their learning. Current approaches have emerged from two separate traditions: North American work on learning strategies and strategy training, and European work on learner training. Sheerin (1997: 59–60) prefers the term 'learner development' to 'training' because the latter 'implies the imparting of a defined set of skills and it also implies something that is done by someone to someone else'. She defines learner development as 'cognitive and affective development involving increasing awareness of oneself as a learner and an increasing willingness and ability to manage one's own learning'. In the 1990s, North American and European approaches have tended to merge and the use of terms such as strategy training and learner training no longer reflects any clear distinction in approach. I use the term *learner development* here to cover the broad range of practices that have grown out of these two traditions.

The primary goal of all approaches to learner development is to help learners become 'better' language learners. Current approaches

Concept 10.1   **Approaches to learner development**

Approaches to learner development can be classified into six main categories:

1. Direct advice on language-learning strategies and techniques, often published in the form of self-study manuals for independent learners. Advice tends to be prescriptive and is not necessarily based on research. One of the earliest examples of this kind of manual was produced for missionaries travelling abroad (Brewster and Brewster, 1976).

2. Training based on 'good language learner' research and insights from cognitive psychology. Weaver and Cohen (1997) is a recent example of a teacher's manual based on extensive strategy research, which includes suggestions for a 30-hour training course.

3. Training in which learners are encouraged to experiment with strategies and discover which work well for them. Ellis and Sinclair's (1989) learner-training manual is based on the assumption that the aim of training is 'to help learners consider the factors that affect their learning and discover the learning strategies that suit them best' (p. 2).

4. Synthetic approaches drawing on a range of theoretical sources. Dickinson's (1992) book on learner training draws on North American strategy research, European research on autonomy and self-directed learning, research on language awareness and insights from second language acquisition research.

5. Integrated approaches treating learner training as a by-product of language learning. Legutke and Thomas (1991: 284), for example, argue that the aim of learner training is not to train the learners first and then teach them a language, but to 'teach them to communicate in the L2 while helping them to learn and think about their learning'.

6. Self-directed approaches in which learners are encouraged to train themselves through reflection on self-directed learning activities. Holec (1987) and Esch (1997) have described self-directed programmes of this kind.

In current practice, there is general agreement that learner development activities should not be separated from language-learning activities. The extent to which learners should 'be trained' or 'train themselves' remains an area of debate within the field of autonomy.

also tend to view the development of autonomy as an integral part of this goal. Cohen (1998: 67), for example, argues that:

> *Strategy training*, i.e. explicitly teaching students how to apply language learning and language use strategies, can enhance students' efforts to reach language program goals because it encourages students to find their own pathways to success, and thus it promotes learner autonomy and self-direction.

The relationship between strategy use and autonomy is complex, however, and the claim that learner development programmes can both improve language-learning performance and foster autonomy needs to be treated with caution.

10.1   Learner development and language learning

In early work on the 'good language learner', it was assumed that effective strategies could be identified by observing the strategies used by effective learners and that less effective learners could be trained in their use with a resulting increase in their learning efficiency (Naiman et al., 1978; Rubin, 1975; Stern, 1975). Although subsequent research has led to some qualification of these assumptions, McDonough's (1999) review of research suggests that the basic hypotheses that effective strategies can be identified and that learners can learn how to use them remains valid (Quote 10.1).

> **Quote 10.1** McDonough on the effectiveness of strategy training
>
> A second conclusion is also patent, which is that teaching strategies is not universally successful, but the latest research is showing that, in certain circumstances and modes, particularly when incorporated into the teacher's normal classroom behaviour, and thus involving teacher training as well as learner training, success is demonstrable.
>
> McDonough (1999: 13)

Cohen (1998: 65) states that the underlying premise of strategy training is that 'language learning will be facilitated if students become more aware of the range of possible strategies that they can consciously select during language learning and language use'. In an important critique of strategy training, however, Rees-Miller (1993, 1994) raised four major objections to its underlying assumptions:

1. There is no empirical evidence for a causal relationship between awareness of strategies and success in learning.
2. Some of the characteristics associated with success in learning, such as being active in the learning process, cannot be defined as specific behaviours and may therefore be unteachable.
3. Case studies of unsuccessful learners suggest that the use of strategies employed by successful learners is insufficient in itself to lead to more effective learning.
4. Successful learners do not necessarily use recommended strategies and often use non-recommended strategies.

Rees-Miller argued that in view of the lack of evidence for its effectiveness, resources spent on strategy training might be better directed elsewhere.

In reply to Rees-Miller's argument, Chamot and Rubin (1994) cited a number of research studies showing correlation between strategy use and improved language-learning performance. However, they also reported that research had shown that the effectiveness of particular strategies is influenced by variables such as proficiency level, task, text, language modality, background knowledge, context of learning, target language and learner characteristics. The use of strategies varies from one good learner to another 'indicating that the good language learner cannot be described in terms of a single set of strategies but rather through the ability to understand and deploy a personal set of effective strategies' (p. 772). This more cautious view of the potential of strategy training also informs the recent surveys by Cohen (1998) and McDonough (1999).

Although Rees-Miller (1994) rightly points out that correlation between strategy use and improved performance does not necessarily indicate a causal effect, the balance of evidence suggests that strategy training can to lead to improvement in learning performance given the right circumstances. According to Chamot and Rubin (1994), five components important in strategy training are:

- discovery and discussion of strategies that learners are already using for specific learning tasks;
- presentation of new strategies by explicitly naming and describing them;
- modelling of strategies;
- explaining why and when the strategies can be used;

- providing extensive practice with authentic tasks and opportunities for students to discuss their own applications of the strategies and their effectiveness.

Chamot and Rubin's emphasis on the importance of task-based practice is reflected in Cohen's (1998: 65) argument that 'the most efficient way for learner awareness to be heightened is by having teachers provide strategies-based instruction to students as part of the foreign language curriculum'.

10.2 Learner development and autonomy

There appears to be good evidence that learner development programmes can be effective in improving language-learning performance, provided they take account of factors of context, learning preference and learning style and are not limited to teaching an approved set of strategies. It has also been claimed that learners who acquire the ability to use strategies flexibly, appropriately and independently are, in effect, autonomous (Quote 10.2). The contention that learner development programmes lead to greater autonomy needs to be treated with caution, however, as their effectiveness in this respect appears to depend upon the forms they take.

> **Quote 10.2** Wenden on learner development and autonomy
>
> In effect, 'successful' or 'expert' or 'intelligent' learners have learned how to learn. They have acquired the learning strategies, the knowledge about learning, and the attitudes that enable them to use these skills and knowledge confidently, flexibly, appropriately and independently of a teacher. Therefore, they are autonomous.
>
> Wenden (1991: 15)

Reviewing research by Bereiter and Scardamalia (1989), which shows the failure of strategy instruction to produce significant long-term changes in performance among 'poor' learners, Murayama (1996: 9) argues:

> The crucial point in teaching strategies is what kind of objectives learners have in *their* mind when learning the target strategies. The teacher sets a target for the class so as to help them acquire knowledge or skills. The students, however, do not necessarily share the teacher's intention.

In particular, if the teacher simply explains the strategies and the learners' role is simply to listen and answer the teacher's questions, they may be acquiring little more than the skills of listening to information and answering questions. According to Murayama, 'if learners consider learning to be a task, no strategies can make learning more efficient' (p. 10). The problem of learner development for autonomy can thus be seen as a problem of changing the learner's view of learning from one of completing tasks set by others to one of constructing knowledge for themselves. To the extent that this may involve deep change in the learners' psychological orientation towards the learning process and the content of learning, the acquisition of a set of strategies leading to gains in learning performance is not necessarily equivalent to the development of autonomy.

In an earlier paper, I also suggested that learner development programmes often involve an implicit moulding of the learner to approved patterns of behaviour that is inimical to the development of autonomy (Benson, 1995a). An analysis of learner training materials showed that they tend to 'position' learners in five ways:

- through direct modes of address (notably the second person singular 'you');
- through direct advice inserted into overtly non-prescriptive text;
- by limiting the learning options from which learners are invited to choose;
- by guiding students to the discovery of hidden norms of behaviour (often those located at the centre of a range of options);
- through visual and verbal images of successful learners.

While learners are not obliged to accept implicitly approved behaviours, they may nevertheless be left with the feeling that they are poor language learners if they do not conform to the expectations of the learner development programme. It was also observed that learner-training materials tend to treat learners as 'decontextualised' individuals and do little to address the relationship between the process of learning a language and the role of the language in the learners' lives. Inviting learners to explore their reasons for language learning and to criticise conventional methods of learning may be more conducive to the development of autonomy than a focus on awareness of strategies and skills.

An example of a learner development project designed to help Japanese learners take advantage of opportunities to learn English in their everyday life is reported by Ryan (1997: 218):

> Despite the richness of the environment in terms of resources for learning English, many learners in Japan are unaware of the possibilities of using them beyond the obvious step of enrolling in a language class.

Each module of the project focuses on a particular kind of resource and is divided into three phases:

1. Consciousness-raising discussion of available resources.
2. Presenting and practising techniques to exploit resources.
3. Introduction to the theoretical constructs of language acquisition underlying the selection of resources and techniques.

In this way, the project connects theoretical constructs of learner development and language learning to the learners' everyday experience of the target language.

Esch (1997) argues for an approach in which learners train themselves through reflection and discussion on learning activities. Questioning the effectiveness of training courses in fostering autonomy on the grounds that 'there are no "autonomous language learning skills" to be trained' (p. 165), Esch argues that:

> At one level, as Ellis and Sinclair (1989) clearly demonstrate, it is possible to organize such courses systematically, and the outcome should be to produce learners who are better aware of the learning process and of the various techniques available for language learning. At the other level, the fostering of autonomy in language learners by means of workshops where learners 'train' one another is more difficult but possible as long as it does not become a routine. Control by the teachers, if it returns through the back door, will produce some short-term language learning gains but will not help learners reap the benefits of taking charge of their own learning.
>
> (p. 175)

One of the main features of Esch's approach to learner training for a group of independent learners of French at the University of Cambridge was that the participants largely determined the content and conduct of the training workshops themselves. Each week the group met for one hour to carry out an activity they had planned the previous week and to discuss work they had carried out individually between meetings. The adviser attached to the group simply observed and recorded what was said. Esch ascribes the success of the workshop to three factors: 'the students were self-selected; the feedback was essentially given in the course of conversations but always seemed to be to the point because it was a conversational topic shared by the whole group; the syllabus was selected by the members of the group from the second week onwards' (p. 165).

Instruction and reflection need not necessarily be counterposed, however. Cohen (1998: 66–7) advocates explicit instruction in strategy use, but he also argues that strategy training should help learners to:

- self-diagnose their strengths and weaknesses in language learning;
- become more aware of what helps them to learn the language they are studying most efficiently;
- develop a broad range of problem-solving skills;
- experiment with both familiar and unfamiliar learning strategies;
- make decisions about how to approach a language task;
- monitor and self-evaluate their performance;
- transfer successful strategies to new learning contexts.

Cohen also argues that one goal of strategy training is 'to promote learner autonomy and learner self-direction by allowing students to choose their own strategies and to do so spontaneously, without continued prompting from the language teacher' (p. 70). The approach suggested by Cohen is clearly one that aims to avoid the pitfalls of an overemphasis on explicit instruction in learner development.

10.3 The effectiveness of learner-based approaches

While resource-based and technology-based approaches to the development of autonomy focus on providing learners with *opportunities* for self-directed learning, learner-based approaches aim to *enable* learners take greater control over their learning by directly providing them with the skills they need to take advantage of these opportunities. The key research questions in relation to learner-based approaches to autonomy concern the extent to which learner development programmes actually succeed in this aim.

Research evidence suggests that explicit instruction in strategy use can enhance learning performance. It does not, however, show that it is necessarily effective in enabling learners to develop the capacity for *autonomous* learning. The risk involved in explicit instruction is that learners will develop a set of techniques for learning management, without developing the corresponding abilities concerned with control over cognitive and content aspects of their learning that will allow them to apply these techniques flexibly and critically. Reflective training models appear to be more effective in fostering autonomy because they integrate these three aspects of control and allow the learners to develop an awareness of the appropriateness of strategies to the overall self-direction of their learning. It must emphasised, however, that there is to date relatively little empirical evidence that such models are as effective as explicit instruction in terms of enhancing learning performance.

Attitudes towards the effectiveness of various approaches to learner development are in part a question of whether the focus falls upon language-learning performance or autonomy. On balance, however, the research evidence suggests that approaches involving a combination of explicit instruction and learner reflection may be more effective in achieving both of these goals than those based on one of these methods alone. Learner development programmes are also likely to be more effective to the extent that they are integrated with opportunities to exercise control in the context of the learner's ongoing experience of learning a language both outside and inside the classroom.

Chapter 11

Classroom-based approaches

Further reading

Wright, T. (forthcoming) *Teaching and Researching Classroom Management*
(ALIA series).

In Chapters 11, 12 and 13, we will consider approaches to fostering
autonomy which focus on changes to the relationships found within
conventional educational structures: classroom practice, control of the
curriculum and the role of the teacher. In each case, it is assumed that
the key factor in the development of autonomy is the opportunity
for students to make decisions regarding their learning within a collaborative and supportive environment. As Candy (1991) argues, this

---

Quote 11.1 Candy on learner control

It is perhaps useful to think of teachers and learners as occupying positions
on a continuum from teacher-control at one extreme to learner-control at
the other, where the deliberate surrendering of certain prerogatives by the
teacher is accompanied by the concomitant acceptance of responsibility
by the learner or learners. In the sense that there can be a dynamically
changing equilibrium in this arrangement, it is reminiscent of the famous
image of the teacher on the one end of a log, with the learner on the
other end.

Candy (1991: 9)

---

opportunity arises when teachers 'deliberately surrender' their pre-rogative of making most or all of the significant decisions concerning the students' learning.

In the context of language learning, Allwright (1978: 105) has argued that the complexities of the language-learning process make teacher control of classroom learning a high-risk strategy. The teacher who takes exclusive responsibility for classroom management is 'professionally irresponsible', because 'a serious weakening of the value of the classroom experience for the learners is virtually inevitable'. In Allwright's view, autonomy is fostered when teachers examine the decisions that they normally regard as their prerogative and consider whether the learners should take them instead. Typically, these decisions concern the plan-ning of classroom activities and the evaluation of their outcomes.

11.1 Planning classroom learning

Several experimental programmes suggest that learner control over the planning of classroom activities can produce positive results in terms of both autonomy and language learning. Littlejohn (1982), for example, conducted an experiment with small groups of volunteer students study-ing beginner-level Spanish without a teacher. Post-course questionnaire results suggested that small-group independent study led to increased motivation. Participants reported that they often felt inhibited in teacher-led classrooms by the expertise of the teacher and by the pres-ence of other students with whom they felt in competition. Without the teacher they felt more free to speak, to make mistakes and to con-tribute their own experiences, leading to a feeling of being supported in their learning difficulties. In a later study, Littlejohn (1983), reported similar benefits when students were given a degree of control over the content of their learning within a teacher-directed classroom environ-ment (Concept 11.1).

In an experiment in which 16 student teachers worked with teachers in five London schools to introduce learner-selected collaborative group work in modern language classes, Harris and Noyau (1990) observed that the learners reported an increase in motivation and learning. Teachers involved in the project also observed that girls and higher-ability students appeared to adapt to collaborative work more quickly. Lamb (1997) reported on an initiative in compulsory modern

Concept 11.1   An experiment in learner-control

In an experiment with two groups of university students in Bahrain, who were repeating a 14-week English course they had failed the previous year, Littlejohn (1983) introduced significant elements of learner control into a teacher-directed environment. Groups of students were asked to review grammar sections in the previous year's textbook and to report on what the sections required them to do and how difficult or easy they found them. The teacher then asked for volunteers to research an area of grammar, present their findings to the class and provide exercises, tasks and games for practice. From the eighth week of the course, two of the six weekly hours were devoted to student-directed classes in which groups of 5–6 students decided upon and carried out activities by themselves, calling on the assistance of the teacher when necessary. On retaking the examination they had failed the previous year, the experimental groups showed improvements equal to or greater than those of similar students in three teacher-directed groups. Littlejohn also reports that the participants developed a greater sense of responsibility for their learning, a more active role in the classroom, greater involvement with course texts and a willingness to use additional resources.

language classes in an English comprehensive school to encourage self-management in learning. Although general learning goals were determined by the National Curriculum and specific goals were made explicit in units of work, learners selected the order in which they worked on subgoals and selected their own tasks for language practice from a bank of resources. Lamb reported a majority preference for independent study over teacher-directed work, increased motivation and improved examination results.

A number of experiments in learner control over planning have involved peer teaching. Fitz-Gibbon and Reay (1982), for example, asked 14 year olds to tutor 11 year olds in French in an inner city comprehensive school in England. Before the experiment, the majority of the older students reported that they disliked the French language and French language classes. After the experiment, the researchers asked the participants to rank school subjects according to how much they liked them and found a significant positive shift in the rank for French.

Assinder (1991) introduced peer teaching to a group of 12 students taking the current affairs module of an English for Further Studies course in Sydney. The group was divided into two and each group regularly prepared video-based lessons and teaching materials for the other group. Based on post-course questionnaires and her own observations, Assinder reported gains in motivation, participation, 'real' communication, in-depth understanding, responsibility for learning, commitment to the course, confidence, mutual respect, the number of skills and strategies used and accuracy in written outcomes. In a model of peer teaching developed for advanced learners of French at the University of Brighton (Carpenter, 1996), pairs of students took turns to prepare and conduct three-hour classes based around authentic texts. On the basis of post-course questionnaires, Carpenter reported gains in motivation and use of learning strategies. She also reported problems, including lack of participation by some students and uneven quality of learner-prepared classes, and suggested that peer teaching may be more effective when students have advanced skills in the target language and feel comfortable with their peers.

Results of experiments in which learners are asked to set their own goals and plan activities within the classroom suggest that increased learner control is beneficial to language learning in the short term. However, the factors contributing to learning gains are often difficult to determine. In peer-teaching experiments, for example, the experience of teaching may be a significant factor in learning gains. Transfer of control also often involves an increase in student–student interaction and increased opportunities to use and process the target language in group work. Most experiments report clear gains in motivation and in factors related to autonomy such as responsibility for learning and strategy use. These gains are difficult to measure, however, and the use of teacher observations and post-course questionnaires may lead to results that favour the goals of the experiment. Learner variables such as proficiency in the language and gender may also be related to the effectiveness of experiments in learner control.

One clear outcome of the research is the change in the role of the teacher that results from initiatives to increase learner control over learning content and procedures. Assinder (1991: 223), for example, reports a significant change in her role in peer-taught classes, describing herself as a 'resource' for language queries, 'on-the-spot checker' and a 'sounding-board' for ideas, opinions and interpretation. By drastically reducing the time spent talking in class and on preparation, she was also able to increase time spent gathering data on individual student difficulties and to hold more individual counselling sessions.

11.2   Evaluating classroom learning

Further reading

Oscarson, M. (1997) Self-assessment of foreign and second language
proficiency. In C. Clapham and D. Corson (eds) *Language Testing and
Assessment*. Encyclopedia of Language and Education, Volume 7. Dordrecht:
Kluwer, pp. 175–87.

Self-assessment has been a prominent theme, both in the literature
on autonomy and in the literature on language testing. Although self-
assessment has been linked to the idea of autonomy in the language-
testing field, greater emphasis has been placed on the reliability of
summative self-assessments of language proficiency. Oscarson (1989),
however, distinguishes between assessment as an internal self-directed
activity and assessment as an external other-directed activity. From
the perspective of autonomy, the formative aspects of internal assessment are of greater significance than learners' ability to match their
own assessments with external assessments of their proficiency. In self-
directed learning, the distinction between self-assessment of learning
outcomes and self-monitoring of the learning process is also blurred,
since self-assessment is ongoing and influences planning. In this sense,
self-assessment includes reflection on goals, learning activities and
appropriate assessment criteria.

Oscarson (1989) identifies four main benefits of formal self-assessment
for learners:

1. Self-assessment trains learners to evaluate the effectiveness of their
communication, which is beneficial to learning in itself.

2. It raises learners' awareness of the learning process and stimulates
them to consider course content and assessment critically.

3. It enhances their knowledge of the variety of possible goals in language learning, which leaves them in a better position to exercise
control over their own learning and to influence the direction of
classroom activities.

4. It expands the range of assessment criteria to include areas in which
learners have special competence, such as the evaluation of their
own needs and affective dimensions of the learning process.

Blanche (1988) also observes that in a number of studies self-assessment
is seen to increase learners' motivation.

Several studies show that the correlation between learners' judgements in relation to tutors' judgements can be high, especially when students have been given training (Bachman and Palmer, 1989; Oscarson, 1989; Rolfe, 1990). Thomson (1996) asked students of Japanese at the University of New South Wales to plan, execute and self-assess a short self-directed programme of learning. She found that the learners were capable of carrying out the assessment, but also noted some variation in the levels of their self-ratings according to gender and ethnic background. Asian female students, especially, appeared prone to rate themselves lower than other groups. In a review of several self-assessment studies, Cram (1995: 273) observes that the 'accuracy' of self-assessment varies according to several factors, including the type of assessment, language proficiency, academic record, career aspirations and degree of training. Oscarson's (1997) review of research on self-assessment suggests that learners are capable of assessing their own language proficiency reliably under appropriate conditions.

Self-assessment for certification purposes appears to be rare. However, self-assessment was used as an element in collaborative assessment among a group of trained language teachers studying for a Postgraduate Diploma at the University of Edinburgh (Dickinson, 1988; Haughton and Dickinson, 1989). On completing an assignment the students assigned themselves a grade using agreed criteria. This grade was compared to a tutor's grade and a final grade was negotiated in cases of difference, with a second tutor acting as final arbiter. Collaborative assessment is also used in the credit-bearing Autonomous Learning Modules at Helsinki University (Karlsson et al., 1997) and Leblanc and Painchaud (1985) have used self-assessment for initial placement on university-level courses.

For formative purposes, however, the reliability of learners' assessments of their proficiency seems to be of less importance than their capacity to engage in the process of self-assessment (Concept 11.2). Nunan (1994 – reported in Nunan, 1996) investigated what happened when a group of 30 undergraduate EAP students were encouraged to self-monitor and self-evaluate using guided learning journals. Nunan observed that opportunities to reflect led to greater sensitivity to the learning process over time. Lor's (1998) study of learners' reflective journal entries suggests, however, that many learners experience difficulty in reflecting upon and evaluating their learning spontaneously and often fail to see the value of self-evaluation. In an earlier study of learning logs, Schärer (1983) also observed that students needed considerable assistance and that the use of log books could even have a discouraging effect on weaker learners.

Concept 11.2   **An experiment in learner control**

Smolen et al. (1995) report an interesting initiative to introduce a cycle of goal setting, planning and self-assessment within a portfolio assessment framework in a US middle school ESL classroom. On Mondays students wrote weekly goals on index cards and on Fridays they wrote a reflective statement on the back of the cards describing how well they had achieved their goals. They also selected a sample from their working portfolio and wrote a reflective statement explaining why their sample was important to them, placing both in a 'showcase' portfolio. In addition to the goal cards, students kept a time planning sheet and a daily learning log. The researchers observed that, initially, students tended to write simplistic goals and reflective statements. In particular, reflective statements tended to address 'whether or not they had completed their goal instead of their thoughts on why and how they had completed it and what they learned' (p. 23).

Focusing on reading strategies, the teacher then developed a programme of modelling and discussion, which culminated in a student-designed poster listing strategies that students could use in reading. The researchers found that, as a result of this process, several students incorporated strategy use within their goals and reflective evaluations. Focusing on goals incorporating prediction strategies, the researchers observed that reflective statements illustrated 'an ability to evaluate their predictions and identify why their predictions were correct and incorrect'. Assessing the value of the initiative, they claim that establishing personal goals based on self-evaluation of their work significantly affected student involvement in the portfolio process, encouraged students to make decisions about what to focus on next in their learning and positively affected their view of themselves as learners and decision makers.

Cram's (1995) review of research suggests that students' willingness and ability to engage in self-assessment practices increases with training. She also argues that self-assessment works best in a supportive and predictable environment, in which 'teachers would place high value on independent thought and action; learners' opinions would be accepted non-judgementally and external rewards would be minimised' (p. 295). Cram emphasises teacher preparation as a crucial factor in the success of self-assessment and includes in her paper a detailed outline of a teacher-training workshop.

A number of instruments have been developed for self-assessment, including self-marked tests, progress cards on which students can record whether they have reached predetermined objectives, self-rating scales on which students estimate their proficiency in various areas of language or their ability to perform communicative tasks, and diaries or logs (for example, see Ellis and Sinclair, 1989; Lewis, 1990; McNamara and Deane, 1995; Oscarson, 1989). Portfolios have also been seen as a useful tool for self-monitoring and self-assessment (Gottlieb, 1995; Smolen et al., 1995). From the perspective of autonomy, it seems to be particularly important that self-assessment instruments encourage formative self-monitoring and a cyclical approach to the re-evaluation of goals and plans. A record of work form used at the University of Hong Kong, for example, encourages learners (a) to distinguish between what they have done and what they have learned in an activity and (b) to account for the value of the activity in planning further work (Figure 11.1).

As Holec (1985b: 142) points out, the purpose of assessment for the learner differs from its purpose for the teacher. From the learner's

---

Date: .... **Period covered:** ....

What I have done

(Describe activities and write down the titles of any materials you have used)

What I have learned

(Summarise what you think you have learned in a few words)

Reflections

(Comment on how useful and enjoyable your activities were. Any problems?)

Future plans

(Note down next activities and when you will do them. Also note any changes to your goals or plans)

Figure 11.1   **A 'record of work' form used at the University of Hong Kong**

perspective, assessment is valuable because 'the learner needs to know at all times whether, on the one hand, his performances correspond to what he was aiming at and, on the other, whether he has made any progress towards his chosen objective'. The aim of self-assessment is, therefore, 'to provide the learner with all the information he needs to control his learning process and progress'. In order to achieve this aim, self-assessment procedures must be 'relevant to the learner in question and to the particular learning in which he is engaged'. They must be carried out on relevant performances, using relevant criteria and relevant standards. It is because of this need for relevance that assessment of self-directed learning must be carried out by learners themselves.

Research shows that learners are, under appropriate conditions and with appropriate training, able to self-assess their language performance, but it does not yet tell us very much about how learners make the process of self-assessment relevant to their own learning goals. Reports on initiatives that integrate self-assessment within a programme of learning are rare in the literature and there remains scope for research on the cyclical relationship between self-assessment and planning in the development of autonomy.

11.3   The nature of control in the classroom

Research suggests that transfer of significant elements of control over learning within the classroom has tangible benefits for learners. However, many of the experiments in learner control of planning and assessment reported in the literature represent isolated events, which often illustrate the constraints upon a fuller implementation of learner control over the processes involved in institutional learning. As Auerbach (1995: 9) points out, the assumption that control is a commodity shared by teachers and learners may underestimate the degree to which day-to-day decisions and classroom roles are conditioned by broader institutional, social and discursive practices (Quote 11.2 overleaf).

Within the day-to-day practice of institutional learning, teachers are largely responsible for planning learning activities and the assessment of students. The teacher's role in planning and assessment, however, as most teachers know, is invariably constrained by external tests and curricular guidelines. Moreover, as Shohamy (1997) points out, 'tests are not isolated events, rather they are connected to a whole set of psychological, social and political variables that have an effect on

> **Quote 11.2** Auerbach on power and control in the classroom
>
> *Close your eyes and imagine an ESL classroom.* My guess is that the picture in your mind's eye includes a teacher, a group of learners, some desks, chairs, a blackboard, books, papers, four walls and a door. Have you drawn anything outside the walls of the classroom? Are there any visible ways in which relations of power or authority show up in your picture? If the learners' relation to the social order outside the classroom is not immediately apparent in your picture, you are probably not alone. Although issues of power and politics are generally seen as inherent in language policy and planning on a macrolevel, classrooms themselves may be seen as self-contained, autonomous systems, insulated from external political concerns. The actual teaching that goes on behind closed doors is often conceived of as a neutral transfer of skills, knowledge or competencies, to be left in the hands of trained professionals whose job it is to implement the latest methods or techniques.
>
> Auerbach (1995: 9)

curriculum, ethicality, social classes, bureaucracy, politics and language knowledge'. In the words of Holec (1985b: 142), there is 'the vague but definite feeling that evaluation is an instrument of power which should not be put in just anybody's hands'. The washback effect of public tests often constrains the teacher's role in planning to one of implementing a predefined curriculum, or, at worst, to 'teaching for the test'. Unless the learners are involved in programmes of study without external assessment requirements, the degree to which self-assessment and learner control of classroom activities can be implemented is likely to be severely constrained.

For some within the field of critical pedagogy, the emphasis in the literature on autonomy on control over the management of learning mystifies the degree to which relations of power in the classroom are shaped by broader social and discursive practices. Some advocate a participatory approach in which teachers join with students to critique and challenge the power structures that condition language learning and struggle to overcome their own marginalisation within the system (Auerbach, 1995). For others, the emphasis on autonomy in language learning should be upon the development of control over language and the students' 'voice' or 'identity' as it is constructed within a second language (Pennycook, 1997; Pierce, 1995).

Critical approaches to language teaching are not necessarily incompatible with attempts to introduce learner control into the classroom, however. It may be that learners who are successful in taking a degree of control over the management of their learning are more likely to develop a critical perspective on learning than those who are not. At the same time, attempts to transfer control may be enhanced by critical discussion and evaluation of institutional, social and ideological constraints on autonomy within the curriculum. An initiative to introduce learner control over planning and evaluation into a course, for example, could well be enhanced by critical discussion of the purposes of existing procedures. Critical awareness of these purposes could help learners towards a more realistic understanding of the value and limitations of control over classroom activities.

11.4 The effectiveness of classroom-based approaches

Classroom-based approaches attempt to foster autonomy by involving learners in decision-making processes concerned with the day-to-day management of their learning. Accounts of experiments in which learners are encouraged to take a degree of control over the planning and assessment of classroom learning are mostly positive and tend to show that learners are able to exercise control over these aspects of their learning given the opportunity to do so and appropriate support. It also seems likely that this capacity is developed more effectively within the classroom, where learners are more readily able to collaborate with other learners and draw on the support of teachers, than outside it.

The important questions about classroom-based approaches to autonomy concern the extent to which control over management of classroom activities leads to the development of control over cognitive and content aspects of learning. Learners may develop the capacity to control cognitive aspects of their learning through the opportunity to take decisions in the classroom, but this will depend in part on the extent to which their decisions are limited by or go beyond learning procedures with which they are already familiar. Similarly, they may develop the capacity to define and determine the content of their learning, but this again depends on the extent to which decisions are constrained by pre-determined learning content. The risk in implementing learner control in the classroom when the scope of decision making is constrained is that the learners will feel that their decisions have little real consequence or that they are being given responsibility without genuine freedom.

One clear outcome of the research is that any attempt to transfer control over one aspect of learning is likely to have complex effects on the system of learning as a whole. Flexibility in the guidelines for the implementation of a curriculum often creates spaces in which individual teachers can allow learners a degree of control over aspects of their classroom learning. However, if the curriculum itself lacks flexibility, it is likely that the degree of autonomy developed by the learners will be correspondingly constrained.

Chapter 12

Curriculum-based approaches

Curriculum-based approaches to autonomy extend the principle of learner control over the management of learning to the curriculum as a whole (Quote 12.1). The principle of learner control over the curriculum has been formalised in the idea of the process syllabus, in which learners are expected to make the major decisions concerning the content and procedures of learning in collaboration with their teachers. It is also apparent in a number of approaches to curriculum negotiation that do not carry the name of the process syllabus, but follow many of the ideas and practices implicit in it.

Quote 12.1 Crabbe on autonomy and the curriculum

The particular question posed is whether the minute-by-minute classroom practice indirectly *fosters* or discourages autonomy. Do events in the classroom challenge or reinforce learners' expectations of their role, do they model individual learning behaviour, do they highlight choices within the curriculum? The important point behind these questions is that autonomy as a goal needs to pervade the whole curricular system and not simply be an occasional part of it.

Crabbe (1993: 208)

12.1 The process syllabus

> **Further reading**
>
> Breen, M.P. and Littlejohn, A. (eds) (2000) *The Process Syllabus: Negotiation in the Language Classroom.* Cambridge: Cambridge University Press.

The idea of the process syllabus emerged in the 1980s as a development of ideas concerned with communicative language teaching and task-based learning (Quote 12.2). The communicative syllabus is based on the notion that, in the course of classroom learning, learners naturally tend to recreate the existing syllabus or create their own. Advocates of the communicative syllabus proposed that language-learning content should not be predefined, but selected and organised within the communicative processes that take place in the classroom itself (Breen and Candlin, 1980). In task-based learning, tasks 'serve as compelling and appropriate means for realising certain characteristic principles of communicative language teaching' (Candlin, 1987: 5). Treated as the basis for action in the classroom, tasks provide both the focus for authentic communication and the occasion for language learning as learners experience and process unpredictable language input in the course of tackling them.

> **Quote 12.2** Breen on the process syllabus
>
> The process syllabus focuses upon three processes: communicating, learning and the purposeful social activity of teaching and learning in the classroom. It is primarily a syllabus which addresses the decisions which have to be made and the working procedures which have to be undertaken for language learning in a group. It assumes, therefore, that the third process – how things may be done in the classroom situation – will be the means through which communicating and learning can be achieved.
>
> Breen (1987a: 166)

The process syllabus adds to these proposals the element of negotiation of learning content and procedures as the means through which communication and learning are achieved. In Breen's (1987a) detailed proposal for the process syllabus, the syllabus designer has two major roles: to provide a plan of the decisions to be made and to provide a bank of classroom activities to facilitate the implementation of the decisions that are made. The content of classroom learning and activities are determined through an ongoing cycle of negotiation and evaluation. The process syllabus is thus aligned to what Legutke and Thomas (1991) call the 'strong version' of communicative language teaching, in which content and procedures, and language learning and language use, are intimately linked.

Simmons and Wheeler (1995: 17) state that the process syllabus has been viewed in two ways: as a 'negotiated component of the syllabus' and as 'an opportunity to enable full learner participation in the decision-making processes associated with selection of content, agreement on procedures, choice of activities and tasks, direction of working and ongoing evaluation'. The first, weaker version of the process syllabus often involves project work, in which learners determine the content, methods of inquiry and outcomes of real world research (Legutke and Thomas, 1991; Ribé and Vidal, 1993). Learners exercise control over the content of the project and the forms of input and output. Collaboration and communication among learners over the solution of real world problems is viewed as an opportunity for language learning. A similar principle also informs approaches to language learning based on Kolb's (1984) experiential model of learning (Kohonen, 1992) and Johnson and Johnson's (1994) cooperative model (Macaro, 1997).

The stronger version of the process syllabus does not presuppose any particular content or approach to learning, since these are to be negotiated and renegotiated throughout the course. Clarke (1991: 13) has argued that this version is 'extremely unlikely to be appropriate in anything but a few very unlikely circumstances'. Budd and Wright (1992) and Simmons and Wheeler (1995) report successful short-term implementation of the process syllabus model in university and migrant classrooms (see 16.4, case study). However, it remains the case that there are few published accounts or evaluations of the strong version of the process syllabus in action. Those that we have mainly show gains related to the students' ability to participate in classroom negotiation and awareness of their own learning processes.

12.2   Examples of curriculum-based approaches

Although there are few accounts of the process syllabus in action in the form proposed by Breen (1987a), the literature on autonomy includes a number of accounts of initiatives in which learners have taken responsibility for decision making at the level of the curriculum as a whole.

12.2.1 Autonomy in secondary school: Denmark

The work of Leni Dam and her colleagues in Danish secondary school classrooms is widely regarded as one of the most successful examples of autonomy in language learning in action to date. Their work began in a series of in-service training workshops, discussed in Breen et al. (1989), and has been described in detail by Dam and Gabrielsen (1988) and Dam (1995). The model is classroom based and does not involve self-access, educational technology or formal procedures for learner development. Instead, it takes advantage of relatively loose national curriculum guidelines that allow individual teachers to transfer to the learners the responsibility for decisions about the ways in which broad curriculum objectives and public examination requirements are met. The model is also long term and developmental. In the classrooms of Dam and her colleagues, students are involved in decisions about their learning of English throughout their secondary school careers.

At the heart of the model is a self-evaluation cycle, implemented both within lessons and at various stages during the school year, in which learning plans are evaluated and revised. The model is thus based on reflection and negotiated curriculum management and, in Dam and Gabrielsen's (1988: 20) words, 'is best described as attempting a change in the context and quality of learning through systematic work on teacher and learner roles'. Examples of typical classroom activities reported in Dam (1995) also show an emphasis on collaborative work and the processing of authentic samples of target language input gathered from outside the classroom into creative written and spoken output to be shared with the class as a whole.

Often described as an experiment, the curriculum model of autonomy developed by Dam and her colleagues is now well established and has been judged successful in terms of student performance over a number of years (see 16.5, case study). The model is close to the model of the process syllabus in its conception, and provides evidence that the conditions under which such a syllabus can be successful need not be as extraordinary as Clarke (1991) suggests.

12.2.2 Talkbase: Thailand

The curriculum model for autonomy – developed in pre-sessional English courses at the Asian Institute of Technology (AIT) and implemented in a course called Talkbase – draws upon theories of communicative language teaching and the process syllabus, but is distinctive in its emphasis on 'communicative people' rather than 'communicative language'. Hall and Kenny (1988) describe three major features of the Talkbase course:

- it focuses on the learners and what they actually want to say,
- tasks and content are often largely determined by the students themselves,
- in methodological terms, the focus is on process rather than content.

Talkbase differs from the ideal model of the process syllabus in that the nature of the students' work is determined by initial input from the teacher. However, as described by Hall and Kenny (1988: 29):

> The course has nothing in the way of a traditional timetable where slots have to be filled, but provides instead a set of inter-related activities organised in weekly units. Here the intended outcome of each week's work forms a major input to that of the following, with a cumulative build-up for the learners in understanding and practice, as compartmentalization gives way to wholeness.

A typical example of initial teacher input is the instruction, 'Drying: Find out what you can about the above subject and come back this afternoon prepared to talk about what you have found and how you have found it.' The instruction is deliberately ambiguous and open to multiple interpretations in terms of content and procedure. Subsequent tasks are largely determined by the results of earlier tasks presented in report-back sessions.

The approach taken at AIT is distinguished from project-based approaches by the idea that the students should be involved in initiating 'a piece of work'. In contrast to a project, which is viewed as an exercise leading to a finished outcome, the process and outcome of a piece of work are not determined in advance. According to Kenny and Laszewski (1997: 130–1),

> A piece of work itself makes demands upon the learner because its outcomes depend on the learner's interpretation of what needs to be achieved. The learners, in exercising their autonomy, become self-critical as they apply existing knowledge and skill toward achieving their identified ends.

The approach to pre-sessional courses developed at AIT is well established and has been judged successful both by the institution that sponsors it and by outside visitors. According to Hall and Kenny (1988: 25), the most notable result of the course is a 'startling increase in confidence and ability' among students who enter the course with little experience of speaking English.

12.2.3   Autonomous Learning Modules: Finland

The Autonomous Learning Modules (ALMS), run by the Helsinki University Language Centre for first-year undergraduate students following an EFL course as part of a compulsory foreign language requirement, are of particular interest as an example of a radical approach to autonomy within a framework of institutional assessment (Karlsson et al., 1997). In contrast to the Denmark and Thailand models, the ALMS course is based on self-access and makes no reference to the idea of the process syllabus. In contrast to other approaches to self-access, however, the ALMS course also involves the notion of a curriculum that is largely determined and evaluated by the students.

Although it is almost entirely self-directed, the 13-week ALMS course is a credit-bearing course, in which the organisers have resolved a number of difficult organisational problems concerning assessment and timetabling. The motivation for the project initially arose from some teachers' dissatisfaction with more conventional courses and an interest in self-access. Its implementation was prompted, however, by institutional concerns with economy of teacher contact time. The ALMS programme functions as an alternative to an 80-hour classroom course and involves 60 hours of contact with teachers and counsellors per student. The programme has thus taken advantage of institutional pressures to shift the curriculum in the direction of greater autonomy.

The programme begins with a compulsory six-hour learner awareness session covering six areas:

- Reflections about language learning.
- Consciousness-raising of language learning strategies.
- Analysis of students' own strategies.
- Analysis of language needs, present and future.
- The students' own objectives.
- Making preliminary plans and thinking about areas of interest.

Although established learner development techniques and instruments such as the Strategy Inventory for Language Learning (SILL) are used, the emphasis in this part of the course is on reflection and learners' awareness of their own use of strategies and planning.

In the second phase of the course, students are introduced to some of the resources available to them including support groups, the self-access studio and the ALMS room (which contains support materials for the programme), record-keeping documents, reading and reference materials and a mailbox and bulletin board. At this stage, students are also asked to make an initial contract covering their goals, objectives, time allocation, use of resources and materials, methods of learning and partners. They are also introduced to the idea of keeping a log, which serves as a record of work (for final assessment), as a vehicle for reflection and as a basis for discussion in counselling.

Students participating in the ALMS course come into contact with teachers in two roles: the ALMS counsellor and the Faculty Language Teacher. The ALMS counsellor is primarily responsible for helping the students with the idea and practice of autonomous learning and takes charge of the learner awareness and individual counselling sessions. The Faculty Language Teacher is primarily responsible for issues related to assessment and takes charge of the session in which students write their contracts and a final individual session in which it is decided whether or not each student passes the course. Teachers also take responsibility for support groups, which are run according to a flexible timetable in the central part of the course. Support groups on various skills and topics are timetabled according to an initial estimate of student demand. Participation is voluntary and the nature of the teacher's role varies according to the type of group, but is always intended to be one of support.

Students also participate in three compulsory counselling sessions. In the first session, students are asked what they understand by autonomous learning and how they are realising it in practice. There is also discussion of personal objectives and goals where adjustments can be made to learning contracts. The second session focuses on the students' progress on the basis of entries in the logs. In the third session, the students are expected to outline what they have achieved during the course and how they have developed as language learners and the counsellor and each student together come to a decision as to whether the student has satisfied the course requirements.

In the ALMS course, students work with teacher support, but without the structure of regular classroom sessions with a single teacher. The problem of structure is addressed through self-access facilities, learner-training sessions, counselling, support groups and record-keeping procedures for planning, monitoring and evaluation. The curriculum model represented by the ALMS course thus integrates a number of the techniques conventionally associated with the promotion of autonomy into a complex structure that appears to work well for students, teachers and the institution. A full evaluation of the project has yet to be published, but Karlsson et al. (1997) report that pilot studies showed improvements in motivation and a heightened consciousness of the learning process.

12.3 The effectiveness of curriculum-based approaches

Curriculum-based approaches to autonomy are often judged effective according to their ability to survive. The fact that the models discussed in the previous section have become established and have been judged successful by those who organise and teach them is some evidence of their success. One of the strengths of these models is that they address the issue of control holistically, placing equal emphasis on the development of self-management skills, and control over cognitive and content aspects of learning. For this reason, however, the factors contributing to their success or failure are often difficult to determine.

Curriculum-based approaches can also be described as 'deep-end' approaches, in which learners are expected to develop the capacity for control over learning by exercising their autonomy at a number of levels. They are also characterised by the freedom given to students at an early stage of the course and by the degree of responsibility expected of them. It is evident, however, that the more successful curriculum-based approaches to autonomy do not simply leave the students to 'sink or swim'. Invariably, their effectiveness depends upon implicit or explicit scaffolding structures that support learners in decision-making processes. Without these structures, curriculum-based approaches would do little to help students to develop their capacity to take control over learning.

In the examples discussed in this section, the role of the teacher in the negotiation of learning objectives and procedures is also crucial. As Hall and Kenny (1988: 22) describe it, this role is 'a little like that of the director of a drama workshop whose job it is to get the best out of the players whilst at the same time encouraging the development of the drama'. In this sense, curriculum-based approaches do not imply an abdication of the teacher's role. On the contrary, as in all approaches to the implementation of autonomy, the attitudes, skills and dedication of the teacher are key factors.

Chapter 13

Teacher-based approaches

In evaluating any form of practice designed to promote autonomy, there is a risk that the implementation of autonomy will be seen as a matter of the application of one or more methods of teaching and learning. In practice, however, particular approaches often constitute no more than a framework for interaction between teachers and learners and their effectiveness often depends on their implementation by teachers on a day-to-day basis. In the recent literature on autonomy there has been an increasing tendency to focus on the teacher's role in autonomous learning. In teacher-based approaches the emphasis is, therefore, placed on the teacher's professional development and on teacher education.

13.1 Teacher roles

Wright (1987), following Barnes (1976), characterises teacher roles in terms of a continuum from transmission to interpretation teaching (Quote 13.1 overleaf). The role of the teacher within autonomous learning clearly falls within the framework of interpretation teaching. Terms proposed to describe the role of the teacher within this framework include facilitator, helper, coordinator, counsellor, consultant, adviser, knower and resource. Voller (1997), in a detailed review of the literature on teacher roles in autonomous learning, reduces these to three: *facilitator*, in which the teacher is seen as providing support for learning; *counsellor*, where the emphasis is placed on one-to-one interaction; and *resource*, in which the teacher is seen as a source of

> **Quote 13.1** Wright on teacher roles
>
> ...*transmission* teachers believe in subject disciplines and boundaries between them, in content, in standards of performance laid down by these disciplines that can be objectively evaluated; that the teacher's role is to evaluate and correct learners' performance; that learners will find it hard to meet the standards; *interpretation* teachers believe that knowledge is the ability to organize thought, interpret and act on facts; that learners are intrinsically interested and naturally inclined to explore their worlds; that the teacher's role is to set up dialogues in which learners reorganize their states of knowledge; that learners already know a great deal and have the ability to refashion that knowledge.
>
> Wright (1987: 62)

knowledge and expertise. Voller (1997: 102) itemises the functions and qualities associated with these roles under the headings of technical and psycho-social support. The key features of technical support are:

- helping learners to plan and carry out their independent language learning by means of needs analysis (both learning and language needs), objective setting (both short- and long-term), work planning, selecting materials, and organising interactions;
- helping learners to evaluate themselves (assessing initial proficiency, monitoring progress, and peer- and self-assessment);
- helping learners to acquire the skills and knowledge needed to implement the above (by raising their awareness of language and learning, by providing learner training to help them to identify learning styles and appropriate learning strategies).

The key features of psycho-social support are:

- the personal qualities of the facilitator (being caring, supportive, patient, tolerant, empathic, open, non-judgemental);
- a capacity for motivating learners (encouraging commitment, dispersing uncertainty, helping learners to overcome obstacles, being prepared to enter into a dialogue with learners, avoiding manipulating, objectifying or interfering with, in other words controlling, them);
- an ability to raise learners' awareness (to 'decondition' them from preconceptions about learner and teacher roles, to help them perceive the utility of, or necessity for, autonomous learning).

The functions and qualities in these lists imply not only the ability to implement particular methods of teaching and learning, but also a commitment to the idea of autonomy manifested in the teacher's global approach towards professional practice. As Breen and Mann (1997) argue, in order to foster autonomy among learners, teachers must believe in the learners' capacity to assert their own autonomy and be prepared to live through the consequences for their own practice. In order to create spaces for learners to exercise their autonomy, teachers must recognise and assert their own.

13.2   Teacher autonomy

Further reading

Sinclair, B., McGrath, I. and Lamb, T. (eds) (2000) *Learner Autonomy, Teacher Autonomy: Future Directions*. London: Longman.

The idea of teacher autonomy arises in part from a shift in the field of teacher education from a focus on the teacher as a conduit for methods devised by experts to a focus on the teacher as a self-directed learner and practitioner (Quote 13.2). It also arises from a growing awareness among teachers involved with learner autonomy of the importance of their own role in the process of helping learners take greater control over their learning. Thavenius (1999: 159) argues:

> **Quote 13.2** Freeman on teacher autonomy
>
> Is learning to teach a matter of replicating how other teachers do things? Or does it depend on coming to grips with one's own ways of thinking and doing things in the classroom? In this book, we take the position that learning to teach is a process that, while it can be informed by the knowledge and insight of others, remains principally the responsibility and work of the learner.
>
> Freeman and Cornwell (1993: xii)

> Developing learner autonomy involves a lot more for the teacher role than most teachers realize. Although they may be ambitious and even eager to start helping their students developing autonomy and awareness of the language learning process, they may still be ignorant of what this means for the teacher role. It is not just a matter of changing teaching techniques, it is a matter of changing teacher personality.

According to McGrath (2000), teacher autonomy involves ideas of professional freedom and self-directed professional development. In order to foster autonomy among learners, teachers must be both free and able to assert their own autonomy in the practice of teaching.

Little (1995a: 178) argues that the starting point for teacher autonomy is the recognition that, regardless of the content of the curriculum, the teacher cannot help but 'teach herself', because 'the curriculum that she presents to her learners is hers and no one else's'. However closely teachers follow curriculum guidelines, they necessarily communicate their own unique interpretations of them to their students. The process of fostering autonomy in learning is thus a process of negotiation uniquely conditioned by the teacher's individuality (p. 179):

> Before embarking on this process of negotiation, the teacher must decide on the areas in which she will seek to promote learner autonomy. She must decide, in other words, whether and to what extent it is possible for the learners to determine their own learning objectives, select their own learning materials and contribute to the assessment of their learning process. In this she will be guided by the institutional framework within which she is working, and the age, educational background and target language competence of her learners.

In other words, autonomy among learners develops uniquely within each setting and is in part a product of the teacher's proactive and on-line assessment of the capacities and preferences of the students. Teacher autonomy can therefore be understood in part as the recognition of one's own professional freedom in the implementation of curriculum guidelines. For McGrath (2000), the initial step towards teacher autonomy in this sense takes place when the teacher adopts an evaluative stance towards the elements of the teaching and learning context over which she has a degree of control.

Several researchers have argued that teacher education should not only equip teachers with a knowledge of issues related to learner autonomy. It should also mirror practices designed to foster autonomy among learners. Little (1995a: 180) argues:

... teacher education should be subject to the same processes of nego-tiation as are required for the promotion of learner autonomy in the language classroom. Aims and learning targets, course content, the ways in which course content is mediated, learning tasks, and the assessment of learner achievement must all be negotiated; and the basis of this nego-tiation must be a recognition that in the pedagogical process, teachers as well as students can learn, and students as well as teachers can teach.

For Lamb (2000), teacher education that aims to foster teacher autonomy should also involve critical reflection on the inequalities of knowledge and experience implicit in professional assumptions about teaching and learning.

In a detailed account of the development of an in-service training pro-gramme for school teachers in Denmark, Breen et al. (1989) illustrate the complexity of these principles as they describe the development of the programme through transmission, problem solving and classroom decision making, and investigation phases. The researchers describe how, in the final phase of the programme, they came to see the trainers as participating in the learning with the trainees, the workshops as exploratory activities in which the teachers acted as informants for the trainees, and the trainees' classrooms as the key training resource. Their account suggests that teacher education for teacher autonomy involves a further step in which teacher *educators* reflect upon their own roles in the training process.

At the University of Minho in Portugal, Vieira (1997, 1999) has also developed a methodology for in-service training with autonomy as the major focus. The assumption behind the methodology is that there is an integral relationship between reflective teaching and autonomy in learning. The aim of the programme, which is inquiry-oriented and classroom-based, is to articulate teacher and learner development within a single framework by exploring the relationship between reflective teaching and learner autonomy. The programme involves one or more trainers working collaboratively with school teachers and involves a loosely negotiated structure beginning with reflection on approaches to teacher education and school pedagogy and moving on to preparation, implementation and reporting phases of action research. Arguing that teacher training and learner training should follow similar principles, Vieira (1997: 65) outlines five training principles:

- focusing on the trainee: curricula and training sessions should be built from personal needs and theories;

- focusing on training processes – particularly on critical reflection and experimentation – and not only on training outcomes;
- enquiring about pedagogical knowledge and practices in order to be able to describe/inform/confront/reconstruct personal theories and action;
- integrating theory and practice by valuing the role of experience-derived knowledge;
- promoting introspective reflection.

Vieira points out that reflective approaches to teacher education run the risk of meaning anything at all, provided there is a reflection component within them. Vieira's programme is distinctive in that it takes autonomy as the focal point for reflection and action research. Vieira argues that this is justified because autonomy provides legitimate criteria for the evaluation of educational practices and necessarily entails a critique of institutional and social contexts of teaching and learning.

13.3　The effectiveness of teacher-based approaches

In general, teacher-based approaches to autonomy involve an emphasis on the teacher's role in the implementation of various forms of practice. They suggest that the teacher's commitment to the idea of autonomy and professional skills will be a crucial factor in their effectiveness. As yet, however, we have few accounts of teacher education programmes directed at teacher autonomy and we know little about their effectiveness in practice. Research on teacher autonomy is likely to become increasingly important, however, as teacher educators take up the challenge of translating curriculum guidelines incorporating the idea of autonomy into large-scale teaching programmes. This challenge is liable to be complex, because it involves recognition of the special character of trainee and in-service teachers as both teachers and learners.

Chapter 14

Conclusion

In this chapter I have reviewed evidence for the effectiveness of a variety of practices in promoting autonomy and better language learning. I have also attempted to show how different approaches place emphasis on different aspects of control. One general conclusion that can be drawn is that no single method of fostering autonomy can be judged the best. Nor can their effectiveness be judged independently of the forms in which they are implemented or contextual factors such as the background and level of the learners and the culture of the learning institution. If autonomy implies control over learning management, cognitive processes and the content of learning, however, it seems likely that it will be fostered most effectively through a combination of approaches. In particular, it appears important that issues of control are addressed at the level of the curriculum as a whole. Certainly, the programmes that appear most able to provide evidence of their effectiveness are those that, like the programmes discussed in Chapter 13, adopt a holistic approach to the development of autonomy.

A second general conclusion is that the research evidence on the effectiveness of various forms of practice in fostering autonomy is much weaker than the research evidence relating to the validity of the concept of autonomy itself. Although we are able to report a number of apparently successful innovations and programmes, it must be emphasised that the empirical evidence for their success is often anecdotal or confined to learner and teacher reports of satisfaction. In particular, it is difficult on the basis of current research evidence to substantiate the claim that we know how to foster autonomy in ways that reliably lead to language-learning gains. In part, this is a consequence of the fact that autonomy cannot be the result of the application of a method. The development of autonomy depends upon the will of the learners and our own adaptability to the contexts of teaching and learning in which we find ourselves. At the same time, it must be acknowledged that too much of what we know about the implementation of autonomy is based on the reflections of experienced practitioners and too little on hard empirical evidence. In Section III we will look in more detail at the ways in which this balance can be redressed through action research.

Section

III Researching Autonomy

Chapter 15

Research methods and key areas of research

The three chapters in this section will . . .

- describe potential areas for action research in the field of autonomy;
- discuss six case studies of exemplary research on autonomy;
- explain how practising teachers can contribute to our knowledge of autonomy and its implementation through action research.

15.1 Action research

> **Further reading**
>
> Burns, A. (1999) *Collaborative Action Research for English Language Teachers.* Cambridge: Cambridge University Press.

Sections I and II of this book have outlined areas of theoretical and practical interest within the field of autonomy in language learning. Chapters 15 and 16 look more closely at some of the key research issues in the field and at the kinds of research projects teachers might carry out as part of their everyday work and professional development.

In its broadest sense, research is a process of inquiry in which answers are sought to questions of interest to the researcher. These answers may be sought through reflection, logical reasoning or analysis of data.

A great deal of the research on autonomy to date has been based on reflection and reasoning. Often, researchers draw conclusions about the nature of autonomy and the practices associated with it from reflection on their own and others' experiences of fostering autonomy. Far less research has been based on systematic analysis of data. This section therefore focuses on data-based action research of the kind that any teachers with sufficient time and energy could carry out within the context of their own practices.

Action research is defined by Wallace (1998: 1) as 'the systematic collection and analysis of data relating to the improvement of some area of professional practice' (Concept 15.1). It is often considered the most accessible form of research for teachers, because its goal is the solution of problems encountered in everyday practice. Action research is also particularly suited to the field of autonomy because it is, in effect, a form of autonomous learning, which can help us to develop our own

---

Concept 15.1   Action research

Action research has five distinctive characteristics.

1. It addresses issues of practical concern to the researchers and the community of which they are members.
2. It involves systematic collection of data and reflection on practice.
3. It is usually small scale and localised and often involves observation of the effects of a change in practice.
4. It often involves analysis of qualitative data and description of events and processes.
5. Its outcomes include solutions to problems, professional development and the development of personal or local theories related to practice.

In language education, the action researcher is often a teacher acting in the role of teacher-researcher. In collaborative action research, teachers work together on shared problems. Burns (1999: 12) states that the goal of collaborative action research is 'to bring about change in social situations as the result of group problem solving and collaboration'. She argues that collaboration increases the likelihood that the results of research will lead to change in institutional practices. As autonomy implies *learner* control, a key question in collaborative action research in the field is the extent to which learners should also be partners in and beneficiaries of the research.

---

autonomy as teachers. In contrast to experimental research, action research does not necessarily require the 'subjects' of the research to be kept in the dark about the researchers' purposes. The ultimate aim of action research on autonomy is to help learners to become more autonomous. There is, therefore, no reason why learners should not be treated as partners in the action research process.

This chapter highlights some of the areas within the field of autonomy where research is most needed. Chapter 16 presents six case studies of data-based research projects in the field and suggests how future researchers might build upon their methods and results.

15.2 Key areas of research

Almost all research in the field of autonomy is based on, and has implications for, one of the three hypotheses stated at the beginning of this book.

1. The concept of autonomy is grounded in a natural tendency for learners to take control over their learning. As such, autonomy is available to all, although it is displayed in different ways and to different degrees according to the unique characteristics of each learner and each learning situation.

2. Learners who lack autonomy are capable of developing it given appropriate conditions and preparation. The conditions for the development of autonomy include the opportunity to exercise control over learning. The ways in which we organise the practice of teaching and learning therefore have an important influence on the development of autonomy among our learners.

3. Autonomous learning is more effective than non-autonomous learning. In other words, the development of autonomy implies better language learning.

The first of these hypotheses is concerned with the nature of autonomy and its component parts. The second concerns the possibility of fostering autonomy among learners. The third is concerned with the effectiveness of our efforts to foster autonomy in terms of language learning. Each of these hypotheses defines a distinct area of research.

15.2.1   Autonomy and its component parts

In this book, autonomy has been described in terms of control over learning management, cognitive processes and the content of learning. Research on the nature of autonomy is usually descriptive and seeks to document the behavioural and psychological attributes associated with these aspects of control (Quote 15.1). Research can help us to understand whether the capacity to control learning comes naturally to learners or whether it needs to be acquired through formal processes of training. It can also help us to understand what to focus on when we seek to foster autonomy and evaluate the results of our efforts.

Quote 15.1   Riley on researching autonomy

A blind man has friends who talk to him about the world which they can see but which he cannot. Amongst the things that interest him most are what his friends call 'bubbles' . . . Intrigued, the blind man asks his friends to make him some bubbles, which they do, but since he cannot see them he is obliged to try to touch them. But not only are they difficult to locate, when he *does* succeed in finding one, his touch destroys it. For him 'bubbles' will remain a matter of hearsay and a slight sensation of dampness on his fingertips. He simply does not have the appropriate tools for observing or experiencing the objects in question.

   Do we? That is, if we extrapolate from my analogy to our present area of interest, do we possess the methodological and conceptual tools which are appropriate to the study of autonomy, self-directed learning and self-access? Or are we teachers and researchers in this field condemned to stumble around like the blind, gesticulating wildly and destroying the very thing we want to understand?

Riley (1996: 251)

Research reviewed in Chapter 4 suggests that learners naturally exercise a degree of control over their learning independently of our efforts to encourage them. If this is the case, fostering autonomy may essentially be a question of helping learners to develop behavioural and psychological characteristics that come more or less naturally to them. However, because so much of the research in the field of language learning has been concerned with the effectiveness of teaching, we still know relatively little about the ways in which learners exercise control over their learning as a natural feature of the process of second language acquisition. In spite of the importance of the issue of culture in debates on autonomy, there has also been very little research on the ways in which control over learning and attitudes towards it vary cross-culturally (see 16.1, case study).

Control over learning may be exercised within the classroom or outside it. Classroom research has established that language learners tend to follow their own agendas during lessons, while second language acquisition research suggests that language acquisition depends less on formal instruction than on independent processing of linguistic input. Much of this research focuses on short-term processes of learning within the classroom. As yet we know little about the ways in which learners go about setting their own agendas in the longer term or how classroom learning fits in with these agendas. The nature of out-of-class learning and its relationship to classroom learning is a relatively new area of research within the field of autonomy, in which there is much to be learned (see 16.2, case study). Studies of language-learning careers may also cast light on the roles of self-instructional and naturalistic learning processes in the acquisition of proficiency. Although longitudinal studies are often impractical for practising teachers, much can be learned from introspective or retrospective accounts of learning gathered through diaries or interviews.

Control over learning may also be displayed in relation to factors such as motivation, anxiety and beliefs about language learning. Although a great deal of research has been conducted in each of these areas, relatively little is known about the ways in which learners go about motivating themselves, dealing with their anxieties and modifying their beliefs independently of teachers. Similarly, although the research base on learners' use of metacognitive strategies in the self-management of learning is strong, much less is known about the role of social and affective strategies. Much could be learned in this area through classroom observation and diary or interview studies.

The fields of research that hold out most promise for the investigation of control of the cognitive processes involved in learning are those concerned with attention, reflection and metacognitive knowledge. Second language acquisition research in these areas often uses experimental techniques and complex theoretical constructs from the field of psychology. However, a great deal can be learned from observational studies that pose relatively straightforward questions. In the area of reflection, for example, we do not yet have a clear understanding of what language learners reflect upon, the circumstances that cause them to reflect, the ways in which they go about reflection, or the role of speech and writing in reflection. Observation of classroom reflection sessions and analysis of learner journals or records of work can provide valuable information on these issues (see 16.3, case study).

Control over the content of learning is one of the least-well researched areas in the field of autonomy. Research in this area calls for a particular focus on decisions made by learners in relation to broad areas of focus in learning (e.g. speaking, writing, etc.) and on the ways in which learners create opportunities for learning in language use. It also calls for investigation of the purposes of learning from the learner's point of view at particular stages of the learning process and their relationship to socially and educationally accepted purposes.

15.2.2   Fostering autonomy

In Section II, practices associated with autonomy were placed under the headings of resource-based, technology-based, learner-based, classroom-based, curriculum-based and teacher-based approaches. Although a great deal of research has been conducted in each of these areas, there is surprisingly little empirical evidence available for the effectiveness of any particular approach. The need for research that seeks to demonstrate the relationship between particular forms of practice and the development of autonomy is therefore ongoing and is not confined to any one area. The most pressing need in each area is for empirical research that will support or undermine the theoretical assumptions on which forms of practice are based (see 16.4, case study).

The effectiveness of practice is of immediate interest to teachers who would like to know whether their own efforts in fostering autonomy are 'working' or not, and how they can be improved. In choosing areas of research, practising teachers are therefore likely to be guided by their own teaching contexts and goals. Action research is an ideal approach and is likely to be most successful when it addresses specific questions.

One of the reasons that we lack hard evidence on the effectiveness of practices designed to promote autonomy concerns the level of generality of research questions. In principle, researchers on autonomy would like to be able to answer questions such as, 'Is self-access effective in promoting autonomy?' In practice, however, research that aims to answer questions of this kind often fails to provide hard evidence for three reasons.

First, as we saw in Section II, a practice such as self-access generally involves a number of elements that are likely to influence its effectiveness. The ways in which these elements are combined constitutes the particular form in which self-access is implemented. The effectiveness of self-access in general cannot be separated from the effectiveness of the particular form in which it is implemented or from the effectiveness of its individual elements. For this reason, research is most likely to produce results when it focuses on a particular variable within the practice under study. In the classical action research model, the researcher first investigates the effects of existing practice and then investigates the effects of the same practice when one variable is changed. In research on self-access, for example, the researcher might investigate the effects of the introduction of a counselling service, a more transparent system of access, or greater learner involvement in the management of the centre.

The second reason concerns the measurement of autonomy (Concept 15.2 overleaf). Although autonomy has been described in this book in terms of observable features of control, we still lack global measures that allow us to judge whether a learner has become more autonomous or not. Research is likely to be most effective, therefore, when it focuses upon directly and indirectly observable behaviours associated with control rather than the construct of autonomy itself. While it is difficult to judge whether learners have become more autonomous or not in a global sense, it is possible to judge whether they are able to produce more effective learning plans, participate more in decision-making processes, reflect more deeply on their learning, and so on.

The third reason concerns the context in which a form of practice occurs. The effects of any change in practice are inevitably conditioned by the context in which it is introduced. The effects of introducing a counselling service into a self-access centre, for example, are likely to be influenced by a number of factors including the age, proficiency level and cultural background of the target learners, their previous learning experiences and goals, the role of self-access in their learning, the characteristics of the self-access centre and the experience and attitudes of the counsellors. Although these factors may not be the focus of the research, they are likely to be important in the interpretation of results. Any action research project should therefore include an 'ethnographic' dimension in which researchers should gather as much contextual information as possible and seek to convey the look and feel of the form of practice investigated.

The conditions for successful action research on the effectiveness of practices aiming to foster autonomy can be summed up by comparing two research questions:

• Is self-access effective in fostering autonomy?
• Does the introduction of a counselling service help Mainland Chinese postgraduate students working independently in a university self-access centre in Hong Kong to produce effective learning plans?

Concept 15.2 **Measuring autonomy**

How do we know if our learners have become more autonomous? Although we cannot observe the *capacity* to control their learning directly, we can observe the *exercise* of this capacity in various aspects of learning. Measuring gains in autonomy, therefore, involves identifying behaviours associated with control and judging the extent to which learners display them. The following are examples of the kinds of questions that can be asked:

- Do learners make and use learning plans?
- Do they participate in classroom decisions?
- Do they reflect upon their learning?
- Do they initiate exchanges in the target language?

Evidence for these behaviours may be direct or indirect. A written learning plan and a portfolio of learning outcomes related to the plan would, for example, be a source of direct evidence of a learner's ability to plan learning. A statement recorded in an interview that a learner regularly plans learning activities before carrying them out would be indirect evidence. Although direct evidence is often more reliable than indirect evidence, indirect evidence can be important in judging whether the learner has a sense of control when displaying certain behaviours.

Although it is possible to reduce the idea of control over learning to observable behaviours, in practice researchers also need to exercise judgement when interpreting data. Although planning is an aspect of control, the fact that a learner makes and executes a plan does not necessarily mean she has exercised control over learning. The researcher may judge, for example, that the plan was incoherent or carried out in a mechanical way. Or she may judge that the plan was coherent and showed evidence of reflection and purpose. Although there are no objective criteria to measure degrees of control, it is important that the criteria used are made clear in research reports, so that readers may exercise their own judgement.

When the effects of a change in practice are at issue, it is important that the aspects of control investigated are relevant to the change in practice. It is equally important that data are collected before and after the change. Knowing that learners are able to control their learning after a change in practice is of little value unless we know what they were able to do before the change was implemented.

The first question is likely to be unanswerable through action research. The second can be answered through careful analysis of transcripts of counselling sessions, the students' learning plans and records of work, and interviews in which the students are asked about the effectiveness of the counselling sessions and their learning plans. Answers to the second question can also provide evidence that will ultimately help us to answer the first more general question. Cumulative evidence related to specific questions about self-access might lead us to conclude that self-access is, in general, effective or ineffective in promoting autonomy. More importantly, it will help us to understand which elements of self-access are most effective and which components of autonomy are most effectively addressed through self-access. By including specific elements of the learning context in the research question, the researcher will also help others to interpret the evidence for themselves and perhaps replicate the research in other contexts.

15.2.3   Autonomy and better language learning

For many of its advocates, the argument for autonomy is concerned primarily with the ability to learn effectively in terms of personal goals. The development of autonomy implies a qualitative change in the learner's orientation towards learning in the direction of personal relevance. Although autonomy may ultimately lead to greater proficiency in language use, whether autonomous learners learn *more* than non-autonomous learners is a secondary issue. In recent years, however, the contribution of practices associated with autonomy to language proficiency has become a critical issue for two reasons. Firstly, researchers are increasingly beginning to understand that there is an intimate relationship between autonomy and effective learning. To date, however, this relationship has largely been explored at the level of theory, and lacks substantial empirical support. Secondly, world-wide concern with accountability in education is increasingly obliging teachers to demonstrate the effectiveness of their practices in terms of proficiency gains. Programmes that prioritise the quality of the learning process over the quantity of language learned have become increasingly difficult to justify. If researchers can show that practices aiming at greater autonomy also lead to greater proficiency, in whatever terms this is measured, their arguments will be strengthened.

For both practical and theoretical reasons, therefore, there is a pressing need for empirical research on the relationship between the development of autonomy and the acquisition of language proficiency.

The hypothesis that practices intended to foster autonomy lead to better language learning can be demonstrated empirically at two levels (Concept 15.3). At the first level, research can attempt to show that a particular form of practice associated with autonomy produces gains in proficiency that are equal to or greater than other forms of practice. Evidence that students following a programme aiming to foster autonomy do as well in assessed tasks as those following regular programmes, for example, can help to validate the programme both to its organisers and to funding authorities. Research of this kind typically attempts to measure gain in terms of conventional quantitative indicators of proficiency. At the second level, research can attempt to describe the ways in which proficiency develops as a result of the distinctive qualities of practices designed to promote autonomy. Research of this kind may aim to develop indicators of proficiency specific to autonomous learning and descriptions of the ways in which the development of autonomy and proficiency interact (see 16.5, case study).

Comments made on the design of action research projects focusing on gains in autonomy apply equally to research on proficiency gains.

Concept 15.3   **Measuring language-learning improvement**

The measurement of language-learning gains in the context of autonomy is a complex matter, which involves two potentially separate questions: Has the learner become a more proficient language user? Has the learner become a more effective language learner? Proficiency gains can be measured using standard testing instruments. However, these may not capture the kinds of improvement that are to be expected with the development of autonomy, where gains in proficiency may be uneven or not immediately apparent.

Gains in the learners' ability to learn languages involve questions of the following kind:

- Are learners able to learn from interaction with authentic target language texts?
- Are they able to create situations of learning for themselves?
- Are they able to monitor and self-assess their own performance?

As yet we lack reliable testing instruments to measure abilities of this kind. Often evidence of ability to learn will rely on direct observation of learners at work, on analysis of records of work and learning outcomes, or on learners' self-reports.

However, research on proficiency gains faces two additional problems. The first concerns the selection of relevant measures of proficiency. Conventional measures typically focus on knowledge of taught content and the learner's ability to demonstrate mastery of taught skills. In programmes aiming to develop autonomy, however, the linguistic content and skills to be acquired will often be determined by the learners and will be difficult to predict in advance. Such programmes may also seek to develop learning skills that are absent from conventional programmes, such as the ability to learn from authentic interaction with the target language, to create situations for learning and to self-assess performance. Although researchers may be under pressure to demonstrate effectiveness in terms of more conventional proficiency indicators, it is important that the criteria used to evaluate practices associated with autonomy are relevant to the goals and expectations of the programme. As Breen and Mann (1997: 141) argue, 'we are very likely to have to struggle for what *we* want to count as evidence for the benefits of what we are trying to do'. The development of relevant criteria and tools for assessing proficiency gains in programmes designed to foster autonomy can therefore be considered a major aim of research.

The second problem concerns the life cycle of programmes aiming to foster autonomy. Conventional language-teaching programmes are often designed so that incremental gains in proficiency can be demonstrated at any point during the programme. Programmes aiming at autonomy, however, will often involve phases in which the learners are expected to re-examine established approaches to learning and adjust to new methods of work. It is also likely that the natural tendency for language learners to regress periodically in order to move forwards at a later stage will be more pronounced in programmes that allow greater freedom in learning. It is therefore important that evaluations of programmes aiming to foster autonomy are sensitive to the temporary disruptions in the learning process that their goals imply. Research that is able to document changes in the quality of learning in such programmes may be less effective in demonstrating short-term gain, but will contribute a great deal to our understanding of the relationship between the development of autonomy and the development of proficiency.

To sum up, there is a pressing need for research that explores the relationship between the development of autonomy and the development of language proficiency. From a practical point of view, such research can help to validate forms of practice that aim to foster autonomy in terms of language-learning gains. From a theoretical point of view, it can help us to test and elaborate the theoretical hypothesis that autonomy in language learning is equivalent to better language learning. At this stage, however, research is likely to be most valuable if it establishes proficiency criteria and assessment tools relevant to autonomous learning and documents the ways in which the development of autonomy and proficiency interact.

Chapter 16

Case studies

Chapter 15 has highlighted issues in the field of autonomy that can profitably be addressed by action research and offered guidance on research design. The remainder of the chapter presents six case studies of research projects illustrating good practice in data-based research on autonomy and the potential for action research in the field. Each case study begins with a background section that explains how the research was related to the researcher's practical concerns. This is followed by a summary of its aims, methodology, results and conclusions. Each case study concludes with a commentary on the contribution of the research to the theory and practice of autonomy and suggestions for further research. These suggestions do not represent the sum total of possibilities for research in the field, which remains open to new ideas and approaches. Indeed, it is hoped that readers will be stimulated to explore new areas of research and methodologies that will contribute to our knowledge of autonomy both in theory and practice.

16.1 Case study: ethnicity and attitudes towards autonomy

16.1.1 Project

Press, M.-C. (1996) 'Ethnicity and the autonomous language learner: different beliefs and different strategies'. In E. Broady and M.-M. Kenning (eds) *Promoting Learner Autonomy in University Language*

Teaching. London: Association for French Language Studies/CILT, pp. 237–59.

Marie-Christine Press's research project was carried out as part of an M.A. in Applied Linguistics course. The results were written up in the form of a dissertation. Press collected data on the learners' age, sex, previous education and ethnicity. The results of her research were later published in a shortened form – with a focus on ethnicity – in a collection of papers on autonomy in university language teaching.

16.1.2 Background

Marie-Christine Press became interested in the relationship between ethnicity and attitudes towards autonomy while teaching Asian students studying foreign languages at the University of Westminster in the UK. She began with the observation that Asian students tended to demand more direct input from teachers than other students and were more reluctant to use the university self-access centre, which played an important role in their courses. Although the Asian students appeared highly motivated, they did not display the kind of self-direction that she associated with motivated learners. In order to test her intuitions and provide better support for these students, Press designed a questionnaire to investigate the relationship between students' ethnicity and their attitudes towards autonomy. A better understanding of this relationship is of practical value to teachers working with multi-ethnic groups. It is also of theoretical value in the context of the debate over the cultural appropriateness of autonomy to non-western contexts (see 1.3.3).

16.1.3 Aims

Press's study was guided by three research questions:

1. Could students of different ethnic backgrounds have different expectations and needs in regard to foreign language learning?
2. Would they consequently tend to use different learning strategies?
3. Would different strategies need to be highlighted in learner-training activities for students with different preferred approaches?

It was also hoped that the study would provide insight into the broader question of whether the concept of autonomy is culturally biased towards European students.

The study drew upon theories concerned with the relationship between ethnicity and second language acquisition. Following Gardner

(1985, 1988), Press assumed that cultural beliefs and expectations are likely to influence attitudes to second language learning and that learner beliefs are rooted in sociocultural traditions. The literature on ethnolinguistic vitality, which views the ethnicity of individuals as a function of the degree to which they are attached to the ethnolinguistic groups of which they are members (Giles and Byrne, 1982), led her to include learners' definitions of their own ethnicity as a factor in the research.

The study focused on two hypotheses:

1. Students of Asian origin would have a greater belief in the importance of rote learning and rule-based study (in addition to the value of general study strategies) than other students.

2. A strong attachment to their ethnic identities would lead students to adopt 'instrumental' approaches to language learning, rather than 'integrative' approaches adopted by students who wish to become closer to native speakers of the target language.

Implicit within these hypotheses was the assumption that rote learning, rule-based study and instrumental approaches to language learning were less conducive to autonomous learning than more communicative and integrative approaches.

16.1.4   Methodology

Press designed a three-part questionnaire (Concept 16.1 overleaf) to elicit data on ethnolinguistic identity, beliefs about language learning and preferred strategies. The first part of the questionnaire asked students to identify their own ethnicity and elicited attachment to ethnic identity through the questions 'How often do you think of yourself as British?' and 'How often do you think of yourself as a member of your national or ethnic group?'. The second part elicited beliefs about language learning, by asking the students to what extent they agreed with 22 beliefs identified in an earlier study by Wenden (1987). The third part of the questionnaire elicited the students' preferred strategies by asking how often they would use each of three alternative strategies from Oxford's (1990) taxonomy in 13 different situations.

The questionnaire was completed in class time by 70 male and 30 female students. Since Press was principally interested in the extent to which ethnic groups were homogeneous in their beliefs and preferred strategies, the main statistical test used in the analysis of the data was the one-way ANOVA (analysis of variance) test, which allows researchers to see whether variability between groups is greater than variability within groups.

Concept 16.1 **Questionnaire research**

Questionnaires can be used to collect biographical and learner self-report data on preferences, beliefs, behaviours or evaluations. In analysing questionnaire data, it is important to bear in mind that the answers given represent evidence of what the respondents say they believe or do, rather than evidence of what they actually believe or do, which can only be gathered through direct observation of processes and their outcomes.

Researchers should also be aware that respondents may misunderstand questionnaire items or interpret them in different ways to the researcher, particularly when they are put in a foreign language. Questionnaires are often subject to repeated tests of their reliability and validity. Oxford and Burry-Stock (1995) is a good account of the ways in which the Strategy Inventory for Language Learning has been validated cross-culturally.

Press (1996) used a questionnaire to correlate biographical variables with data on learners' beliefs and strategy use. Correlations of this kind call for complex statistical tests that are now made less complex by computer statistical analysis packages. Researchers in the field of applied linguistics often call on statistical experts to help them to choose appropriate tests and interpret the results. Hatch and Lazaraton (1991) is a good source of information on statistical tests for applied linguistic research.

Statistical tests are useful in establishing the significance of results for other researchers, but they are not always required in action research. Researchers frequently use questionnaires as an initial source of data to identify research questions that are followed up with in-depth interviews or other qualitative methods.

16.1.5 Results

The results from the questionnaire items aimed to identify students' ethnicity showed that the students did not neatly divide themselves into ethnic groups. Students identified their own ethnicity using 20 different labels and some students answered 'none'. Press reduced the 20 labels to 4, using those most often used by the students themselves ('Asian', 'Black', 'British' and 'White') and added an 'Others' category. The Asian category comprised 11 students of Chinese, Japanese, Indian and Pakistani background, some of whom were born in Britain and some of whom were not. The results showed that the Asian students thought of themselves as British more frequently than the Black, White or Other groups.

The results from questions related to learner beliefs tended to confirm Press's intuition that the Asian students would prefer more traditional modes of learning, since they showed a stronger belief in the importance of repetition, memorisation and systematic error correction than other groups. To this extent, the study confirmed her hypothesis that the Asian students were likely to resist independent study and self-access.

The Asian students also reported greater use of visualisation and memory strategies, were motivated by written tests and made greater use of general study strategies than other groups. They reported that they were more motivated by group work and by praise than other groups and that they were most eager to ask for help with new language. These results supported Press's earlier impressions of Asian students as eager students motivated by praise.

The Black students were identified as having the strongest attachment to their group. However, the hypothesis that students with strong attachment to their group would display instrumental motivation was not confirmed. The Black students did not display stronger instrumental motivation than other groups. Indeed, it was the British group who showed the strongest instrumental motivation, while the Black and Asian groups showed some strong integrative traits, especially the wish to be closely identified with the target language and its speakers.

16.1.6   Conclusions

Press's study concluded that, for the students in her study, there was some correlation between ethnicity and preferred approaches to learning, although the correlation was complex and not necessarily as she hypothesised. The broad conclusion that she drew was that there cannot be one method of language learning for all students. A particular mode of learning designed to promote autonomy will not necessarily work equally well for students of different cultural backgrounds. Press argued for a more sensitive interpretation of the concept of autonomy and suggested that the priority in learner training programmes might be given to self-knowledge, which could enable learners of diverse cultural backgrounds to make informed choices about the modes of learning which suit them best.

16.1.7   Commentary

Press's study has both practical and theoretical implications. Designed to verify informal observations she had made of her students, the study produced unexpected results that could be fed back into her own teaching. The results of the study showed that both the construct of ethnicity and its relationship to autonomy becomes more complex when subjected to data-based analysis. This led her to conclude that the best approach to learner training would be one that allows students to explore their own needs and preferences rather than one tailored to the assumed needs of different ethnic groups.

Press's study also contributes hard evidence to the debate on autonomy and culture (3.3), a field of investigation that has to date largely been characterised by theoretical speculation. In particular, it confirms the assumption that students' attitudes towards learning are culturally specific and are likely to influence responses to practices designed to foster autonomy. However, the major contribution of the study lies less in the answers that it provides to specific questions than in its demonstration of the complexity of the issues involved in the relationship between autonomy and culture. In particular, it illustrates the importance of investigating students' own definitions of their cultures and their attachment to them.

16.1.8   Further research

The published account of Press's study includes her questionnaire and a clear account of the procedures used in analysis. The study could therefore be replicated in other contexts. One difficulty in interpreting Press's results arises from the degree of variation within the population investigated. For example, the Asian group in the study consisted of only 11 learners and various nationalities and cultural backgrounds were represented within the group. Although Press aimed to identify groups within a multicultural population and understand the differences between them, the same methodology could be applied to populations that are, on the face of it, more homogeneous. Replications of the study with larger groups of students who share the same nationality would contribute a great deal to our understanding of the relationship between autonomy and culture.

The methodology used by Press could equally be applied to cultural variables other than ethnicity. Although discussions of autonomy and culture have tended to be dominated by concerns with nationality and ethnicity, factors such as gender, age, educational level and previous educational experience may influence learner responses to practices associated with autonomy. One of the important features of Press's approach to the collection of ethnolinguistic data is the way that it allows the learners to identify the categories by which they would describe themselves and their degree of attachment to those categories. The same approach could be followed in adapting her questionnaire items to other cultural variables.

One conclusion that can be drawn from Press's study is that the relationship between learner variables and attitudes to autonomy is highly complex. This opens up a number of interesting avenues for smaller-scale research, building on her approach to the identification of cultural variables. Press's research uses data on a broad range of beliefs and preferences to make inferences about learners' attitudes towards autonomy. However, culturally conditioned responses to the specific forms of practice associated with autonomy may be more relevant to the organisation of teaching and learning than responses to the construct of autonomy in general.

Smaller-scale research projects could therefore produce equally important results with a narrower focus. A research project to find out how learners of different cultural backgrounds respond to a self-access project, for example, could first isolate the elements within the practice that are intended to contribute towards the development of autonomy, such as goal setting, making a learning plan, selecting resources and self-evaluation. It could then investigate student attitudes to each of these elements both before and after the project. Although such a project would focus on a narrowly defined set of issues specific to the context in which the learners are studying, its results could contribute to a more fine-grained understanding of the relationship of cultural factors to the practice of autonomy. The cultural variables and area of practice to be investigated are likely to be determined by the particular situation in which the researchers are working. However, the cumulative results of such research could tell us a great deal more about the relationship between autonomy and culture than we know at present.

16.2   Case study: out-of-class learning

16.2.1   Project

Yap, S.S.L. (1998) *Out-of-class use of English by secondary school students in a Hong Kong Anglo-Chinese school.* MA Dissertation, University of Hong Kong.

Shirley Yap's research project was carried out in the final stages of her MA in Applied Linguistics and the results were written up in the form of a dissertation.

16.2.2   Background

In a recent measure to strengthen mother-tongue education, the Hong Kong government has required secondary schools to teach through the medium of Chinese unless they can clearly demonstrate the ability of staff and students to teach and learn through the medium of English. At the time of the research, Shirley Yap taught in a Hong Kong girl's secondary school that had been successful in its bid to continue to teach in English. The school now aims to create an 'English-rich' environment by promoting the use of English inside and outside the classroom. In response to the challenges faced by her school, Yap decided to investigate the extent to which her own students used English outside the classroom and their perceptions of the importance of out-of-class use of English to their learning.

16.2.3   Aims

Yap's study addressed three research questions:

1. Do students create opportunities to use English outside the classroom and, if so, how?
2. Is there a difference between more proficient and less proficient learners in their approach to out-of-class use of English?
3. How important are these activities, in the students' own opinions, in helping them improve their English?

The overall aim of the study was to produce a description of her students' out-of-class learning and its importance to their overall learning efforts.

16.2.4   Methodology

The subjects of the study were 18 female students, aged 17–19, studying in the Arts stream. The researcher was the teacher of their English Literature class. Two research instruments were used:

- a self-report questionnaire constructed from a taxonomy of out-of-class learning activities derived from a review of the literature (e.g. Littlewood and Liu, 1996; Pickard, 1995) and conversations with her students;
- a semi-structured interview, based on the questionnaire results, conducted with four higher proficiency and four lower proficiency students.

As a measure of proficiency, Yap used the students' results in the public examination taken the year before.

Yap approached her data as a source of indirect evidence on the learners' participation in out-of-class activities (Concept 16.2). The interview data were analysed using a method known as 'meaning condensation' (Kvale, 1996), in which the transcripts were read repeatedly and summarised in order to bring out key themes.

Concept 16.2   **Qualitative data as a source of indirect evidence**

Unable to observe evidence of out-of-class learning directly, Yap (1998) relied on indirect evidence from a questionnaire and interviews. Her questionnaire furnished data on the types and frequency of out-of-class learning for a large group of students. Interview data helped her come to a deeper understanding of the factors involved in out-of-class learning. In the following extract, a student mentions a feeling of 'happiness' resulting from her use of English outside the classroom:

> Um..and I have an experience to speak with foreigners just because they are friends of my uncle. But um..um..at that time I was young, just Form 2, er..I am brave to talk to them. And um..er..it is quite good because when you know that they know what you are talking about, you are happy, actually.

Yap found that the majority of the learners in her study mentioned feelings of happiness, enjoyment or satisfaction and concluded that regular participation in out-of-class learning is in part dependent on these feelings.

16.2.5   Results

Yap's study produced useful findings in relation to her three research questions:

1. She found that all of the students created opportunities to use English outside the classroom. However, they showed a preference for activities focusing on receptive, rather than productive skills. It appeared that students found speaking English out of class particularly daunting and also that their opportunities for speaking and writing were fewer than their opportunities for reading and listening to English. When students did speak English out of class, they tended to do so inside school rather than outside. They also showed a preference for situations in which they were able to use short

formulaic utterances (greetings, apologies, etc.) than longer more freely constructed utterances (complaining, comforting, warning), in which they were likely to switch to Cantonese.

2. She found no correlation between out-of-class use of English and proficiency. Low-proficiency and high-proficiency students used English outside class to similar degrees and in similar ways.

3. She also found that both low- and high-proficiency students tended to value out-of-class learning equally. Students tended to attach higher value to activities that involved native-speaker input and were considered 'serious', providing opportunities for extra practice and insights into western culture. At the same time, students appeared to value activities that were 'fun' or gave them a pleasurable sense of achievement.

16.2.6   Conclusions

Yap observed that six of the eight students interviewed reported that their out-of-class use of English was self-initiated. They did it because they enjoyed and valued it, not because they were encouraged to do it by teachers or parents. Often they were personally committed to and proud of their efforts to use English outside the classroom. From this she concluded that efforts to promote out-of-class learning should build upon the activities that students already value. She suggested that teachers should create opportunities for students to share information about the strategies they use. Noting that her students appear to value opportunities to speak English, but often lack the confidence and opportunity to do so, Yap also suggested that teachers in her school might focus on providing students with speaking opportunities as part of the 'English-rich' environment in her school.

16.2.7   Commentary

Yap's study gave her insights into an area of her students' learning to which she had previously had little access. She was surprised to discover the degree to which her students displayed creativity and determination in their use of English out-of-class. At the same time, the study gave her a number of ideas on how she and her fellow teachers could promote more effective out-of-class learning, building on the strengths and preferences that the students already displayed. The study also provided broader insights into the nature of out-of-class learning. It was noted in Chapter 4 that we know very little about the ways in which naturalistic learning, self-instruction and classroom learning interact. Yap's study suggests that even classroom learners within a relatively other-directed system take considerable responsibility for the overall direction of their language learning. Yap's study also suggests that affective factors are an especially important factor in learners' choice of, and attitudes to, the value of out-of-class activities.

16.2.8   Further research

Out-of-class language learning is a new area of study of great importance to the theory and practice of autonomy. The dearth of studies in this area highlights the fact that research has tended to focus on the development of autonomy in institutional settings without establishing a firm knowledge base on the ways in which learners take control of their learning as a natural feature of the learning process. Research in this area is likely to tell us not only what learners do outside the classroom, but also how their classroom learning fits into their broader orientations towards language and language learning. The activities in which learners engage can be documented through questionnaire studies. However, as Yap's study shows, deeper insights into the factors that influence choice of activities and the value attached to them can be gained through retrospective interviews. One of the problems with retrospective interviews is that the nature of experience may be distorted by time. An alternative approach is to ask students to keep journals in which they describe activities and their feelings about them.

Equally important are studies focusing on the ways in which learners create learning opportunities out of class and the ways in which they actually learn from them. Journals or portfolios in which students collect the outcomes of out-of-class activities appear to be a promising source of data for research of this kind. In an ongoing study of Hong Kong university students' out-of-class learning of Japanese, Itakura (1999) asked learners to use a notebook to record their thoughts about the activities they carried out. She also asked them to glue the materials they used into their notebooks. In keeping their notebooks, the learners showed considerable creativity in the design of learning tasks based on authentic samples of Japanese. At the same time the construction of the notebook entries revealed much about the processes of self-instruction involved in their out-of-class learning and their relationship to classroom learning.

16.3 Case study: reflection

16.3.1 Project

Lor, W. (1998) *Studying the first-year students' experience of writing their reflection journals with the use of a web-based system.* MA dissertation. University of Hong Kong.

Winnie Lor's research project was part of an MA in Applied Linguistics. The results were written up in her dissertation and were later presented at a conference on reflective practice.

16.3.2 Background

Several researchers have identified the capacity to reflect on one's own learning processes as a key psychological component of autonomy (see 5.2.2). To date, however, we know relatively little about how learners reflect on language learning or what happens when they are encouraged to do so by teachers. As an English teacher at the University of Hong Kong, Winnie Lor also observed that the concept of reflection might have different meanings in different cultural contexts. In Chinese, for example, the word 'reflection' carries a connotation of 'evaluating one's moral acts'. She also observed that Hong Kong students, coming from a school system in which examination pressure encourages memorisation and rote learning, are often said to be weak in critical thinking skills. She therefore decided to investigate what would happen when these students were asked to reflect upon their learning in the context of an out-of-class learning project.

16.3.3 Aims

Lor's study aimed to describe the process of reflection among students who were asked to reflect upon their out-of-class learning using the format of a written journal. It focused on two main research questions:

- What kinds of things do students reflect upon?
- To what extent could their journal entries be described as reflective?

The study was essentially descriptive, aiming to answer 'what' questions rather than 'how' or 'why' questions. The outcome of the research was intended to be a set of descriptive categories that would allow a better understanding of the process of reflection among her students.

16.3.4   Methodology

The subjects of the study were first-year Arts students following a compulsory English language course, including an assessed out-of-class learning project. As part of this project, students were encouraged to fill in 'record-of-work' forms, which included a space for reflection on learning activities, to be submitted in a portfolio at the end of the project (see Figure 11.1). Instead of using these record-of-work forms, however, Lor invited her students to send her bi-weekly entries for a 'reflection journal' via a web-based system. This system allowed the students to write their entries in their own time and to review previous entries before making new ones. It also allowed the researcher to collect data in an easily accessible computerised form. The database for the study finally consisted of journals from 12 students who wrote 10 entries or more. Lor deliberately avoided training the students or explaining how she expected them to reflect on their learning. Her regular responses to their entries were designed to encourage the students to continue writing, but not to influence the ways in which they wrote.

Lor approached the journal entries as direct evidence of the learners' ability to reflect on their learning experiences (Concept 16.3). In analysing the data, Lor used a 'grounded theory' approach (Glaser and

---

Concept 16.3   **Qualitative data as a source of direct evidence**

Lor (1998) used the entries in learners' reflection journals as a source of direct evidence of their ability to reflect on their learning. In the following extract from her data, a student reflects upon her problems in independent learning:

> I find that it is very hard to keep up learning English on one's own. First there is homework to consider. Then there is revision of lectures and tutorials. It is difficult to find enough time to seriously engage oneself in learning English properly on one's own. Sometimes even if time permits, it is hard to motivate oneself to do some independent learning. I find it exceedingly hard to allot a specific period of time to work on my independent programme, though I know that would be the most effective way.

Lor was able to use such data as direct evidence of learner reflection. Interpreting this extract, she notes how an external obstacle to independent learning (lack of time) turns into an internal obstacle (her own lack of motivation and problems with time management) in the course of her reflection.

Strauss, 1967), in which she aimed to generate theory through the systematic review and categorisation of data. Categories and their interrelationships were elaborated in the process of interpretation. This approach was thought to be particularly relevant to the initial investigation of an issue about which relatively little is known.

16.3.5   Results

Addressing the question of what the students reflected upon, Lor identified six categories, which she termed 'objects of reflection':

- learning events or situations;
- the learner's role in the learning process;
- the learner's feelings about learning and learning events;
- learning gains;
- difficulties encountered in the process of learning;
- decisions and plans.

These six objects of reflection were further reduced to four domains: context, affect, cognition and intention.

Lor observed that most of the entries were organised around particular learning events. In most cases these events were planned in advance and reflection on unplanned learning was infrequent. She also observed that the students' reflections did not often lead to more systematic plans or changes in plan. In many cases, learners recorded positive feelings about activities, and took these feelings as a reason to continue with the same kinds of activities. In rarer cases, learners recorded feelings of discomfort that caused them to produce a longer entry in which an experience was re-evaluated and re-framed.

Addressing the question of degrees of reflectivity, Lor observed that the journal entries were often short and that there was little sense of continuity across entries. In most cases, each entry covered a distinct event or topic and there was little reference to earlier entries. Using her own categories of context, affect, cognition and intention, Lor identified two dimensions of reflectivity: integration and transformation. A journal entry or sequence of entries can be considered as more integrated if it brings together the domains of context, affect and cognition, explores relationships between them and bases intentions on reflections within those domains. Reflection can be considered transformative if it displays evidence that the learner is reworking experiences, considering alternatives and changing her perception of experiences.

16.3.6 Conclusions

Lor concluded that the students in her study found the process of reflection in journal writing difficult. They were often unsure what they should write and looked to her for guidance. With some exceptions, their journal entries were neither well integrated nor transformative. She also observed that exceptional cases of deeper reflection were often triggered by experiences that challenged perceptions of language learning. From this she concluded that encouraging students to reflect more deeply on their learning does not necessarily imply training learners in strategies for reflection. Rather, teachers should aim to provide students with challenging experiences that provoke deeper reflection and with opportunities to discuss the processes of learning that arise from them.

16.3.7 Commentary

From her study, Lor gained a great deal of knowledge about her students and their capacity to reflect upon learning. The study also contributes significantly to our understanding of the process of reflection among language learners, in particular in relation to the role of affective factors in learners' thinking about learning. Often reflection is treated as a matter of the intellect alone. Lor's study suggests, however, that for many language learners positive or negative feelings are often the starting point for conscious reflection. It also suggests that the process of planning independent learning activities is crucially affected by affect. Reflections upon positive feelings can confirm the learner's sense of the rightness of a plan. Negative feelings about learning experiences can become an occasion for deeper reflection leading to changes in plan.

16.3.8 Further research

Lor's study highlights two key areas for further research in the area of reflection and autonomy: the nature of learner reflection in natural contexts of learning and ways in which deeper reflection can be encouraged. Reflection is essentially an internal process that cannot be observed directly. As such, devices such as journals or reflection sessions are artefacts of research that allow us to observe the outcomes of reflection. At the same time it is likely that the externalisation of thought in writing or in speech facilitates reflection by allowing learners to distance themselves from their experiences and thoughts. In this sense, research on reflection and the promotion of reflective learning are intimately linked.

Lor chose to use learning journals on independent learning as a source of data and devised a highly original method of collecting entries through the web. Learners can also be asked to write down their thoughts about classroom activities and their value immediately after they have happened, or end-of-class discussions can be recorded and transcribed. Lor's study focused on the content of reflection and therefore emphasised the identification of themes. The question of how learners reflect is equally important and can be approached through discourse analysis of learner talk and writing, focusing for example on the construction of reflective passages or narratives about learning experiences.

Important issues in the promotion of reflective learning include the medium and form in which reflection is externalised. In Lor's study, as in many other diary studies, the learners wrote in the medium of the target language. This raises the question of whether reflection may be deeper if it is conducted in the learners' first language. It also raises the question of whether reflection in the target language has its own benefits in terms of developing the learners' capacity to think and express themselves in that language. The outcomes of written and spoken reflection, as well as the outcomes of private reflection, learner–teacher dialogue and learner–learner dialogue, could also be compared. Lor's model for the identification of objects of reflection and degrees of reflectivity is a useful starting point for comparisons of this kind and could be refined through further empirical research. As Lor points out, there is also a need for longer-term studies that investigate how the capacity for reflection develops as learners become more familiar with a particular mode of externalising their reflections.

16.4 Case study: decision making in the process syllabus

16.4.1 Project

Simmons, D. and Wheeler, S. (1995) *The Process Syllabus in Action.* Sydney: National Centre for English Language Teaching and Research.

This project was carried out as part of the researchers' professional work in the Australian Adult Migrant Education Project. The results were published in the form of a research monograph, one of a series published by the National Centre for English Language Teaching and Research at Macquarie University, Sydney.

16.4.2 Background

In 12.1, the process syllabus was discussed as a form of practice, which, although not explicitly linked to the concept of autonomy, shares its central concern with learner control. It was also noted that there had been few studies of the 'strong version' of the process syllabus in action. Diane Simmons and Sylvia Wheeler decided to investigate how one model of the process syllabus worked in their own institution, the National Centre for English Language Teaching and Research (NCELTR) at Macquarie University, Sydney. Their research both contributed to the ongoing development of the model and produced a description and analysis of the process of syllabus negotiation, about which we know more in theory than in practice.

16.4.3 Aims

The major aim of the study was to evaluate how the reality of the process syllabus in action compares with the idealised model proposed in the literature (Breen, 1987a). Twelve research questions were posed, of which four were directly related to the issue of learner control.

1. To what extent do individual differences affect learners' full participation in the negotiation process?
2. Are learners able to adopt syllabus design roles that are traditionally reserved for teachers?
3. What types of decisions do learners make in the negotiation process?
4. What are the pitfalls associated with the negotiation process?

Through these questions, the researchers aimed to understand the learners' roles in decision-making and its implications for the practicability of the process syllabus.

16.4.4 Methodology

The researchers decided to use a case study approach, in which the life cycle of a unit is examined so that generalisations can be made about the wider population to which it is related. The informants for the study were 14 adult migrants following an intensive 18-week English for Professional Employment course in Australia designed for students with professional qualifications and intermediate to advanced level English. The group was multilingual and its members shared eight different languages. The study covered the nine-week classroom input component of the course and the focus of attention was the 'action meeting', which was held each Monday morning to determine the week's work.

In a case study approach, researchers gather as much relevant data as possible, much of it unstructured (Concept 16.4). Data sources for this project included audiotapes of the action meetings, needs analysis, biographical and end-of-course questionnaires and learner diaries. Transcripts of the action meetings were the major source of data on the questions relevant to the negotiation process. The researchers counted the number of words spoken and turns taken in meetings. Discourse analysis of the transcripts also identified 'incidents' that were classified in terms of the types of decisions made, the functions of the activities in which participants were involved and their roles as 'emitters' (sources) or 'targeters' (recipients) of messages. A descriptive account of the action meetings showing 'what the negotiation process looked like, sounded like and what people actually did' was also produced (Simmons and Wheeler, 1995: 36).

Concept 16.4 **Analysing unstructured data**

Data collected in the form of interview transcripts, learner diaries, transcripts of classroom events and so on are often called 'unstructured data'. It is up to the researcher to impose some kind of structure on the data through coding. Coding involves reading and re-reading data and assigning codes to sections of it that are significant in terms of the researcher's focus. The categories used in coding often emerge as the researcher reads.

In their study of self-instruction, Rosewell and Libben (1994: 672–3) were interested in finding evidence of 'self-determined volitional behaviour that the learner engages in to affect the course of his or her learning'. Using learner diaries as data, the researchers searched for examples of 'autonomously-controlled tasks' (ACTs). These were divided into Pedagogical and Functional ACTs. Pedagogical ACTs were divided into five operations: addition, deletion, transposition, repetition and change. The operation of addition, for example, involved inserting a new task within a sequence of tasks defined by the self-instructional materials. The following is an example of a piece of data coded as addition:

> I've made a vocabulary sheet for Chapter 1. I hope this helps me remember all the words. Cheat sheets . . . I can't live without them.

At a later stage of analysis, the researchers counted the instances of various kinds of ACTs in their data and correlated them with the learner's level of achievement.

16.4.5   Results

The study produced a number of interesting results on questions related to learner control. The researchers found that individual differences were a significant factor in participation in the action meetings. Initially, the more fluent Indian and Sri Lankan participants tended to dominate the meetings. East Asian participants reported that they were quiet in meetings either because of their lack of confidence in speaking English or because of their tendency to be careful and thoughtful in decision-making situations. In later meetings, however, the level of contribution of individual speakers evened out as the less fluent speakers tended to take on roles such as chairperson and the more fluent speakers tended to withdraw.

The principal task assigned to the action meetings was to make decisions on participation, procedure and subject matter of the ongoing course by reviewing the previous week's timetable and proposing a timetable for the following week. The fact that the group succeeded in this task each week is taken as evidence that they were able to take on tasks of syllabus design traditionally reserved for teachers, and that 'collectively the learners were able to take responsibility for their own learning and to share in the decision making process of the group as a whole' (Simmons and Wheeler, 1995: 55). Action meetings tended to address group needs rather than individual needs. Individual needs were addressed through active negotiation for independent learning time and small group projects. The researchers also observed that individual students took on resource and facilitating roles for the group as a whole by, for example, acting as computer instructors, arranging guest speakers and reporting back on information gathered outside class.

With reference to Breen's (1987a) proposed model of the process syllabus, it was observed that the majority of action meeting decisions concerned participation, procedure, content and alternative working procedures. Fewer decisions on alternative activities were made. In particular, participants appeared to treat timetable slots that had already been allocated to named teachers for named subject matter (e.g. 'Australian English', 'Communication in the Workplace') as non-negotiable, confining their discussion to free timetable slots. Methodology and classroom procedures were also not discussed. The participants thus established their own framework of negotiable and non-negotiable areas of the course, which fell short of full participation in syllabus planning, but nevertheless appeared to satisfy their collective needs.

The end-of-course evaluation questionnaire showed that the participants were positive about the action meetings and 11 of the 13 respondents proposed no changes to the model. The two changes proposed both suggested that training at an early stage in the course would have been helpful. Other individual comments indicated that some students felt that their lack of fluency and confidence in English had inhibited their participation and that the teachers could have played a stronger role in the negotiation process.

16.4.6   Conclusions

In addressing issues concerning learners' ability to participate in decision making, the researchers were in part responding to Clarke's (1991) suggestion that a strong version of the process syllabus would only be practicable in unusual circumstances. In response, Simmons and Wheeler (1995: 63) argue that:

> The results indicate that this syllabus model rather than being a radical alternative to more traditional syllabus types is, in fact, a practical alternative. The study revealed the students were 100% in favour of the opportunity to get involved in their own course management and on the whole they viewed the experience as a very positive one.

However, it was also observed that positive evaluation of the action meeting model was related to the participants' backgrounds as professionals, their common interest in seeking professional employment and their relatively high level of English proficiency. One participant reported, for example, that the model 'treats the students as mature people, assuming that they are people with initiative'. Another stated that he felt 'encouraged to speak about my opinions during other meetings as well' (p. 61). These comments suggest that the process model may be particularly appropriate in situations where classroom negotiation provides a realistic opportunity to 'rehearse a performance for some later time and place' (Littlejohn, 1983: 11).

16.4.7   Commentary

Simmons and Wheeler's study produced data that could be fed back into the planning and organisation of future implementations of the process syllabus within their institution. It also produced results that are of general interest for a theory on the effectiveness of practices associated with autonomy, especially in relation to the practicability of transferring control to learners.

One of the main contributions of the study is its development of a systematic research methodology to assess the extent of decision making and the types of decisions made by learners in situations where they are encouraged to take a degree of control. Rather than rely on participants' self-reports, the researchers attempted to establish objective measures of control. Their use of meeting transcripts to identify the level of contribution of individual participants, the direction of messages and the types of decisions made is of particular value. Although the case study approach can be used to generalise results to similar situations, the researchers were also careful to relate their conclusions to contextual factors involving the nature of the course and the identities of the participants. The result was a fine-grained description of the decision-making process and its limitations in the context of their institution that is of considerable value to other researchers in the field.

16.4.8   Further research

Research on the ways in which learners participate in decision making and the factors that influence their participation is clearly important to the theory and practice of autonomy. Simmons and Wheeler investigated a situation in which the learners were expected to exercise a high degree of control over the course. As such, the researchers were able to adopt an open-ended approach, which sought to describe the decision-making process as a whole. Since the contextual variables operating upon the course are stated clearly, replication studies paying attention to contextual differences are possible. The opportunity to implement a strong version of the process syllabus is rare and for many teachers a more limited version is often the only realistic option. Smaller-scale studies of decision-making processes in situations where learners are encouraged to take a more limited degree of control over their learning are nevertheless valuable. Transcripts of events in which decisions are expected to be made are an ideal source of data, although transcription is time-consuming. Observation notes taken by a researcher who is not directly involved in them are more economical of time and often equally useful. Where the decision-making process is individual rather than collective, learning journals or records of work can also be analysed for evidence of decision making. Rosewell and Libben's (1994) study of self-instruction is a good example of the use of discourse analysis techniques to reveal evidence of decision making in learning journals.

Several factors in the course that Simmons and Wheeler investigated appear to favour implementation of learner control: the learners had relatively high levels of education and proficiency in the language of negotiation; they shared common professional backgrounds and the common goal of seeking employment; the course had no examination element; and linguistic gain was not a priority. Other factors appear to be less favourable: the participants had diverse linguistic and cultural backgrounds and a range of proficiency levels in spoken English. Individual differences among learners also appeared to affect their level of participation in the decision-making process. Smaller-scale research projects could focus more closely on these variables. Press's (1996) study, reported earlier in this chapter, could provide a model for identifying learner variables and the strength of their attachment to them in such research.

16.5   Case study: language acquisition in autonomous classrooms

16.5.1   Project

Dam, L. and Legenhausen, L. (1996) 'The acquisition of vocabulary in an autonomous learning environment – the first months of beginning English'. In R. Pemberton et al. (eds) *Taking Control: Autonomy in Language Learning*. Hong Kong: Hong Kong University Press, pp. 265–80.

The Language Acquisition in an Autonomous Learning Environment (LAALE) research project was begun in 1992 and is a collaboration between researchers in Denmark and Germany. Results from various phases of the project have been published in books and journals and reported at numerous conferences. This case study reports on the first phase of the project, which was presented at a conference on autonomy in Hong Kong and published in a collection of papers arising from it.

16.5.2   Background

As we saw in 12.2, Leni Dam and her colleagues in Denmark have, for a number of years, been taking groups of students from beginner level English to the end of secondary school in classrooms where the content and methods of learning are largely determined by the students themselves. Although this model has demonstrated its effectiveness in terms of the development of autonomy, Dam was concerned to show that it is equally effective in terms of language learning. In 1992, Dam, together with Lienhard Legenhausen, began the Language Acquisition in an Autonomous Learning Environment (LAALE) project, which aims to study the language development of a class of 21 young Danish learners learning English 'the autonomous way' in comparison to parallel classes following more traditional methods in Denmark and Germany.

16.5.3   Aims

The broad aim of the LAALE project is to show that autonomous learning is effective in terms of language proficiency. LAALE is a longitudinal study, starting from beginner level and focusing on a different language area at each stage of the project. The early phases of the project focused on productive vocabulary (7.5 weeks), receptive vocabulary and spelling (15 weeks), grammatical structures and writing (30 weeks) and oral proficiency (1 year 5 months). This case study covers the first two phases of the project. In these phases the researchers examined the vocabulary introduced into the classroom and the vocabulary development of students in the Danish autonomous (DA) class in comparison to students in more traditional textbook-based classrooms in the same Danish school (DT) and in one German school (GT). The researchers acknowledge that the DT and GT classes cannot strictly be considered as control groups because independent measures of comparability are lacking. They are treated, rather, as a point of reference for the DA group.

16.5.4   Methodology

In the first few weeks of the DA class, new language was largely introduced by the learners themselves. The learners were encouraged to bring in samples of English they had encountered in their everyday life, which were shared with other learners through group work and wall displays. They were also given picture dictionaries and asked to find words that they would like to know or remember and to use them in private diaries and in texts and games produced for other students. New language was also introduced by the teacher through nursery rhymes, songs and fairy tales and in the form of phrases that were useful in classroom organisation. In the DT and GT classrooms new language was largely introduced through the class textbook or by the teacher.

In order to document the process of vocabulary acquisition during the first four weeks of learning, the researchers made a list of all the English words made public in the DA classroom and of the ways in which they were introduced. This list was compared with the vocabulary lists for the textbook used in the GT classroom and the Leuven English Teaching (LET) list of the most common words in English (Engels et al., 1981). After 7.5 and 15 weeks of learning, vocabulary tests were administered to all three groups: the first was an informal elicitation of all the words the learners were able to recall spontaneously, and the second a 175-item test of long-term retention focusing on receptive skills and spelling.

16.5.5   Results

The vocabulary introduced in the DA classroom in the first four weeks amounted to 400 words, compared to 124 words introduced by the textbook used in the GT classroom and 800 words required by the state curriculum for the whole of the first year. The researchers also noted that the words introduced into the DA classroom represented a different distribution of semantic fields than those introduced by the GT textbook. For example, the DA students introduced comparatively more words for people, animals and colours and comparatively fewer words for numbers and objects used in school.

The 400 items introduced into the DA class were also compared to the most common words of English identified in the LET lists. These 400 items covered 32% of the 500 most common words and 62% of the 100 most common words. In contrast, the GT textbook covered 19% of the 500 most common words and 30% of the 100 most common words after twice the number of lessons. The researchers were unable to compare the 400 words made public in the DA classroom with similar lists for the DT and GT classes. The figures from the GT textbook may well underestimate the number of words introduced in the GT classroom since additional vocabulary is sure to have been encountered in the course of lessons.

The two vocabulary tests administered after 7.5 and 15 weeks aimed to discover how many new words the students had retained. In the first test students were asked to write down as many English words as they could. The results for the DA group (average number of words recalled = 62) were significantly higher than those for the GT group (average number of words = 47) and DT group (average number of words recalled = 34). Since the Danish students were in mixed ability groups, they showed a greater range of individual results than the GT grammar school classes. Nevertheless, the average number of words recalled by the class as a whole, by the top ten and by the bottom ten students in the DA group, all exceeded the average for the GT class.

The second test aimed to test the learners' long-term passive retention of the 400 vocabulary items introduced in the first four weeks. The results showed that the DA group were slightly better on auditory recognition, while the GT group were better when writing and spelling were involved. The results for the DA group also showed that retention of words presented in songs and rhymes was higher, especially among weaker students. However, because the GT group could only be tested on the subset of the 400 items that were introduced in their textbook, the two groups could not be compared reliably.

16.5.6   Conclusions

Dam and Legenhausen's conclusions were cautiously but clearly stated (Concept 16.5). The first two phases of their research aimed to provide evidence that autonomous learning was effective in terms of vocabulary acquisition, which is one conventional indicator of successful language learning. The researchers claimed that the results demonstrated that vocabulary acquisition in the autonomous approach was successful and compared favourably with results from textbook-based approaches.

Concept 16.5   **Reporting conclusions**

In research reports, a clear statement of conclusions and their limitations can help other researchers to interpret and build upon the research. Dam and Legenhausen's summary of their conclusions is an excellent example of a concise statement of what their research tells us:

> The results of the two vocabulary tests convincingly demonstrate that vocabulary acquisition in the autonomous approach is very successful and compares favourably with results from more traditional textbook-based approaches. The number of words that 'emerge' in the first few months and are publicly shared by the whole learner group exceeds the requirements of official syllabus guidelines for German grammar school classes (i.e. higher ability classes). The mastery and availability of an extended vocabulary might also be due to the fact that the autonomous approach succeeds in making learners aware of the English language surrounding them in their L1 environment and in integrating this knowledge into their developing L2 competence. A subset of the words that are available to these learners would thus not be classified as 'newly acquired' but as words which they have 'become aware of'. Traditional approaches might turn out to be less successful in this regard.
>
> Dam and Legenhausen (1996: 280)

They also suggested that this may have been due to the fact that the autonomous approach made the learners more aware of the English language surrounding them and helped them to integrate this knowledge into their developing L2 competence.

16.5.7   Commentary

Dam and Legenhausen's research is an important attempt to establish the effectiveness of autonomous approaches to teaching and learning in terms of language proficiency using quantitative measures. The researchers use a variation of the conventional experimental method based on the analysis of the effects of different treatments on comparable groups. Using a conventional indicator of proficiency – vocabulary acquisition – they provide some evidence that, for the group of learners under study, Dam's approach to the implementation of autonomy is effective. Research on gains in proficiency is unusual in the field of autonomy in language learning and Dam and Legenhausen's main contribution has been to show that such research is possible. Published results from later phases of the study tell us much about the ways in which autonomy and language proficiency interact in the longer term and in relation to other variables such as the acquisition of grammar and spoken communication skills (Legenhausen, 1999a, 1999b, 1999c).

16.5.8   Further research

The LAALE project points to a number of directions in which research on the relationship between autonomy and language proficiency might develop. Dam and Legenhausen acknowledge problems of comparability between the 'autonomous' and 'non-autonomous' groups, which mean that the latter cannot strictly be treated as control groups. In practice, strict comparability in research involving classroom groups observed over relatively long periods of time is rarely possible. Similarly, experimental research is most reliable where the treatment of experimental and control groups differs with respect to a single variable. Practices designed to foster autonomy, however, often differ radically from more traditional methods in more than one respect. Even if it can be shown that the autonomous approach is more effective than the non-autonomous approach overall, it will be difficult to establish which aspects of the practice account for the results.

Replications of Dam and Legenhausen's research methods in situations where classroom groups are more closely comparable and where the character of the innovation designed to promote autonomy is more clearly identifiable could therefore provide useful data. For example, if, in a school where foreign language reading texts are normally assigned by the teacher, one class of students were encouraged to select their own reading texts, pre- and post-tests of vocabulary and reading comprehension might provide some indication of different rates of development in proficiency. If the students who chose their own tests showed higher rates of development, there would be some reason to attribute the effect to an innovation specifically designed to promote autonomy. If, however, the innovation involved the students selecting and discussing their reading texts in groups, it would be difficult to separate the effect of freedom of choice from the effect of group work. Carefully designed small-scale action research projects that limit the number of variables investigated may, therefore, reveal more about the effectiveness of specific practices associated with autonomy than larger-scale projects.

Although comparative studies of 'autonomous' and 'non-autonomous' classrooms are valuable, research is also needed to establish the ways in which proficiency develops as a consequence of the development of autonomy. Dam and Legenhausen's study shows that the learners in the DA classroom learned more of the words expected at their level than the other groups. It also shows that the additional vocabulary learned by the DA group was qualitatively different to the vocabulary learned by the other groups in that it was relevant to their interests and needs and was acquired through self-motivated learning inside and outside the classroom. In other words, the quantity of vocabulary acquired appears to be directly related to the act of self-selection of words to be learned.

Research that describes more complex language-learning outcomes in the context of the development of autonomy is of particular importance in evaluating the claim that autonomous language learners are, by definition, better language learners. The possibilities for research of this kind can be illustrated by referring back to Simmons and Wheeler's (1995) study of the process syllabus in action. Because of their focus on the decision-making process, Simmons and Wheeler chose not to investigate the claim that participation in syllabus negotiation leads to language-learning gains. In end-of-course evaluations, however, several participants reported that participation in action meetings to determine course content and procedures had helped them to enhance their fluency and confidence in professional contexts. These self-reports could perhaps be verified empirically through further analysis of the action meeting transcripts focusing on, for example, the development of turn-taking skills, the range of speech acts used or instances of repair and negotiation of meaning. Evaluation of gains in proficiency arising from participation in practices associated with autonomy need not be a separate matter from the evaluation of gains in autonomy.

16.6 Case study: developing autonomy

16.6.1 Project

Fowler, A. (1997) 'Developing independent learning'. In A. Burns and S. Hood (eds) *Teachers' Voices 2: Teaching Disparate Learner Groups.* Sydney: National Centre for English Language Teaching and Research, pp. 115–23.

Anne Fowler's project is one of a number of action research projects carried out with the support of the National Centre for English Language Teaching and Research at Macquarie University in Sydney. The results of the project were published, together with others, in a collection of action research reports. The *Teachers' Voices* series is an excellent source of examples of action research reports.

16.6.2 Background

As a teacher in the Australian Adult Migrant Education Programme (AMEP), Anne Fowler began her action research project from her observations of a particular group of students in her charge. Although these students were motivated to learn and willing to work hard, they also expressed a sense of frustration at their lack of progress and in their ability to use and learn English outside the classroom. For many of the students the 'chaotic' organisation of their class materials appeared to be a particular barrier to progress. She therefore decided to make several changes in her teaching approach, designed to develop the students' learning and organisational skills, and to evaluate their effects.

16.6.3 Aims

Fowler aimed to implement and evaluate the usefulness of three strategies:

1. *Portfolios of written work.* The students were asked to organise their written work in a folder, to arrange it according to themes and keep

an ongoing table of contents. The portfolio also included assessment and feedback sheets. At the end of the term, the students selected examples of their work for assessment.

2. *Self-study tapes*. Fowler offered to record individualised self-study tapes once a week to encourage the students to practice speaking outside the classroom.

3. *Independent learning plan*. After discussion of ways to extend learning beyond the classroom, the students were asked to draw up a 'contract' for independent learning and keep a record of their work on a proforma designed by the teacher.

16.6.4   Methodology

In order to evaluate the effectiveness of these strategies, Fowler used several instruments:

- *Portfolio*. The students used a questionnaire as a basis for class discussion on the usefulness of the portfolios and wrote a report.

- *Self-study tapes*. The researcher kept a record of what she had taped each week and noted the students' comments. The students also filled out a questionnaire on the usefulness of the tapes.

- *Independent learning plan*. The students' contracts and records of work were used as data and a questionnaire was also administered.

16.6.5   Results

Fowler found that evaluations of the portfolio system were positive in all but two cases. As positive effects, students mentioned improvements in revision, recall, organisation, self-management and monitoring their development. The most positive evaluations came from the students she had identified as being least well organised before the system was implemented.

The self-study tapes were less effective. Seven of the 13 students chose to use the tapes but, after the fifth week of term, they stopped bringing tapes for recording. Although they were intended to facilitate speaking, the students' responses to the questionnaire showed that they saw them mainly as resources for listening. Fowler concluded that they were not helpful in promoting independent use of English outside class and decided to drop them from the course.

In drawing up their independent learning plans, the students showed considerable creativity. Examples of objectives were:

- Listening to English music and TV
- Reviewing my day's learning before going to sleep at night
- Buying a whiteboard for my kitchen to display what I am learning
- Thinking in English.

Although all the students participated in this initiative, only six kept records of their work and of these six only one continued throughout the course. However, the students' comments on the initiative were positive and reflected growing self-confidence. They appeared to find the experience of trying out new strategies a positive one.

16.6.6 Conclusions

Overall, student self-evaluations showed improvement in the organisation of their learning and self-confidence. Fowler concluded that it was worth continuing with the portfolios and independent learning plans. She also took note of students' comments that time spent organising portfolios in class reduced the time for language-learning activities and adjusted her approach accordingly. At the same time, she felt that the independent learning plans had been less successful than they could have been, because insufficient class time had been spent on discussion of ongoing progress.

16.6.7 Commentary

Of the six case studies reported in this chapter, Fowler's research falls most squarely within the tradition of action research oriented towards the improvement of professional practice. It is less concerned with filling a gap in our general knowledge of issues related to autonomy than with the practical problem of helping a particular group of students to overcome obstacles to progress in their learning. As such it reminds us of the fact that the objective of research on autonomy is not so much the development of theory but more the development of practice. Although the theory of autonomy contributes to its practical implementation, helping students to take greater control over their learning is most often a question of organising the day-to-day curriculum in ways that respond to their developing preferences and needs. By basing her strategies on the solution to a particular problem faced by her learners, and by collecting data on their effects, Fowler was able to make fine adjustments to the curriculum that were sensitive to the progress of the students. At the same time, the learners' involvement in the evaluation of the effectiveness of these strategies contributed to the development of their self-confidence and self-management skills.

16.6.8   Further research

Fowler's project points less to the direction of a research agenda defined in terms of a set of questions that need to be answered, and more to a particular style of research. From the teacher's perspective, all research on the implementation of autonomy is local and begins with the question: 'How can I help my students become more autonomous in the context in which they and I live and work?' Sharing the results of research improves our general knowledge of the theory and practice of autonomy. However, it is important to bear in mind that the practice of autonomy is not equivalent to the implementation of a method based on abstract theory. The theory of autonomy consists of what we know about control over learning and its relationship to the development of learning. As such, it is not so much a theory of learning as a body of knowledge that allows us to approach problems of teaching and learning from the perspective of the learner.

The implementation of autonomy is thus an interpretative process in which the learner's perspective is assigned a privileged position in the solution of problems of teaching and learning. In this sense, research on autonomy is not a specialised field with clearly defined boundaries and subject matters. Research on autonomy takes place whenever the researcher approaches an issue of teaching or learning from the learner's perspective. In this sense the concept of autonomy is relevant to all research on teaching and learning and the important research questions are those that are of most immediate relevance to teachers and learners in the specific contexts in which they work.

Chapter 17

Conclusion

Throughout this book it has been emphasised that, because autonomy takes a variety of forms, there is no single best method of fostering it. In this chapter, three broad areas for research have been proposed. The nature of autonomy and the characteristics of the autonomous learner remain matters for research and debate. We still know relatively little about the ways in which practices associated with autonomy work to foster autonomy, alone or in combination, or about the contextual factors that influence their effectiveness. We are also unable to argue convincingly, on the basis of empirical data, that autonomous language learners learn languages more effectively than others, nor do we know exactly how the development of autonomy and language acquisition interact. Although research has begun to address these issues, the opportunities for researchers to contribute to the knowledge base on autonomy are many.

Autonomy is a theoretical construct, accepted by many as a goal of language education. It is hoped that this book has at least demonstrated the validity of the construct, its validity as a goal and the possibility of moving towards it in practice. Researchers and practitioners need to show, however, that autonomy is not only desirable but also achievable in everyday contexts of language teaching and learning. In the course of writing this book, I have moved progressively from theory to practice and from the evaluation of practice to practical action research. My own reflections on the processes of learning that the writing of this book has involved lead me to conclude that, although theoretical clarification is important, there is an equally pressing need for data-based research that will ground the construct of autonomy in everyday practice. A fuller understanding of the nature of autonomy in language learning, the practices that best foster it among learners and their relation to language acquisition is a goal that we may approach through the accumulation and analysis of research focused on problems of day-to-day practice. Action research grounded in the professional concerns of practising teacher-researchers can contribute much towards the achievement of this goal.

IV Resources

Chapter 18

Resources for research and practice

18.1 Books, journals and newsletters

For a clear and readable introduction to the concept of autonomy in language learning, I recommend two short books by Little (1991) and Dam (1995). Gremmo and Riley (1995) give a useful history of the main concepts in the field. Recent collections of papers providing an overview of current research and practice include Benson and Voller (1997), Crabbe and Cotterall (1999), Dickinson and Wenden (1995), Little et al. (2000) and Pemberton et al. (1996). Although language learning has been one of the main fields in which the theory and implementation of autonomy has developed in recent years, there is also a rich literature on autonomy and self-direction beyond the field of language education. Candy (1991) offers a comprehensive and highly readable survey of the field.

Autonomy in language learning has been associated with several areas of practices, among which self-access and learner development have perhaps been the most important. Gardner and Miller (1999) is essential reading for anyone setting up a self-access centre. Papers by Sheerin (1997) and Sturtridge (1997) and the collection of papers by Esch (1994) are also recommended. Dickinson (1992) and Wenden (1991) are good introductions to issues of learner development for autonomous language learning and Cohen (1998) can be recommended as an up-to-date survey of research on learning strategies and strategy training. Dam (1995) is an excellent introduction to issues of autonomy in the classroom. Recent collections of papers by Breen and Littlejohn

(2000) and Kohonen (2000) are recommended for an overview of the process syllabus and experiential learning.

Among international journals on applied linguistics and language learning, *System* and *ELT Journal* regularly publish papers on autonomy and related topics. *Language Learning Journal* also publishes articles related to autonomy of a shorter and more practical kind. *Mélanges Pédagogiques* is a publication of CRAPEL at the University of Nancy, France, which regularly includes papers on autonomy and self-access.

Several of the professional associations listed in this section publish newsletters. *Independence* is published by the IATEFL Independence SIG in the UK, *Learning Learning* is published by the JALT Learner Development N-SIG in Japan, and *Self-access Language Learning* is published by HASALD in Hong Kong. The AILA Scientific Commission on Autonomy publishes a newsletter called *Learner Autonomy in Language Learning* circulated via e-mail to its members.

18.2   Conferences and workshops

There is no regular international conference on autonomy in language learning. The annual IATEFL and JALT conferences usually include strands on autonomy and learner development organised by the relevant special interest groups. Recent AILA congresses have also included symposia on autonomy organised by the Scientific Commission on Autonomy.

Smaller conferences and workshops on autonomy and related areas of practice are held regularly in various parts of the world and offer an opportunity for researchers to present their work. The AILA Scientific Commission on Autonomy web site has an up-to-date list of forthcoming conferences and workshops.

18.3   Professional associations

Several professional associations have been formed to bring together researchers and teachers interested in autonomy in language learning and related areas of practice. The easiest way to contact these associations is through their web sites.

AILA Scientific Commission on Learner Autonomy

The AILA Scientific Commission publishes a newsletter called *Learner Autonomy in Language Learning*, which is circulated by e-mail and published on the web. Members of the Commission also maintain the Learner Autonomy Project Inventory, a list of current projects on autonomy, which is also circulated by e-mail. The Scientific Commission also regularly organises a symposium on autonomy at AILA Congresses. For current information, visit the Scientific Commission's website at
<http://www.vuw.ac.nz/lals/div1/ailasc/>

HASALD

The Hong Kong Association for Self-access Learning and Development (HASALD) aims to promote self-access and autonomy in language learning in Hong Kong. HASALD organises monthly meetings and occasional conferences and publishes a newsletter called *Self-access Language Learning*. For more information, visit the HASALD web site at
<http://www.engl.polyu.edu.hk/hasald/>

IATEFL Learner Independence SIG

Special interest group of the International Association of Teachers of English as a Foreign Language. The SIG publishes a newsletter called *Independence*, holds regular workshops in various parts of Europe and organises a strand on learner independence at the annual IATEFL conference. For more information, contact the Learner Independence SIG coordinator, c/o IATEFL, 3 Kingsdown Chambers, Kingsdown Park, Whitstable, Kent CT5 2DJ, England or visit the SIG web site at
<http://www.iatefl.org/lisig/lihome.htm>

JALT Learner Development N-SIG

National Special Interest Group of the Japan Association of Language Teachers concerned with learner development and autonomy. The N-SIG publishes a newsletter in English and Japanese called *Learning Learning*, and holds regular workshops in Japan. For more information, visit the N-SIG web site at
<http://odyssey.miyazakimu.ac.jp/html/hnicoll/learnerdev/home E.html>

18.4   E-mail lists

AUTO-L

AUTO-L is an open e-mail discussion list devoted to autonomy in language learning. Subscribers send information, opinions and queries and regular moderated discussions are held. To subscribe, send e-mail to Anita Wenden
    <wldyc@cunyvm.edu>

PLAN

Discussion list on language advising maintained by organisers of the project on language advising based at the University of Hull, UK. To subscribe, send e-mail to
    <mailbase@mailbase.ac.uk>
with the following text in the body of the message
    join plan name surname
    stop

SMILE

Discussion list maintained by the Strategies for Maintaining an Independent Learning Environment project based at the University of Hull, UK. To subscribe, send e-mail to
    <mailbase@mailbase.ac.uk>
with the following text in the body of the message:
    join smile name surname
    stop

18.5   Web sites

Autonomy and Independence in Language Learning

The author of this book maintains a regularly updated site on autonomy in language learning and related issues. The site includes a comprehensive bibliography.
    <http://ec.hku.hk/autonomy/>

Association for Language Awareness

Includes the International Language Awareness Database and links to other language awareness sites.
<http://www.liv.ac.uk/~ms2928/ala/index.htm>

CARLA: second language learning strategies

Web site on language-learning strategy research maintained by the Center for Advanced Research on Language Acquisition at the University of Minnesota.
<http://carla.acad.umn.edu/slstrategies.html>

International e-mail Tandem Network

Web site maintained by the European Union funded project on Autonomous and Intercultural Language Learning in Tandem. Includes resources for tandem learning and an extensive bibliography.
<http://www.slf.ruhr-uni-bochum.de/>

PLAN (Professional Language Advisers Network)

Web site designed to raise awareness of the role of language advisers in self-access centres and to spread good practice in language advising.
<http://www.hull.ac.uk/langinst/plan/>

SMILE (Strategies for Managing an Independent Learning Environment)

Web site supporting the funded project based at the Universities of Hull, Nottingham Trent and Ulster. SMILE targets staff and learners, with particular focus on learner training.
<http://www.hull.ac.uk/langinst/smile/index.htm>

18.6 Bibliographies

Autonomy and Independence in Language Learning
<http://www.booksites.net/benson>
compiled by Phil Benson.

Language Learning in Tandem

<http://www.slf.ruhr-uni-bochum.de/email/idxeng00.html>
compiled by Helmut Brammerts.

Language Learning Strategies

<http://www.res.kutc.kansai-u.ac.jp/~takeuchi/LLS.html>
compiled by Osamu Takeuchi.

18.7 Self-access centres

Many self-access language learning centres maintain web sites containing information about their facilities and services. The following is a selection of those known to the author.

- *University of Cambridge (Independent Learning Centre)*
  <http://www.langcen.cam.ac.uk/studyfac/privstud.htm>
- *Chinese University of Hong Kong (Independent Learning Centre)*
  <http://www.ilc.cuhk.edu.hk/>
- *City University of Hong Kong (Self-access Centre)*
  <http://www.cityu.edu.hk/elc/sac.htm>
- *Hong Kong Polytechnic University (Centre for Independent Language Learning)*
  <http://www.engl.polyu.edu.hk/CILL/>
- *Hong Kong University (Virtual English Centre)*
  <http://ec.hku.hk/vec/>
- *Hong Kong University of Science and Technology, Language Centre (Self-access Centre)*
  <http://lc.ust.hk/~sac/>
- *University of Hull Language Institute (Open Learning Centre)*
  <http://www.hull.ac.uk/langinst/open.htm>
- *University of Illinois Urbana-Champaign (LinguaCenter)*
  <http://deil.lang.uiuc.edu/LinguaCenter/>
- *James Cook University (Self-access Centre)*
  <http://sacwww.jcu.edu.au/mlsac/index.html>

- *Universitat Jaume 1 (Centre d'Autoaprenentatge de Llengües) (in Catalan)*
  <http://sic.uji.es/serveis/slt/cal/>
- *Macquarie University (Independent Learning Centre)*
  <http://www.nceltr.mq.edu.au/ilc.htm>
- *University of Münster (Self-access Centre)*
  <http://www.anglistik.uni-muenster.de/SAC/>

References

Allwright, R.L. (1978) 'Abdication and responsibility in language teaching', *Studies in Second Language Acquisition*, 2 (1): 105–21.

Allwright, R.L. (1984) 'Why don't learners learn what teachers teach? – The interaction hypothesis'. In D.M.S. Singleton and D.G. Little (eds) *Language Learning in Formal and Informal Contexts*. Dublin: Irish Association for Applied Linguistics, pp. 3–18.

Allwright, R.L. (1988) 'Autonomy and individualization in whole-class instruction'. In A. Brookes and P. Grundy (eds) *Individualization and Autonomy in Language Learning*. ELT Documents, 131. London: Modern English Publications and the British Council, pp. 35–44.

Altman, H.B. and James, C.V. (eds) (1980) *Foreign Language Teaching: Meeting Individual Needs*. Oxford: Pergamon.

Aoki, N. and Smith, R. (1999) 'Learner autonomy in cultural context: the case of Japan'. In D. Crabbe and S. Cotterall (eds) *Learner Autonomy in Language Learning: Defining the Field and Effecting Change*. Frankfurt: Peter Lang, pp. 19–27.

Assinder, W. (1991) 'Peer-teaching, peer-learning: one model', *ELT Journal*, 45 (3): 218–29.

Aston, G. (1993) 'The learner's contribution to the self-access centre', *ELT Journal*, 47 (3): 219–27.

Aston, G. (1997) 'Involving learners in developing learning methods: exploiting text corpora in self-access'. In P. Benson and P. Voller (eds) *Autonomy and Independence in Language Learning*. London: Longman, pp. 204–14.

Auerbach, E.R. (1995) 'The politics of the ESL classroom: issues of power in pedagogical choices'. In J.W. Tollefson (ed.) *Power and Inequality in Language Education*. Cambridge: Cambridge University Press, pp. 9–33.

Bachman, L.F. and Palmer, A.S. (1989) 'The construct validation of self-ratings of communicative language ability', *Language Testing*, 6: 14–29.

Bailey, K.M. (1983) 'Competitiveness and anxiety in adult second language learning: looking at and through the diary studies'. In H. Seliger and M. Long (eds) *Classroom Oriented Research in Second Language Acquisition*. Rowley, Mass.: Newbury House, pp. 67–103.

Barkhuizen, G.P. (1998) 'Discovering learners' perceptions of ESL classroom teaching/learning activities in a South African context', *TESOL Quarterly*, 32 (1): 85–108.

Barnes, D. (1976) *From Communication to Curriculum*. London: Penguin.

Barnett, L. and Jordan, G. (1991) 'Self-access facilities: what are they for?', *ELT Journal*, 45 (4): 305–12.

Benson, P. (1994) 'Self-access systems as information systems: questions of ideology and control'. In D. Gardner and L. Miller (eds) *Directions in Self-access Language Learning*. Hong Kong: Hong Kong University Press, pp. 3–12.

Benson, P. (1995a) 'A critical view of learner training', *Learning Learning: JALT Learner Development N-SIG Forum*, 2 (2): 2–6.

Benson, P. (1995b) 'Self-access and collaborative learning', *Independence* 12: 6–11. (Reprinted in A.C. McClean (ed.) *SIG Selections 1997: Special Interests in ELT*. London: IATEFL, pp. 55–9.)

Benson, P. (1996) 'Concepts of autonomy in language learning.' In R. Pemberton et al. (eds) *Taking Control: Autonomy in Language Learning*. Hong Kong: Hong Kong University Press, pp. 27–34.

Benson, P. (1997a) 'The philosophy and politics of learner autonomy'. In P. Benson and P. Voller (eds) *Autonomy and Independence in Language Learning*. London: Longman, pp. 18–34.

Benson, P. (1997b) 'The semiotics of self-access language learning in the digital age'. In V. Darleguy et al. (eds) *Educational Technology in Language Learning: Theoretical Considerations and Practical Applications*, Lyons: INSA (National Institute of Applied Sciences), pp. 70–8.

Benson, P. (2000) 'Autonomy as a learners' and teachers' right'. In B. Sinclair et al. (eds) *Learner Autonomy, Teacher Autonomy: Future Directions*. London: Longman, pp. 111–17.

Benson, P. and Lor, W. (1998) *Making Sense of Autonomous Language Learning: Conceptions of Learning and Readiness for Autonomy*. English Centre Monograph, No. 2. Hong Kong: University of Hong Kong.

Benson, P. and Lor, W. (1999) 'Conceptions of language and language learning', *System*, 27 (4): 459–72.

Benson, P. and Voller, P. (eds) (1997) *Autonomy and Independence in Language Learning*. London: Longman.

Bereiter, C. and Scardamalia, M. (1989) 'Intentional learning as a goal of instruction'. In L.B. Resnick (ed.) *Knowing, Learning and Instruction*. Hillsdale, NJ: Lawrence Erlbaum, pp. 361–92.

Bialystok, E. (1994) 'Analysis and control in the development of second language proficiency', *Studies in Second Language Acquisition*,16: 157–68.

Blanche, P. (1988) 'Self-assessment of foreign-language skills: implications for teachers and researchers', *RELC Journal*, 19: 75–93.

Block, D. (1996) 'A window on the classroom: classroom events viewed from different angles'. In K. Bailey and D. Nunan (eds) *Voices from the Language Classroom*. Cambridge: Cambridge University Press, pp. 168–94.

Bonham, L.A. (1991) 'Guglielmino's self-directed learning readiness scale: what does it measure?' *Adult Education Quarterly*, 41 (2): 91–9.

Booton, P. and Benson, P. (1996) *Self-access: Classification and Retrieval*. Manchester: British Council.

Boud, D. (1988) 'Moving towards autonomy'. In D. Boud (ed.) *Developing Student Autonomy in Learning*. Second Edition. London: Kogan Page, pp. 17–39.

Boud, D., Keough, R. and Walker, D. (eds) (1985) *Reflection: Turning Experience into Learning*. London: Kogan Page.

Bowers, R. (1995) 'WWW-based instruction for EST'. In T. Orr (ed.) *English for Science and Technology: Profiles and Perspectives*. University of Aizu, Japan: Centre for Language Research, pp. 5–8.

Boyd, W. (1956) *Émile for Today: the Émile of Jean Jacques Rousseau*. London: Heinemann.

Breen, M.P. (1986) 'The social context of language learning: a neglected situation', *Studies in Second Language Acquisition*, 7: 135–58.

Breen, M.P. (1987a) 'Contemporary paradigms in syllabus design', *Language Teaching*, 20 (3): 157–74.

Breen, M.P. (1987b) 'Learner contributions to task design'. In *Language Learning Tasks*. Lancaster Working Papers in English Language Education, Volume 7. London: Prentice Hall.

Breen, M.P. (1991) 'Understanding the language teacher'. In R. Phillipson et al. (eds) *Foreign/Second Language Pedagogy Research*. Clevedon: Multilingual Matters. pp. 213–33.

Breen, M.P. and Candlin, C.N. (1980) 'The essentials of a communicative curriculum in language teaching', *Applied Linguistics*, 1 (2): 89–112.

Breen, M.P., Candlin, C.N., Dam, L. and Gabrielsen, G. (1989) 'The evolution of a teacher training programme'. In R.K. Johnson (ed.) *The Second Language Curriculum*. Cambridge: Cambridge University Press, pp. 111–35.

Breen, M.P. and Littlejohn, A. (eds) (2000) *The Process Syllabus: Negotiation in the Language Classroom*. Cambridge: Cambridge University Press.

Breen, M.P. and Mann, S. (1997) 'Shooting arrows at the sun: perspectives on a pedagogy for autonomy'. In P. Benson and P. Voller (eds) *Autonomy and Independence in Language Learning*. London: Longman, pp. 132–49.

Brewster, E.T. and Brewster, E.S. (1976) *Language Acquisition Made Practical: Field Methods for Language Learners*. Pasadena: Lingua House.

Broady, E. and Kenning, M-M. (eds) (1996) *Promoting Learner Autonomy in University Language Teaching*. London: Association for French Language Studies in association with CILT.

Brockett, R.G. and Hiemstra, R. (1991) *Self-direction in Adult Learning: Perspectives on Theory, Research, and Practice*. London: Routledge.

Brookes, A. and Grundy, P. (eds) (1988) *Individualization and Autonomy in Language Learning*. ELT Documents 131. London: Modern English Publications/British Council.

Brookfield, S. (1981) 'Independent adult learning', *Studies in Adult Education*, 13: 15–27.

Brookfield, S. (1993) 'Self-directed learning, political clarity, and the critical practice of adult education', *Adult Education Quarterly*, 43 (4): 227–42.

Budd, R. and Wright, T. (1992) 'Putting a process syllabus into practice'. In D. Nunan (ed.) *Collaborative Language Learning and Teaching*. Cambridge: Cambridge University Press, pp. 208–29.

Burns, A. (1999) *Collaborative Action Research for English Language Teachers*. Cambridge: Cambridge University Press.

Campbell, C. and Kryszewska, H. (1992) *Learner-based Teaching*. Oxford: Oxford University Press.

Candlin, C.N. (1987) 'Towards task-based language learning'. In C.N. Candlin and D. Murphy (eds) *Language Learning Tasks*. London: Prentice Hall, pp. 5–22.

Candy, P.C. (1991) *Self-direction for Lifelong Learning*. San Francisco: Jossey-Bass.

Carpenter, C. (1996) 'Peer teaching: a new approach to advanced level language teaching'. In E. Broady and M-M. Kenning (eds) *Promoting Learner Autonomy in University Language Teaching*. London: Association for French Language Studies/CILT, pp. 23–38.

Carvalho, D. (1993) *Self-access: Appropriate Materials*. Manchester: British Council.

Chamot, A.U., Küpper, L. and Impink-Hernandez, M.V. (1988) *A Study of Learning Strategies in Foreign Language Instruction: Findings of the Longitudinal Study*. MacLean, VA: Interstate Research Associates.

Chamot, A.U. and Rubin, J. (1994) 'Comments on Janie Rees-Miller's "A critical appraisal of learner training: theoretical bases and teaching implications": Two readers react', *TESOL Quarterly*, 28 (4): 771–6.

Chapelle, C. (1997) 'CALL in the year 2000: still in search of research paradigms', *Language Learning and Technology*, 1 (1): 19–38.

Chapelle, C. and Green, P. (1992) 'Field independence/dependence in second language acquisition research', *Language Learning*, 42: 47–83.

Clarke, D.F. (1991) 'The negotiated syllabus: what it is and how is it likely to work?', *Applied Linguistics*, 12 (1): 13–28.

Cockburn, A. and Blackburn, R. (eds) (1970) *Student Power: Problems, Diagnosis, Action*. London: Penguin.

Cohen, A.D. (1998) *Strategies in Learning and Using a Second Language*. London: Longman.

Coleman, J.A. (1997) 'Residence abroad within language study', *Language Teaching*, 30: 1–20.

Cooley, L. (1993) 'Using study guides: an approach to self-access', *Hong Kong Papers in Linguistics and Language Teaching*, 16: 93–101.

Corder, S.P. (1967) 'The significance of learners errors', *International Review of Applied Linguistics* 4: 161–9.

Cotterall, S. (1995a) 'Developing a course strategy for learner autonomy', *ELT Journal*, 49 (3): 219–27.

Cotterall, S. (1995b) 'Readiness for autonomy: investigating learner beliefs.' *System*, 23 (2): 195–206.

Cotterall, S. (1999) 'Key variables in language learning: what do learners believe about them', *System*, 27 (4): 593–13.

Crabbe, D. (1993) 'Fostering autonomy from within the classroom: the teacher's responsibility', *System*, 21 (4): 443–52.

Crabbe, D. and Cotterall, S. (eds) (1999) *Learner Autonomy in Language Learning: Defining the Field and Effecting Change*. Frankfurt: Peter Lang.

Cram, B. (1995) 'Self-assessment: from theory to practice. Developing a workshop guide for teachers'. In G. Brindley (ed.) *Language Assessment in Action*. Sydney: Macquarie University, NCELTR, pp. 271–306.

Crittenden, B. (1978) 'Autonomy as an aim of education'. In K.A. Strike and K. Egan (eds) *Ethics and Educational Policy*. London: Routledge & Kegan Paul.

Crookes, G. and Schmidt, R.W. (1991) 'Motivation: reopening the research agenda', *Language Learning*, 41 (4): 469–512.

Dakin, J. (1973) *The Language Laboratory and Language Learning*. London: Longman.

Dam, L. (1995) *Learner Autonomy 3: from Theory to Classroom Practice*. Dublin: Authentik.

Dam, L. and Gabrielsen, G. (1988) 'Developing learner autonomy in a school context – a six-year experiment beginning in the learners' first year of English.' In H. Holec (ed.) *Autonomy and Self-directed Learning: Present Fields of Application*. Strasbourg: Council of Europe, pp. 19–30.

Dam, L. and Legenhausen, L. (1996) 'The acquisition of vocabulary in an autonomous learning environment – the first months of beginning English.' In R. Pemberton et al. (eds) *Taking Control: Autonomy in Language Learning*. Hong Kong: Hong Kong University Press, pp. 265–80.

De Graff, R. (1997) 'The EXPERANTO experiment: effects of explicit instruction on second language acquisition', *Studies in Second Language Acquisition*, 19: 249–76.

Deci, E.L. (1978) 'Applications of research on the effects of rewards'. In M. Lepper and D. Greene (eds) *The Hidden Costs of Reward: New perspectives on the Psychology of Human Motivation*. Hillsdale: NJ: Lawrence Erlbaum, pp. 193–203.

Deci, E.L., Vallerand, R.J., Pelletier, L.G. and Ryan, R.M. (1991) 'Motivation and education: the self-determination perspective', *Educational Psychologist*, 26: 325–46.

Deller, S. (1990) *Lessons form the Learner: Student-generated Activities for the Language Classroom*. London: Pilgrims Longman Resource Books.

Dewey, J. (1916/1966) *Democracy and Education and Introduction to the Philosophy of Education*. New York: Free Press. (First published, 1916.)

Dewey, J. (1933) *How we Think*. Chicago: Regney.

Dickinson, L. (1987) *Self-instruction in Language Learning*. Cambridge: Cambridge University Press.

Dickinson, L. (1988) 'Collaborative assessment: an interim account'. In H. Holec (ed.) *Autonomy and Self-directed Learning: Present Fields of Application*. Strasbourg: Council of Europe, pp. 121–8.

Dickinson, L. (1992) *Learner Autonomy 2: Learner Training for Language Learning*. Dublin: Authentik.

Dickinson, L. (1995) 'Autonomy and motivation: a literature review.' *System*, 23 (2): 165–74.

Dickinson, L. (1997) 'Culture, autonomy and common sense'. In *Autonomy 2000: The Development of Learning Independence in Language Learning*. Conference Proceedings. Bangkok: King Mongkut's Institute of Technology Thonburi.

Dickinson, L. and Carver, D. (1980) 'Learning how to learn: steps towards self-direction in foreign language learning', *ELT Journal*, 35 (1): 1–7.

Dickinson, L. and Wenden, A. (eds) (1995) Special issue on autonomy. *System*, 23 (2).

Dörnyei, Z. (1998) 'Motivation in Second and Foreign Language Learning', *Language Teaching*, 31: 117–35.

Ellis, G. and Sinclair, B. (1989) *Learning to learn English: a Course in Learner Training*. Cambridge: Cambridge University Press.

Ellis, R. (1994) *The Study of Second Language Acquisition*. Oxford: Oxford University Press.

Engels, L.K., Van Beckhoven, B., Leenders, T. and Brasseur, I. (1981) *LET Vocabulary-List: Leuven English Teaching Vocabulary-List based on Objective Frequency Combined with Subjective Word-Selection*. Department of Linguistics, Catholic University of Leuven. Leuven: Acco.

Esch, E. (1996) 'Promoting learner autonomy: criteria for the selection of appropriate methods'. In R. Pemberton et al. (eds) *Taking Control: Autonomy in Language Learning*. Hong Kong: Hong Kong University Press, pp. 35–48.

Esch, E. (1997) 'Learner training for autonomous language learning'. In P. Benson and P. Voller (eds) *Autonomy and Independence in Language Learning*. London: Longman, pp. 164–76.

Esch, E. (ed.) (1994) *Self-access and the Adult Language Learner*. London: CILT.

Fernández-Toro, M. and Jones, F.R. (1996) 'Going solo: learners' experiences of self-instruction and self-instruction training'. In E. Broady and M.-M. Kenning (eds) *Promoting Learner Autonomy in University Language Teaching*. London: Association for French Language Studies/CILT, pp. 185–214.

Field, L.D. (1989) 'An investigation into the structure, validity and reliability of Guglielmino's Self-directed Learning Readiness Scale', *Adult Education Quarterly*, 39 (3): 125–39.

Fitz-Gibbon, C.I. and Reay, D.G. (1982) 'Peer-tutoring: brightening up FL teaching in an urban comprehensive school', *British Journal of Language Teaching*, 20 (1): 39–44.

Fowler, A. (1997) 'Developing independent learning'. In A. Burns and S. Hood (eds) *Teachers' Voices 2: Teaching Disparate Learner Groups*. Sydney: National Centre for English Language Teaching and Research, pp. 115–23.

Fox, J. (1994) 'Demystifying IT in second language learning.' In E. Esch (ed.) *Self-Access and the Adult Language Learner*. London: CILT, pp. 19–27.

Freeman, D. and Cornwell, S. (eds) (1993) *New Ways in Teacher Education*. Alexandria, VA: TESOL.

Freire, P. (1970) *Pedagogy of the Oppressed*. New York: Herder & Herder.

Freire, P. (1974) *Education for Critical Consciousness*. London: Sheed and Ward.

Gardner, D. (1994) 'Student-produced video documentary: Hong Kong as a self-access resource', *Hong Kong Papers in Linguistics and Language Teaching* 17: 45–54.

Gardner, D. (1996) 'Self-assessment for self-access learning', *TESOL Journal*, 5 (3): 18–23.

Gardner, D. and Blasco Garcia, R. (1996) 'Interactive video as self-access support for language-learning beginners.' In R. Pemberton et al. (eds) *Taking Control: Autonomy in Language Learning*. Hong Kong: Hong Kong University Press, pp. 219–32.

Gardner, D. and Miller, L. (1999) *Establishing Self-Access: From Theory to Practice*. Cambridge: Cambridge University Press.

Gardner, R.C. (1985) *Social Psychology and Second Language Learning*. London: Edward Arnold.

Gardner, R.C. (1988) 'The socio-educational model of second language acquisition: assumptions, findings and issues', *Language Learning*, 38 (1): 101–26.

Gardner, R.C. and Lambert, W.E. (1972) *Attitudes and Motivation in Second Language Learning*. Rowley, Mass.: Newbury House.

Garrison, D.R. (1992) 'Critical thinking and self-directed learning in adult education: an analysis of responsibility and control issues', *Adult Education Quarterly*, 42 (3): 136–148.

Geddes, M. and Sturtridge, G. (eds) (1982) *Individualisation*. London: Modern English Publications.

Gibbons, M., Bailey, A., Comeau, P., Schmuck, J., Seymour, S. and Wallace, D. (1980) 'Toward a theory of self-directed learning: a study of experts without formal training', *Journal of Humanistic Psychology*, 20 (2): 41–56.

Gibbs, B. (1979) 'Autonomy and authority in education', *Journal of Philosophy of Education*, 13: 119–32.

Giles, H. and Byrne, J.L. (1982) 'An intergroup approach to second language acquisition', *Journal of Multilingual and Multicultural Development*, 3 (1): 17–40.

Glaser, B.G. and Strauss, A.M. (1967) *The Discovery of Grounded Theory: Strategies for Qualitative Research*. New York: Aldine.

Gottlieb, M. (1995) 'Nurturing student learning through portfolios', *TESOL Journal*, 5 (3): 12–14.

Gremmo, M.-J. and Riley, P. (1995) 'Autonomy, self-direction and self-access in language teaching and learning: the history of an idea.' *System*, 23 (2): 151–64.

Guglielmino, L.M. (1977) *Development of the Self-directed Learning Readiness Scale*. PhD Thesis. University of Georgia.

Guglielmino, L.M. (1989) 'Guglielmino responds to Field's investigation', *Adult Education Quarterly*, 39 (4): 235–40.

Guillot, M.-N. (1996) 'Resource-based language learning: pedagogic strategies for Le Monde sur CD-ROM'. In E. Broady and M.-M. Kenning (eds) *Promoting Learner Autonomy in University Language Teaching*. London: Association for French Language Studies/CILT, pp. 139–58.

Hall, D. and Kenny, B. (1988) 'An approach to a truly communicative methodology: the AIT pre-sessional course', *English for Specific Purposes*, 7: 19–32.

Hammond, M. and Collins, R. (1991) *Self-directed Learning: Critical Practice*. London: Kogan Page.

Harding-Esch, E.M. (1982) 'The open access sound and video library of the University of Cambridge: progress report and development', *System*, 10 (1): 13–28.

Harri-Augstein, S. and Thomas, L. (1991) *Learning Conversations: the Self-organised Way to Personal and Organizational Growth*. London: Routledge.

Harris, R. McL. (1990) 'Reflections on self-directed adult learning: some implications for educators of adults', *Studies in Continuing Education*, 11 (2): 102–16.

Harris, V. and Noyau, G. (1990) 'Collaborative learning: taking the first steps'. In Ian Gathercole (ed.) *Autonomy in Language Learning*. London: CILT, pp. 55–64.

Hatch, E. and Lazaraton, A. (1991) *The Research Manual: Design and Statistics for Applied Linguistics*. Boston: Heinle & Heinle.

Haughton, G. and Dickinson, L. (1989) 'Collaborative assessment by masters' candidates in a tutor-based system', *Language Testing*, 5 (2): 233–46.

Hayward, K. (1994) 'Self-access writing centres'. In D. Gardner and L. Miller (eds) *Directions in Self-Access Language Learning*. Hong Kong: Hong Kong University Press, pp. 39–42.

Ho, J. and Crookall, D. (1995) 'Breaking with Chinese cultural traditions: learner autonomy in English language teaching.' *System*, 23 (2): 235–44.

Holec, H. (1980) 'Learner training: meeting needs in self-directed learning'. In H.B. Altman and C.V. James (eds) *Foreign Language Learning: Meeting Individual Needs*. Oxford: Pergamon, pp. 30–45.

Holec, H. (1981) *Autonomy in Foreign Language Learning*. Oxford: Pergamon. (First published 1979, Strasbourg: Council of Europe.)

Holec, H. (1985a) 'On autonomy: some elementary concepts'. In P. Riley (ed.) *Discourse and Learning*. London: Longman, pp. 173–90.

Holec, H. (1985b) 'Self-assessment'. In Robert J. Mason (ed.) *Self-directed learning and Self-access in Australia: from Practice to Theory*. Proceedings of the National Conference of the Adult Migrant Education Programme, Melbourne, June 1984. Melbourne: Council of Adult Education, pp. 141–58.

Holec, H. (1987) 'The learner as manager: managing learning or managing to learn?'. In A. Wenden and J. Rubin (eds) *Learner Strategies in Language Learning*. London: Prentice Hall, pp. 145–56.

Holec, H. (ed.) (1988) *Autonomy and Self-directed Learning: Present Fields of Application*. Strasbourg: Council of Europe.

Holliday, A. (1999) 'Small cultures', *Applied Linguistics*, 20 (2): 237–64.

Horwitz, E.K. (1987) 'Surveying student beliefs about language learning'. In A. Wenden and J. Rubin (eds) *Learner Strategies in Language Learning*. London: Prentice Hall, pp. 119–29.

Horwitz, E.K. (1988) 'The beliefs about language learning of beginning university foreign language students', *The Modern Language Journal*, 72 (3): 283–94.

Horwitz, E.K., Horwitz, M.B. and Cope, J. (1986) 'Foreign language classroom anxiety', *The Modern Language Journal*, 70: 125–32.

Horwitz, E.K. and Young, D. (1991) *Language Learning Anxiety: from Theory and Research to Classroom Implications*. Englewood Cliffs, NJ: Prentice Hall.

Hurd, S. (1994) 'The Language Learning Centre at the University of Central Lancashire: a case study'. In E. Esch (ed.) *Self-Access and the Adult Language Learner*. London: CILT, pp. 126–34.

Illich, I. (1971) *Deschooling Society*. London: Calder & Boyars.

Itakura, H. (1999) 'Learner journals as a means of promoting out-of-class Japanese learning'. Paper presented at AILA Congress, Tokyo, August, 1999.

Johnson, D.W. and Johnson, R.T. (1994) *Learning Together and Alone*. Fourth edition. Boston: Allyn & Bacon.

Johnston, M. (1985) 'ESL development and self-directed learning'. In Robert J. Mason (ed.) *Self-directed Learning and Self-access in Australia: from Practice to Theory*. Proceedings of the National Conference of the Adult Migrant Education Programme, Melbourne, June 1984. Melbourne: Council of Adult Education, pp. 173–214.

Jones, F.R. (1993) 'Beyond the fringe: a framework for assessing teach-yourself materials for ab initio English-speaking materials', *System*, 21: 453–69.

Jones, F.R. (1994) 'The lone language learner: a diary study', *System*, 22: 441–54.

Jones, F.R. (1998) 'Self-instruction and success: a learner profile study', *Applied Linguistics*, 19 (3): 378–406.

Jones, J. (1995) 'Self-access and culture', *ELT Journal*, 49 (3): 228–34.

Karlsson, L., Kjisik, F. and Nordlund, J. (1997) *From Here to Autonomy*. Helsinki University Press.

Karmiloff-Smith, A. (1992) *Beyond Modularity. A Developmental Perspective on Cognitive Science*. Cambridge, MA: MIT Press.

Kelly, G. (1955) *The Psychology of Personal Constructs*. New York: Norton.

Kelly, G. (1963) *A Theory of Personality*. New York: Norton.

Kelly, R. (1996) 'Language counselling for learner autonomy: the skilled helper in self-access language learning.' In R. Pemberton et al. (eds) *Taking Control: Autonomy in Language Learning*. Hong Kong: Hong Kong University Press, pp. 93–113.

Kenning, M.-M. (1996) 'IT and autonomy'. In E. Broady and M.-M. Kenning (eds) *Promoting Learner Autonomy in University Language Teaching*. London: Association for French Language Studies/CILT, pp. 121–38.

Kenny, B. (1993) 'For more autonomy', *System*, 21 (4): 431–42.

Kenny, B. and Laszewski, M. (1997) 'Talkbase in Vientiane'. In B. Kenny and W. Savage (eds) *Language and Development: Teachers in a Changing World*. London: Longman, pp. 129–40.

Kilpatrick, W.H. (1921) *The Project Method*. New York: Teachers College Press.

Kirtikara, K. (1997) 'Autonomy rediscovered'. In *Autonomy 2000: The Development of Learning Independence in Language Learning*. Conference Proceedings. Bangkok: King Mongkut's Institute of Technology Thonburi, pp. 93–100.

Knowles, M. (1975) *Self-directed Learning: a Guide for Learners and Teachers*. New York: Cambridge, The Adult Education Company.

Kohonen, V. (1992) 'Experiential language learning: second language learning as cooperative learner education'. In D. Nunan (ed.) *Collaborative Language Learning and Teaching*, Cambridge: Cambridge University Press, pp. 14–39.

Kohonen, V. (ed.) (2000) *Experiential Learning in Foreign Language Education*. London: Longman.

Kolb, D. (1984) *Experiential learning: Experience as the Source of Learning and Development*. Englewood Cliffs, NJ: Prentice Hall.

Krashen, S. (1982) *Principles and Practice in Second Language Acquisition*. Oxford: Pergamon.

Kvale, S. (1996) *Interviews: an Introduction to Qualitative Research Interviewing*. London: Sage.

Lamb, T. (1997) 'Self-management in the secondary school languages classroom'. In *Autonomy 2000: The Development of Learning Independence in Language Learning*. Conference Proceedings. Bangkok: King Mongkut's Institute of Technology Thonburi, pp. 101–15.

Lamb, T. (2000) 'Finding a voice: learner autonomy and teacher education in an urban context'. In B. Sinclair et al. (eds) *Learner Autonomy, Teacher Autonomy: Future Directions*. London: Longman, pp. 118–27.

Leblanc, R. and Painchaud, G. (1985) 'Self-assessment as a second language placement instrument', *TESOL Quarterly*, 19 (4): 673–87.

Legenhausen, L. (1999a) 'Language acquisition without grammar instruction? The evidence from an autonomous classroom', *Revista Canaria de Estudios Ingleses*, 38.

Legenhausen, L. (1999b) 'The emergence and use of grammatical structures in conversational interactions: comparing traditional and autonomous learners'. In B. Mißler and U. Multhaup (eds) *The Construction of Knowledge, Learner Autonomy and Related Issues in Foreign Language Learning*. Tübingen: Stauffenberg, pp. 27–40.

Legenhausen, L. (1999c) 'Traditional and autonomous learners compared: the impact of classroom culture on communicative attitudes and behaviour'. In C. Edelhoff and R. Weskamp (eds) *Autonomes Fremdsprachenlernen*. Munich: Max Hueber Verlag, pp. 166–82.

Legutke, M. and Thomas, H. (1991) *Process and Experience in the Language Classroom*. London: Longman.

Leow, R.P. (1997) 'Attention, awareness and foreign language behaviour', *Language Learning*, 47 (3): 467–505.

Lewis, J. (1990) 'Self-assessment in the classroom: a case study'. In G. Brindley (ed.) *The Second Language Curriculum in Action*. Sydney: National Centre for English Language Teaching and Research, pp. 187–213.

Lewis, T., Woodin, J. and St. John, E. (1996) 'Tandem learning: independence through partnership'. In E. Broady and M.-M. Kenning (eds) *Promoting Learner Autonomy in University Language Teaching*. London: Association for French Language Studies/CILT, pp. 105–20.

Little, D. (1990) 'Autonomy in language learning.' In Ian Gathercole (ed.) *Autonomy in Language Learning*, London: CILT, pp. 7–15.

Little, D. (1991) *Learner Autonomy. 1: Definitions, Issues and Problems*. Dublin: Authentik.

Little, D. (1994a) 'Interactive videocassette for self-access: a preliminary report on the implementation of Autotutor II', *Computers in Education*, 23 (1–2): 165–70.

Little, D. (1994b) 'Learner autonomy: a theoretical construct and its practical application', *Die Neueren Sprachen*, 93 (5): 430–42.

Little, D. (1995a) 'Learning as dialogue: the dependence of learner autonomy on teacher autonomy.' *System*, 23 (2): 175–82.

Little, D. (1995b) 'Quality in the autonomous classroom: the role of evaluation and assessment'. Paper presented at the Seminar on Quality and Autonomy, Danmarks Lærerhøjskole, Copenhagen, August.

Little, D. (1996) 'Freedom to learn and compulsion to interact: promoting learner autonomy through the use of information systems and information technologies'. In R. Pemberton et al. (eds) *Taking Control: Autonomy in Language Learning*. Hong Kong University Press, pp. 203–18.

Little, D. (1997a) 'Language awareness and the autonomous language learner', *Language Awareness*, 6 (2/3): 93–104.

Little, D. (1997b) 'Responding authentically to authentic texts: a problem for self-access language learning?' In P. Benson and P. Voller (eds) *Autonomy and Independence in Language Learning*. London: Longman, pp. 225–36.

Little, D., Dam, L. and Timmer, J. (eds) (2000) *Focus on Learning rather than Teaching: Why and How?* Dublin: Trinity College, Centre for Language and Communication Studies.

Little, D. and Singleton, D. (1990) 'Cognitive style and learning approach'. In R. Duda and P. Riley (eds) *Learning Styles*. Nancy: Presses Universitaires de Nancy, pp. 11–19.

Littlejohn, A. (1982) *A procedural guide for teacherless language learning groups*. MA dissertation, University of Lancaster.

Littlejohn, A. (1983) 'Increasing learner involvement in course management', *TESOL Quarterly*, 17 (4): 595–608.

Littlejohn, A. (1985) 'Learner choice in language study', *ELT Journal*, 39 (4): 253–61.

Littlejohn, A. (1997) 'Self-access work and curriculum ideologies'. In P. Benson and P. Voller (eds) *Autonomy and Independence in Language Learning*. London: Longman, pp. 181–91.

Littlewood, W.T. (1981) *Communicative Language Teaching*. Cambridge: Cambridge University Press.

Littlewood, W.T. (1996) 'Autonomy: an anatomy and a framework', *System*, 24 (4): 427–35.

Littlewood, W.T. (1997) 'Self-access: why do want it and what can it do?'. In P. Benson and P. Voller (eds) *Autonomy and Independence in Language Learning*. London: Longman, pp. 79–92.

Littlewood, W.T. (1999) 'Defining and developing autonomy in East Asian contexts', *Applied Linguistics*, 20 (1): 71–94.

Littlewood, W.T. and Liu, N.F. (1996) *Hong Kong Students and their English*. Hong Kong: Macmillan.

Lonergan, J. (1994) 'Self-access language centres: implications for managers, teachers and learners.' In E. Esch (ed.) *Self-Access and the Adult Language Learner*. London: CILT, pp. 119–25.

Long, M. (1983) 'Does second language instruction make a difference? A review of the research', *TESOL Quarterly*, 17: 359–82.

Lor, W. (1998) *Studying the first-year students' experience of writing their reflection journals with the use of a web-based system*. MA dissertation. University of Hong Kong.

Louden, W. (1991) *Understanding Teaching*. London: Cassell.

Macaro, E. (1997) *Target Language, Collaborative Learning and Autonomy*. Clevedon: Multilingual Matters.

McCall, J. (1992) *Self-access: Setting up a Centre*. Manchester: British Council.

McDonough, S. (1999) 'Learner strategies', *Language Teaching*, 32: 1–18.

McGarry, D. (1995) *Learner Autonomy 4: The Role of Authentic Texts*. Dublin: Authentik.

McGrath, I. (2000) 'Teacher autonomy'. In B. Sinclair et al. (eds) *Learner Autonomy, Teacher Autonomy: Future Directions*. London: Longman, pp. 100–10.

McNamara, M.J. and Deane, D. (1995) 'Self-assessment activities: toward autonomy in language learning', *TESOL Journal*, 5 (3): 17–21.

MacIntyre, P. and Gardner, R. (1991) 'Methods and results in the study of foreign language anxiety: a review of the literature'. *Language Learning*, 41: 25–57.

Mak, L. (1994) 'From English teacher to producer: how to develop a multimedia computer simulation for teaching ESL'. In D. Gardner and L. Miller (eds) *Directions in Self-Access Language Learning*, Hong Kong: Hong Kong University Press, pp. 145–54.

Makin, L. (1994) 'Learner telesupport: language advising by e-mail.' In E. Esch (ed.) *Self-Access and the Adult Language Learner*. London: CILT, pp. 83–96.

Marshall, K. (1996) 'The rewards and pitfalls of autonomy: a Bangor experience'. In E. Broady and M.-M. Kenning (eds) *Promoting Learner Autonomy in University Language Teaching*. London: Association for French Language Studies/CILT, pp. 39–60.

Martyn, E. (1994) 'Self-access logs: promoting self-directed learning.' In D. Gardner and L. Miller (eds) *Directions in Self-access Language Learning*. Hong Kong: Hong Kong University Press, pp. 65–78.

Martyn, E. and Voller, P. (1993) 'Teachers' attitudes to self-access learning', *Hong Kong Papers in Linguistics and Language Teaching*, 16: 103–10.

Mason, R.J. (ed.) (1985) *Self-directed learning and Self-access in Australia: from Practice to Theory*. Proceedings of the National Conference of the Adult Migrant Education Programme, Melbourne, June 1984. Melbourne: Council of Adult Education.

Matsumoto, K. (1989) 'An analysis of a Japanese ESL learner's diary: factors involved in the L2 learning process', *JALT Journal*, 11: 167–92.

Matsumoto, K. (1996) 'Helping L2 learners reflect on classroom learning', *ELT Journal*, 50 (2): 143–9.

Mayes, T. (1994) 'Hypermedia and cognitive tools.' In E. Esch (ed.) *Self-access and the Adult Language Learner*. London: CILT, pp. 28–36.

Mezirow, J. (1981) 'A critical theory of adult learning and education', *Adult Education*, 32 (1): 3–24.

Mezirow, J. (1991) *Transformative Dimensions of Adult Learning*. San Francisco: Jossey-Bass.

Mezirow, J. et al. (1990) *Fostering Critical Reflection in Adulthood: a Guide to Transformative and Emancipatory Learning*. San Francisco: Jossey-Bass.

Milton, J. (1997) 'Providing computerized self-access opportunities for the development of writing skills'. In P. Benson and P. Voller (eds) *Autonomy and Independence in Language Learning*. London: Longman, pp. 237–48.

Moore, C. (1992) *Self-access: appropriate technology*. Manchester: British Council.

Motteram, G. (1997) 'Learner Autonomy and the Web'. In V. Darleguy et al. (eds) *Educational Technology in Language Learning: Theoretical Considerations and Practical Applications*. Lyons: INSA (National Institute of Applied Sciences), pp. 17–24.

Murayama, I. (1996) 'The status of strategies in learning: a brief history of changes in researchers' views', *Learning Learning: JALT Learner Development N-SIG Forum*, 2 (3): 7–12.

Naiman, N., Fröhlich, M., Stern, H.H. and Todesco, A. (1978) *The Good Language Learner*. Research in Education Series, No. 7, Ontario Institute for Studies in Education.

Nicholas, H. (1991) 'Language awareness and second language development'. In C.V. James and P. Garrett (eds) *Language Awareness in the Classroom*. London: Longman, pp. 78–95.

Norton, B. (1997) 'Language, identity and the ownership of English', *TESOL Quarterly*, 31 (3): 409–429.

Nunan, D. (1987) 'Communicative language teaching: the learner's view'. In B. Das (ed.) *Communicating and Learning in the Classroom Community*. Singapore: RELC, pp. 176–190.

Nunan, D. (1988) *The Learner-centred Curriculum: a Study in Second Language Teaching*. Cambridge: Cambridge University Press.

Nunan, D. (1989) *Understanding Language Classrooms*. London: Prentice Hall.

Nunan, D. (1991) *Language Teaching Methodology*. London: Prentice Hall.

Nunan, D. (1994) 'Self-assessment and reflections as tools for learning'. Paper presented at the Assessment Colloquium, International Language in Education Conference, University of Hong Kong, December.

Nunan, D. (1995a) *ATLAS. Learning-centred Communication*. Boston: Heinle & Heinle/International Thomson Publishing.

Nunan, D. (1995b) 'Closing the gap between learning and instruction', *TESOL Quarterly*, 29 (1): 133–58.

Nunan, D. (1996) 'Towards autonomous learning: some theoretical, empirical and practical issues.' In R. Pemberton et al. (eds) *Taking Control: Autonomy in Language Learning*. Hong Kong: Hong Kong University Press, pp. 13–26.

Nunan, D. (1997) 'Designing and adapting materials to encourage learner autonomy'. In P. Benson and P. Voller (eds) *Autonomy and Independence in Language Learning*. London: Longman, pp. 192–203.

Nunan, D. (ed.) (1992) *Collaborative Language Learning and Teaching*. Cambridge: Cambridge University Press.

O'Dell, F. (1992) 'Helping teachers to use a self-access centre to its full potential', *ELT Journal*, 46 (2): 153–9.

O'Dell, F. (1997) 'Confidence building for classroom teachers working with self-access resources'. In P. Benson and P. Voller (eds) *Autonomy and Independence in Language Learning*. London: Longman, pp. 150–63.

O'Malley, J.M. and Chamot, A.U. (1990) *Learning Strategies in Second Language Acquisition*. Cambridge: Cambridge University Press.

Oscarson, M. (1989) 'Self-assessment of language proficiency: rationale and applications', *Language Testing*, 6: 1–13.

Oscarson, M. (1997) 'Self-assessment of foreign and second language proficiency'. In C. Clapham and D. Corson (eds) *Language Testing and Assessment*. Encyclopedia of Language and Education. Volume 7. Dordrecht: Kluwer, pp. 175–87.

Oxford, R.L. (1990) *Language Learning Strategies: what every Teacher should Know*. Rowley, Mass.: Newbury House.

Oxford, R.L. and Burry-Stock, J.A. (1995) 'Assess the use of language learning strategies worldwide with the ESL/EFL version of the strategy inventory for language learning (SILL)', *System*, 23 (1): 1–23.

Paris, S.G. and Byrnes, J.Y.P. (1989) 'The constructivist approach to self-regulation of learning in the classroom'. In B.J. Zimmerman and D.H. Schunk (eds) *Self-regulated Learning and Academic Achievement*. New York: Springer-Verlag, pp. 169–200.

Pemberton, R., Li, E.S.L., Or, W.W.F. and Pierson, H.D. (eds) (1996) *Taking Control: Autonomy in Language Learning*. Hong Kong: Hong Kong University Press.

Pemberton, R., Toogood, S., Ho, S. and Lam, J. (2001) 'Approaches to advising for self-directed language learning'. *AILA Review*.

Pennycook, A. (1997) 'Cultural alternatives and autonomy'. In P. Benson and P. Voller (eds) *Autonomy and Independence in Language Learning*. London: Longman, pp. 35–53.

Perkins, D.N. and Salomon, G. (1989) 'Are cognitive skills context-bound?', *Educational Researcher*, pp. 16–25.

Pickard, N. (1995) 'Out-of class language learning strategies: three case studies', *Language Learning Journal*, 12: 35–7.

Pierce, B.N. (1995) 'Social identity, investment and language learning', *TESOL Quarterly*, 29 (1): 9–31.

Pierson, H.D. (1996) 'Learner culture and learner autonomy in the Hong Kong Chinese context.' In R. Pemberton et al. (eds) *Taking Control: Autonomy in Language Learning*. Hong Kong: Hong Kong University Press, pp. 49–58.

Prabhu, N.S. (1987) *Second Language Pedagogy*. Oxford: Oxford University Press.

Press, M-C. (1996) 'Ethnicity and the autonomous language learner: different beliefs and different strategies'. In E. Broady and M.-M. Kenning (eds) *Promoting Learner Autonomy in University Language Teaching*. London: Association for French Language Studies/CILT, pp. 237–59.

Ramadevi, S. (1992) *Learner Autonomy in the ESL Classroom: a Study in Curriculum Design*. New Dehli: B.R. Publishing Corporation.

Raz, J. (1986) *The Morality of Freedom*. Oxford: Oxford University Press.

Rees-Miller, J. (1993) 'A critical appraisal of learner training: theoretical bases and teaching implications', *TESOL Quarterly*, 27 (4): 679–89.

Rees-Miller, J. (1994) 'Comments on Janie Rees-Miller's "A critical appraisal of learner training: theoretical bases and teaching implications": The author responds', *TESOL Quarterly*, 28 (4): 776–81.

Reid, J. (1987) 'The learning style preferences of ESL students', *TESOL Quarterly*, 21: 87–111.

Ribé, R. and Vidal, N. (1993) *Project Work*. London: Heinemann.

Richards, K. and Roe, P. (1994) *Distance Learning in ELT*. Modern English Publications/British Council.

Riley, P. (1986) 'Who's who in self-access.' *TESOL France News*, 6 (2): 23–35.

Riley, P. (1988) 'The ethnography of autonomy'. In A. Brookes and P. Grundy (eds) *Individualisation and Autonomy in Language Learning*. ELT Documents 131. London: Modern English Publications in association with the British Council (Macmillan), pp. 12–34.

Riley, P. (1996) 'The blind man and the bubble: researching self-access.' In R. Pemberton et al. (eds) *Taking Control: Autonomy in Language Learning*. Hong Kong: Hong Kong University Press, pp. 251–64.

Riley, P. (1997) 'The guru and the conjurer: aspects of counselling for self-access'. In P. Benson and P. Voller (eds) *Autonomy and Independence in Language Learning*. London: Longman, pp. 114–31.

Riley, P. and Zoppis, C. (1985) 'The sound and video library'. In P. Riley (ed.) *Discourse and Learning*. London: Longman, pp. 286–98.

Robinson, P. (1995) 'Attention, memory, and the "noticing" hypothesis', *Language Learning*, 45: 283–331.

Rogers, C.R. (1969) *Freedom to Learn*. Columbus, Ohio: Charles E. Merrill.

Rogers, C.R. (1983) *Freedom to Learn for the 80s*. New York: Merrill.

Rohrkemper, M.M. (1989) 'Self-regulated learning and academic achievement: a Vygotskian view'. In B.J. Zimmerman and D.H. Schunk (eds) *Self-regulated Learning and Academic Achievement: Theory, Research and Practice*. New York: Springer-Verlag, pp. 143–67.

Rolfe, T. (1990) 'Self- and peer-assessment in the ESL curriculum'. In G. Brindley (ed.) *The Second Language Curriculum in Action*. Sydney: Macquarie University, National Centre for English Language Teaching and Research, pp. 163–86.

Rosewell, L.V. and Libben, G. (1994) 'The sound of one-hand clapping: how to succeed in independent language learning', *Canadian Modern Language Review*, 50 (4): 668–88.

Rowntree, D. (1990) *Teaching through Self-instruction: How to Develop Open Learning Materials*. London: Kogan Page.

Rubin, J. (1975) 'What the "good language learner" can teach us', *TESOL Quarterly*, 9: 41–51.

Ryan, S. (1997) 'Preparing learners for independence: resources beyond the classroom'. In P. Benson and P. Voller (eds) *Autonomy and Independence in Language Learning*. London: Longman, pp. 215–24.

Schärer, R. (1983) 'Identification of learner needs at Eurocentre'. In R. Richterich (ed.) *Case Studies in Identifying Language Needs*. Oxford: Pergamon Press, pp. 106–16.

Schmidt, R.W. (1990) 'The role of consciousness in second language learning', *Applied Linguistics*, 11: 11–26.

Schmidt, R.W. and Frota, S.N. (1986) 'Developing basic conversational ability in a second language: a case study of an adult learner of Portuguese'. In R. Day (ed.) *Talking to Learn: Conversation in Second Language Acquisition*. Rowley, MA: Newbury House, pp. 237–326.

Schunk, D.H. and Zimmerman, B.J. (eds) (1994) *Self-regulation of Learning and Performance: Issues and Educational Applications*. Hillsdale, NJ: Lawrence Erlbaum.

Schunk, D.H. and Zimmerman, B.J. (eds) (1998) *Self-regulated Learning: from Teaching to Self-regulated Practice*. New York: Guilford Press.

Scott, M., Carioni, L., Zanatta, M., Bayer, E. and Quintanilha, T. (1984) 'Using a "standard exercise" in teaching reading comprehension', *ELT Journal*, 38: 114–20.

Sheerin, S. (1991) 'State of the art: self-access', *Language Teaching*, 24 (3): 143–57.

Sheerin, S. (1997) 'An exploration of the relationship between self-access and independent learning'. In P. Benson and P. Voller (eds) *Autonomy and Independence in Language Learning*. London: Longman, pp. 54–65.

Shohamy, E. (1997) 'Critical language testing and beyond'. Paper presented at the American Association of Applied Linguistics Meeting, Orlando, March.

Simmons, D. and Wheeler, S. (1995) *The Process Syllabus in Action*. Sydney: Macquarie University, National Centre for English Language Teaching and Research.

Sinclair, B. (1996) *Activate your English: Pre-intermediate*. Cambridge: Cambridge University Press.

Sinclair, B., McGrath, I. and Lamb, T. (eds) (2000) *Learner Autonomy, Teacher Autonomy: Future Directions*. London: Longman.

Slimani, Y. (1992) 'Evaluating classroom interaction'. In J.C. Alderson and A. Beretta (eds) *Evaluating Second Language Education*. Cambridge: Cambridge University Press, pp. 197–221.

Smolen, L., Newman, C., Wathen, T. and Lee, D. (1995) 'Developing student self-assessment strategies', *TESOL Journal*, 5 (3): 22–7.

Smyth, J. (1991) *Teachers as Collaborative Learners*. Milton Keynes: Open University Press.

Spear, G.E. and Mocker, D.W. (1984) 'The organizing circumstance: environmental determinants in self-directed learning', *Adult Education Quarterly*, 35: 1–10.

Stern, H. (1975) 'What can we learn from the good language learner?' *Canadian Modern Language Review*, 31: 304–18.

Stevens, V. (1995) 'Concordancing with language learners: why? when? what?' *CAELL Journal*, 6 (2): 2–10.

Stevick, E.W. (1990) *Humanism in Language Teaching: a Critical Perspective*. Oxford: Oxford University Press.

Strage, A. (1998) 'Family context variables and the development of self-regulation in college students', *Adolescence*, 55: 17–31.

Sturtridge, G. (1992) *Self-access: Preparation and Training*. Manchester: British Council.

Sturtridge, G. (1997) 'Teaching and language learning in self-access centres: changing roles?'. In P. Benson and P. Voller (eds) *Autonomy and Independence in Language Learning*. London: Longman, pp. 66–78.

Tarone, E. and Yule, G. (1989) *Focus on the Language Learner*. Oxford: Oxford University Press.

Thavenius, C. (1999) 'Teacher autonomy for learner autonomy'. In D. Crabbe and S. Cotterall (eds) *Learner Autonomy in Language Learning: Defining the Field and Effecting Change*. Frankfurt: Peter Lang, pp. 159–63.

Thomas, L.F. and Harri-Augstein, S. (1990) 'On constructing a learning conversation'. In R. Duda and P. Riley (eds) *Learning Styles*. Nancy: Presses Universitaires de Nancy, pp. 207–21.

Thomson, C.K. (1996) 'Self-assessment in self-directed learning: issues of learner diversity.' In R. Pemberton et al. (eds) *Taking Control: Autonomy in Language Learning*. Hong Kong: Hong Kong University Press, pp. 77–91.

Tomlin, R.S. and Villa, V. (1994) 'Attention in cognitive science and second language acquisition', *Studies in Second Language Acquisition*, 16: 183–203.

Tough, A. (1971) *The Adult's Learning Projects*. Toronto: Ontario Institute for Studies in Education.

Underwood, J. (1984) *Linguistics, Computers and the Language Teacher: a Communicative Approach*. Rowley, MA: Newbury House.

Ushioda, E. (1996) *Learner Autonomy 5: The Role of Motivation*. Dublin: Authentik.

Vallerand, R.J. (1997) 'Toward a hierarchical model of intrinsic and extrinsic motivation', *Advances in Experimental Social Psychology*, 29: 271–360.

Vieira, F. (1997) 'Pedagogy for autonomy: exploratory answers to questions any teacher should ask'. In M. Müller-Verweyen (ed.) *Standpunkte zur Sprach- und Kulturvermittlung 7. Neues Lernen, Selbstgesteuert, Autonom*. Goethe Institut, pp. 53–72.

Vieira, F. (1999) 'Pedagogy for autonomy: teacher development and pedagogical experimentation – an in-service teacher training project'. In D. Crabbe and S. Cotterall (eds) *Learner Autonomy in Language Learning: Defining the Field and Effecting Change*. Frankfurt: Peter Lang, pp. 149–58.

Voller, P. (1997) 'Does the teacher have a role in autonomous learning?' In P. Benson and P. Voller (eds) *Autonomy and Independence in Language Learning*. London: Longman, pp. 98–113.

Voller, P., Martyn, E. and Pickard, V. (1999) 'One-to-one counselling for autonomous learning in a self-access centre: final report on an action learning project'. In D. Crabbe and S. Cotterall (eds) *Learner Autonomy in Language Learning: Defining the Field and Effecting Change*. Frankfurt: Peter Lang, pp. 111–26.

Voller, P. and Pickard, V. (1996) 'Conversation exchange: a way towards autonomous language learning.' In R. Pemberton et al. (eds) *Taking Control: Autonomy in Language Learning*. Hong Kong: Hong Kong University Press, pp. 115–32.

Vygotsky, L.S. (1978) *Mind in Society: the Development of Higher Psychological Processes*. Boston: Harvard University Press.

Waite, S. (1994) 'Low-resourced self-access with EAP in the developing world: the great enabler?' *ELT Journal*, 48 (3): 233–42.

Walker, E. (1997) *Foreign language anxiety in Hong Kong secondary schools: its relationship with the age-related factors, schools form and self-perception*. PhD Thesis. University of Hong Kong.

Wallace, M.J. (1998) *Action Research for Language Teachers*. Cambridge: Cambridge University Press.

Wang, M.C. and Peverly, S.T. (1986) 'The self-instructive process in classroom learning contexts'. *Contemporary Educational Psychology*, 11: 370–404.

Warschauer, M. (1996) 'Computer-assisted language learning: an introduction'. In S. Fotos (ed.), *Multimedia Language Teaching*. Tokyo: Logos International, pp. 3–20.

Warschauer, M. and Healey, D. (1998) 'Computers and language learning: an overview', *Language Teaching*, 31: 57–71.

Warschauer, M., Turbee, L. and Roberts, B. (1996) 'Computer learning networks and student empowerment', *System*, 24 (1): 1–14.

Weaver, S.J. and Cohen, A.D. (1997) *Strategies-based instruction: a teacher-training video* (CARLA Working Paper Series 8). Minneapolis: Center for Advanced Research on Language Acquisition.

Weil, S. (1952) *The Need for Roots. Prelude to a Declaration of Duties Towards Mankind*. London: Routledge & Kegan Paul.

Weiner, B. (1984) 'Principles for a theory of student motivation and their application within an attributional framework'. In R. Ames and C. Ames (eds) *Research on Motivation in Education*. Volume 1, Orlando: Academic Press, pp. 15–38.

Wenden, A. (1983) 'Literature review: the process of intervention', *Language Learning*, 33: 103–21.

Wenden, A. (1986a) 'Helping learners think about learning', *ELT Journal*, 40 (1): 3–12.

Wenden, A. (1986b) 'What do second language learners know about their second language learning? A second look at retrospective learner accounts', *Applied Linguistics*, 7 (2): 186–201.

Wenden, A. (1987) 'How to be a successful language learner: insights and prescriptions from L2 learners'. In A. Wenden and J. Rubin (eds) *Learner Strategies in Language Learning*. London: Prentice Hall, pp. 103–14.

Wenden, A. (1991) *Learner Strategies for Learner Autonomy*. London: Prentice Hall International.

Wenden, A. (1995) 'Learner training in context: a knowledge-based approach', *System*, 23 (2): 183–94.

Wenden, A. (1998) 'Metacognitive knowledge and language learning', *Applied Linguistics*, 19 (4): 515–37.

Wenden, A. (ed.) (1999) Special issue on metacognitive knowledge and beliefs in language learning, *System*, 27 (4).

White, C. (1995) 'Autonomy and strategy use in distance foreign language learning: research findings'. *System*, 23 (2): 207–22.

Widdows, S. and Voller, P. (1991) 'PANSI: a survey of ELT needs of Japanese university students', *Cross Currents*, 18 (2): 127–141.

Williams, M. and Burden, R. (1997) *Psychology for Language Teachers*. Cambridge: Cambridge University Press.

Willing, K. (1987) *Learning Styles in Adult Migrant Education*. Adelaide: National Curriculum Resource Centre Research Series.

Wright, T. (1987) *Roles of Teachers and Learners*. Oxford: Oxford University Press.

Yang, N.D. (1998) 'Exploring a new role for teachers: promoting learner autonomy', *System*, 26 (1): 127–35.

Yap, S.S.L. (1998) *Out-of-class use of English by secondary school students in a Hong Kong Anglo-Chinese school*. MA dissertation. University of Hong Kong.

Young, R. (1986) *Personal Autonomy: Beyond Negative and Positive Liberty*. London: Croom Helm.

Zimmerman, B.J. (1998) 'Developing self-fulfilling cycles of academic regulation: an analysis of exemplary instructional models'. In D.H. Schunk and B.J. Zimmerman (eds) *Self-regulated Learning: from Teaching to Self-regulated Practice*. New York: Guilford Press, pp. 1–19.

Zimmerman, B.J. and Schunk, D.H. (eds) (1989) *Self-regulated Learning and Academic Achievement: Theory, Research and Practice*. New York: Springer-Verlag.

Index

O'Malley, J.M. and Chamot, A.U.
  on classification of learning strategies, 81–2
  on classification of metacognitive strategies, 82
Oscarson, M.
  on benefits of self-assessment, 155
out-of-class learning, 62, 63, 185
  possibilities for research, 203
  research case study, 199–203
Oxford, R.
  classification of social and affective strategies, 83

peer teaching, 153–4
Pennycook, A.
  on autonomy and voice, 101
  on the psychologisation of autonomy, 20
personal autonomy, 43–6
personal construct theory, 35–7
Phnom Penh, University of, 122–3
PLAN see Professional Language Advisors Network
planned vs. unplanned learning, 77–8
planning, 77–8, 152–4
power in classroom, 159–61
practice
  definition, 110
preferences, 73–4
Press, M.-C.
  research case study on autonomy and culture, 58, 193–9
problem-solving, 25–7
process syllabus, 164–5
  possibilities for research, 213–14
  research case study, 208–14
Professional Language Advisors Network (PLAN), 232, 233
proficiency see autonomy: and effective learning, autonomy: and proficiency
programmed learning, 11–12
project work, 27, 139–40, 165, 167
psychology of learning, 35–43

Ramadevi, S.
  on control of learning content, 100–1
Raz, J.
  on personal autonomy, 44
Rees-Miller, J.
  on effectiveness of strategy training, 144–5
reflection, 38, 40, 42, 68, 80–1, 87, 90–5, 98, 156, 176, 185
  definition, 90–1
  possibilities for research, 207–8
  research case study, 204–8
representational redescription, 97
research
  case study approach, 209–10
  conclusions, 217

direct and indirect evidence, 188, 201, 205
ethnographic, 187
interviews, 201
qualitative data, 201, 205, 209
questionnaires, 196
statistics, 196
  see also action research, autonomy: research areas
resource-based approaches to autonomy, 113–35, 140
  definition, 113
  effectiveness of, 133–5
  see also authentic materials, distance learning, materials design, self-access, self-instruction
Riley, P., 42
  on autonomy and culture, 55
  on autonomy and individualisation, 12
  on researching autonomy, 184
Riley, P. & Zoppis, C.
  on self-access at CRAPEL, 9
Rogers, C.R., 16, 31–3, 35, 38
  on facilitation, 32
Rosewell, L.V. and Libben, G.
  study of self-instruction, 132, 209
Rousseau, J.-J., 23–5, 35, 59
  on teaching and learning, 24
Rowntree, D.
  on self-instructional materials, 133
Ryan, S.
  study of learner training programme, 147–8

SDLRS see Self-directed Learning Readiness Scale
self-access, 8–10, 113–31, 168–70, 186–9
  curriculum integration, 123–4
  definition, 113–14
  effectiveness of, 133–5
  evaluation of, 115–16
  and individualisation, 11
  learner involvement in, 122–3
  and learner training, 115
  learning vs. practice centre, 123
  management and use, 117–24
  materials for, 124–31
  systems, 119–21
  teacher involvement in, 121–2
  technology in, 117–19, 120
  web sites, 211–12
  see also counselling
Self-access Language Learning, 230, 231
self-assessment, 120, 155–61
  for certification, 156
  and culture, 156
  instruments for, 157–8
  political implications of, 159–61